"*Unity of the Spirit* is an invaluable resource, not only for Cistercian scholars, but for all students of spiritual theology, monasticism, and medieval history. Offering the best of current research on William of Saint-Thierry, this volume makes a significant contribution to the literature on this twelfth-century Cistercian Father. The authors present chapters furthering the scholarship on William's life, works, Christology, relationship with Bernard of Clairvaux, concept of the *unio mystica*, and spirituality. *Unity of the Spirit* makes a handsome tribute to retiring professor E. Rozanne Elder, whose life's work has greatly advanced scholarship on William and Cistercian studies worldwide."

> —Dr. Glenn E. Myers
> Professor of Church History and Theological Studies
> Crown College

"Rosanne E. Elder, PhD, introduced William of Saint-Thierry with his profound theology and spirituality to the English-speaking world in a groundbreaking manner. This festschrift bears witness to her past and ongoing dedication to this twelfth-century monastic theologian. The essays in this volume present William, author of the *Vita Prima*, as an intimate friend of Bernard of Clairvaux. Along with Bernard, William's writings challenge us, today, to engage theology not only academically but also as a personal spiritual pursuit of deification into the mystery of God through *Unity of Spirit*. The contributors to this festschrift reveal various dimensions, 'treasures,' of William's teaching and inaugurate a vision for further scholarly research and spiritual growth."

> —Abbot Thomas X. Davis, OCSO

CISTERCIAN STUDIES SERIES: NUMBER TWO HUNDRED SIXTY-EIGHT

Unity of Spirit

Studies on William of Saint-Thierry in Honor of E. Rozanne Elder

Edited by
*F. Tyler Sergent, Aage Rydstrøm-Poulsen,
and Marsha L. Dutton*

Foreword by
Bernard McGinn

Afterword by
John R. Sommerfeldt

α

Cistercian Publications
www.cistercianpublications.org

LITURGICAL PRESS
Collegeville, Minnesota
www.litpress.org

A Cistercian Publications title published by Liturgical Press

Cistercian Publications
Editorial Offices
161 Grosvenor Street
Athens, Ohio 54701
www.cistercianpublications.org

1	2	3	4	5	6	7	8	9

Library of Congress Cataloging-in-Publication Data

Unity of spirit : studies on William of Saint-Thierry in honor of
E. Rozanne Elder / edited by F. Tyler Sergent, Aage Rydstrom-Poulsen, and Marsha L. Dutton.
      pages cm. — (Cistercian studies series ; number two hundred sixty-eight)
   Includes bibliographical references and index.
   ISBN 978-0-87907-268-1 — ISBN 978-0-87907-051-9 (ebook)
   1. William, of Saint-Thierry, Abbot of Saint-Thierry, approximately 1085–1148?   I. Elder, E. Rozanne (Ellen Rozanne), 1940– honouree.
II. Sergent, F. Tyler, editor.

BX4705.G7464U55   2015
230'.2092—dc23   2015018979

Contents

Foreword

Bernard McGinn

In 1933 Étienne Gilson delivered a course of lectures devoted to Bernard of Clairvaux at the Collège de France. In the same year, he gave an English version of these talks at the University College of Wales in Aberystwith. The lectures, published as *La théologie mystique de Saint Bernard* in 1934 and translated into English in 1940, constitute a major moment in the evolution of what we have come to call Cistercian Studies. Along with his penetrating account of Bernard, Gilson included five appendices on themes and figures relating to the abbot of Clairvaux. The last was entitled "Some Notes on William of Saint-Thierry," whom Gilson described as "a very great theologian, in whom firmness of thought goes hand in hand with a remarkable power of just expression."[1]

To be sure, Gilson was not the first to recognize William's genius. As far back as 1908, the Jesuit Pierre Rousselot had given attention to William's views on the relation of love and knowledge in the path to God in his noted *Pour l'histoire du problème de l'amour au moyen âge*. In 1923, the Benedictine André Wilmart wrote a study concerning the succession and dating of William's works, and in 1932 another Jesuit, Léopold Malevez, dedicated two penetrating articles to William's doctrine of humanity as made in the image and likeness of God. Gilson's own student, Marie-Madeleine Davy, produced a study on the three stages of the spiritual life in William in 1933, the first of her many contributions to the study of the abbot.

---

[1] Étienne Gilson, *The Mystical Theology of Saint Bernard* (Sheed and Ward, 1940; Kalamazoo, MI: Cistercian Publications, 1990), 198.

Nevertheless, Gilson's brief but insightful presentation of William reached a wide audience and helped alert students of theology and spirituality about a major, if neglected, star in the medieval firmament: William, Benedictine abbot of Saint-Thierry and later Cistercian monk of Signy.

Now, more than seventy-five years later, medievalists find it difficult, if not impossible, to neglect the imposing, though often difficult, thought of William, one of the greatest theologians of the twelfth century and, one can argue, of the whole of the Middle Ages. A long line of publications stretching out over more than seventy-five years since Gilson wrote has seen to this. In terms of critical editions of William's works, we no longer have to rely on the faulty texts of Migne's *Patrologia Latina* but can make use of excellent editions found in the Sources Chrétiennes series and in the *Corpus Christianorum, Continuatio Mediaevalis*. Just as important has been the succession of publications by learned scholars, first in Europe and then in North America, who have provided us with insightful studies of William's life and thought. Their names will be familiar to all those interested in the medieval Cistercians—to cite but a few: Marie-Madeleine Davy, Robert Thomas, Jacques Hourlier, Jean Marie Déchanet, Odo Brooke, Theodore Koehler, M. Basil Pennington, Thomas Tomasic, David Bell, and Paul Verdeyen.

The purpose of this volume is to honor a scholar whose contributions to the study of William of Saint-Thierry have been second to none—E. Rozanne Elder. Because so many of Rozanne Elder's published works have dealt with William, it is especially fitting that the focus of the essays that follow concern the abbot of Saint-Thierry. This collection is a joyful occasion for saluting the long and stellar career of someone whose impact on studies of William, as well as on the wider world of Cistercian and monastic scholarship, has shaped the past generation.

As John Sommerfeldt points out in his lively reminiscence "Cîteaux at Kalamazoo" at the end of this volume, Cistercian scholarship in the United States has been intimately connected to Western Michigan University and its Institute for Cistercian Studies for more than four decades. The providential planning of John and the much-lamented Basil Pennington, OCSO, was essential for the beginning of this still-lively chapter in the history of scholarship, as well as in the wider world of the retrieval of medieval spiritual traditions.

The recovery of the Cistercian message for the modern world owes more to Rozanne Elder than to perhaps anyone else due to her tenure as the editorial director of Cistercian Publications and director of the Institute of Cistercian Studies from 1973 to 2009. Although Rozanne has written much, especially on her beloved William of Saint-Thierry, her careful and generous work as editor for scores of volumes of translations, monographs, and collected studies constitute her most remarkable—one might even say un-rivalled—contribution to contemporary Cistercian and monastic studies. It is somewhat astonishing to record that between 1976 and 2011 she edited no fewer than 179 books!

Rozanne's interest in William began, fittingly enough, at Kalam-azoo in 1964 under John Sommerfeldt's tutelage, when she wrote a master's dissertation entitled "'And Yet I Have Loved Him': The Judgment of William of Saint Thierry on Peter Abelard." After two years of teaching at Kalamazoo, she went on to PhD work at the University of Toronto, where in 1972 she defended a brilliant dissertation on "The Image of the Invisible God: The Evolving Christology of William of Saint Thierry." (In the interests of total disclosure, I must admit that I served as the outside examiner for this dissertation—the first time I met Rozanne.) Her dissertation provided the firm starting point for a series of groundbreaking studies on William's view of the nature and work of Christ that appeared over the next few decades. A glance at the bibliography of Rozanne's publications found at the end of this volume, however, will show that her range of writings on William has gone far be-yond the theme of Christology, extending over virtually the whole range of his theology. Rozanne has also written on other aspects of the history and thought of the early Cistercians, as well as on such topics as Marian devotion and the Anglican tradition.

The fact that we are finally getting a better sense of the full theo-logical accomplishment of the abbot of Saint-Thierry is in no small part due to the cogent and penetrating work of Rozanne Elder. This is why it is so right that the essays in this volume focus on William and the many facets of his career. Composed by colleagues, friends, and students of Rozanne, each of these papers pays tribute to her formative work in restoring William to his rightful place in the history of medieval theology. They touch on many aspects, though scarcely all, of William's varied thought: mystical theology (see the essays of Sergent, DelCogliano, Bell), monastic tradition (Ward), exegesis (Sergent, DelCogliano, Tillisch), Christology (Rydstrøm-Poulsen), spiritual anthropology (Stiegman), and hagiography (France, Lange). Altogether, the collection provides a good sense of cutting-edge research on the significance of William and on how much Rozanne Elder has done to shape this ongoing discussion.

Emero Stiegman, a scholar who has made many significant contributions to Cistercian studies over his career, presents a challenging comparison of William and Bernard in his essay, "William of Saint-Thierry's Trinitarian Image or Bernard's Pre-theological Self?" Stiegman argues that the fact that two of William's treatises (*On the Nature and Dignity of Love* and *On Contemplating God*) often circulated along with Bernard's *On Loving God* under the general title *The Book of Love (Liber de amore)* has resulted in a failure to see the real differences between William's doctrinal view of the progress of loving affection (*affectus/affectio*) based on humanity's being made to the image and likeness of the Trinity and Bernard's presentation of the universality of God's love found in the depths of the human self as the starting point for the progress of love to final union. Bernard, then, can be seen as "the prophet of experience," orienting the reader to the "destitute self" that must be filled by God, while in his early work *On the Nature and Dignity of Love*, William begins from a doctrinal view of the trinitarian image in humanity.

The name of David Bell needs no introduction to students of William of Saint-Thierry, since his book *The Image and Likeness: The Augustinian Spirituality of William of Saint Thierry* (Cistercian Publications, 1984) is justly admired as one of the classic modern works on William. In this essay, Bell provides a detailed study and a new translation of one of William's early works, the *Oratio*, a brief prayer (ca. 1122) that Bell convincingly argues is an abortive *meditatio* on pure, or imageless, prayer. Despite its brevity and perhaps unfinished character, the *Oratio* demonstrates one of the important differences between William and his Cistercian contemporaries, such as Bernard and Aelred: his commitment to apophatic theology, perhaps shared only by Isaac of Stella among the other early Cistercians.

Mark DelCogliano's contribution, "A Fresh Look at William of Saint-Thierry's *Excerpts from the Books of the Blessed Ambrose on the Song of Songs*," deals with how William made use of the patristic tradition, specifically in his reading of the Songs of Songs, the *Magna Carta* of Western mysticism. DelCogliano's meticulous and illuminating study is a major addition to the study of the foundations of William's mysticism, as well as being a good illustration of the abbot's exegetical ingenuity. DelCogliano demonstrates how William mostly adheres to Ambrose's texts dealing with the Song, though with significant editorial adjustments, while employing the bishop of Milan's readings as preparation for his own subsequent brilliant interpretation of the biblical book of love in his *Expositio super Cantica Canticorum* of ca. 1135–1138.

The themes of descent, humility, and even humiliation are analyzed in Rose Marie Tillisch's piece on "Humility and Humiliation in William of Saint-Thierry's *Expositio* and Bernard of Clairvaux's Sermons on the Song of Songs." This ambitious comparative essay is both doctrinal and exegetical, showing how Bernard and William made use of texts from the Old Testament (especially Song 1:12) and from the New (Luke 7:36-50; Phil 2:7-8) to construct different, but complementary, understandings of the role of humility and humiliation in the road to salvation. The philological details of this perceptive reading cannot be given here. Suffice it to say that Tillisch's essay is a model for showing the role of comparative exegesis in the history of theology.

The essay of Aage Rydstrøm-Poulsen is especially fitting for this volume because it takes up one of the central themes of Rozanne Elder's work on William, namely, his Christology. Expressing his indebtedness to Elder's 1972 dissertation and subsequent publications, Rydstrøm-Poulsen pushes her argument further by stressing the centrality of the humble descent of the Eternal Word into human nature and the corresponding recognition of our need for humility, something often neglected in studies of William's theology of the stages of the soul's ascent to God. As he summarizes, "According to William the gift of divine love and knowledge of God to humans also means a descent or a humbling of the human."

As Sister Benedicta Ward shows in her essay, "Western Darkness/Eastern Light: William of Saint Thierry and the Traditions of Egypt," there is a certain paradox in the appeals made by William and Bernard to the traditions of the ancient fathers of the desert. As coenobitical monks, the early Cistercians did not imitate the eremitical lifestyle of Antony, Macarius, and the other heroes of the first monasticism, nor did they really know that much about them. The sources for their "ideal of the desert" were Cassian and Athanasius's *Life of Antony*, not the *Sayings of the Fathers*, and their form of imitation was more internal than external. Oddly enough, it was Abelard, whom Bernard and William thought a failed monk at best, who really knew a good deal about the early monks of the desert, as is revealed in his correspondence with Heloise.

Two essays concern the relation of William as biographer-hagiographer to his friend Bernard as seen in the *Vita prima Bernardi*, the work that William left unfinished at his death in 1147. James France presents a study of illustrations taken from the *Vita prima* in his "Bernard Made a Covenant with His Eyes: The Saint and His Biographer, William of Saint-Thierry." The only two known medieval portraits of William are both found in initials at the beginning of manuscripts of the *Vita prima*, showing him along with his subject and friend, Bernard. The *Life* was also the source for many medieval and early modern portrayals of Bernard, as James shows on the basis of illustrations of Bernard's "chastity stories" found in two early sixteenth-century stained-glass programs from Germany.

Marjory Lange provides an insightful analysis of William's rhetorical skill as a hagiographer, or "sacred biographer," in her piece entitled "Mediating a Presence: Rhetorical and Narrative Strategies in the *Vita Prima Bernardi*." After a review of recent discussion of the meaning of the *Vita prima*, including the contributions of Rozanne Elder, Lange analyzes three rhetorical strategies William uses in presenting his picture of Bernard: (1) tactical use of contrasts, (2) gathering together similar events such as miracles in a nonchronological way to heighten their effect, and (3) including himself in the story, so that "William becomes his own rhetorical device" for mediating the meaning of the saint. In short, Lange's essay demonstrates that "William has made Bernard live, as man and as saint, through the strategies he has selected and molded so masterfully."

F. Tyler Sergent's essay on *"Unitas Spiritus* and the Originality of William of Saint-Thierry" provides a survey of one of the key terms of medieval mysticism, *unitas spiritus,* a phrase found in the Vulgate version of Ephesians 4:3 (*soliciti servare unitatem spiritus in vinculo pacis*). Sergent demonstrates that the patristic and early medieval Latin readings of this verse fall into three categories: (1) an interpretation concerning the unity of the Trinity; (2) a reading indicating the union of believers in the Body of Christ; and (3) a mystical reading dealing with the union of Christ and the soul. This last, apparently first found in William and Guerric of Igny, appears to have been created by linking the Ephesians text with 1 Corinthians 6:17 (*qui autem adhaeret Domino, unus spiritus est*). The phrase, as Sergent points out, expresses William's view of deification.

This rich collection of stimulating essays proves that William studies are alive and well in the early years of the twenty-first century, not least because of the teaching, writing, editing, and mentoring of E. Rozanne Elder, to whom this volume is dedicated by her grateful friends, colleagues, and former students. *Ad multos annos!*

Acknowledgments

The editors thank all those who responded enthusiastically to the invitation to create a book honoring Rozanne Elder for all she has done for medieval and Cistercian scholarship, and to Liturgical Press and Cistercian Publications for the enthusiastic decision to publish this volume. It is entirely fitting that the press that Rozanne led so effectively for so many years, almost single-handedly bringing Cistercian authors and thought from the margins of contemporary scholarship into the center, should be the home for this book that celebrates her many distinguished achievements. We also want to acknowledge all those who generously gave papers in Rozanne's honor at the Cistercian Studies Conference of 2009 and those who revised their papers for inclusion in a 2011 issue of *Cistercian Studies Quarterly*, dedicated to Rozanne by the kind permission of its editor, Dom Mark Scott, OCSO.

Many others have assisted with the physical and intellectual work necessary to create the book, and we thank them in particular: José António Brandão, Barbara Duncan, James France, Barbara Grueser, Elizabeth A. Kilburn, Kourtney Kline, Karen McDougall, Daphne Metts, David Smith, Susan Steuer, and Lorraine Wochna. In addition to these people, we thank the Interlibrary Loan Service at Berea College, the office of the Vice President for Research at Ohio University, OhioLink, and Ohio University's Interlibrary Loan Department, all of which made it possible for us to pursue editorial and authorial accuracy.

Finally, and above all, we three thank Rozanne Elder for all she has given each of us individually and communally. When Aage Rydstrøm-Poulsen proposed this project to recognize all that Rozanne has done for so many, he invited Tyler Sergent and Marsha Dutton to join him in accomplishing it. Tyler and Marsha were both honored and grateful at the opportunity, recognizing the way her support has helped to build our careers and valuing her long friendship. With this book we express our gratitude and our admiration for her and her work. May it convey in some small but significant way all that she has done and continues to do and the honor and gratitude due her.

LETTERS OF APPRECIATION

Dom Brendan Freeman, OCSO

No one is taught how to be a leader or administrator on entering a monastery. Rather, each new monk or nun is taught the values of humility, obedience, silence, and how to get along with others. So when I was elected abbot of New Melleray in 1984, I was ill equipped for the demands of the job—the learning curve was going to be steep. The US Regional meeting that year for the seventeen superiors of the Trappist and Trappistine monasteries was held at Gethsemani Abbey; to my surprise I was told that I would be on the board of Cistercian Publications. New Melleray, they told me, was the closest monastery to Western Michigan University, the headquarters of the Medieval Congress, the Institute of Cistercian Studies, and Cistercian Publications. In the communal mind this fact qualified me for the position—the learning curve got steeper.

My first board meeting was held in Kalamazoo, Michigan, in May 1984. Assembled for the meeting were some of the giants of Cistercian scholarship. My contribution to this meeting was to announce the time for the coffee break! After the meeting we would stay for the Cistercian section of the Congress. This event was then and still is organized by Dr. Rozanne Elder. There is nothing comparable to it, with something like forty-five papers given by scholars from around the world on every conceivable topic related to Cistercian monastic life. Many of these scholars, either before or after the Congress, would travel to various monasteries to lecture. Because of Rozanne, all of the monasteries in our region have profited from hearing some of the most renowned scholars in Cistercian studies.

Rozanne's contribution to Cistercian life is ongoing and profound. I believe she has visited all seventeen of our houses lecturing on William of Saint-Thierry. Every year she organizes and directs the Cistercian conference mentioned above. But her most profound contribution has come from her many years as editorial director of Cistercian Publications. This last is the greatest of all. Symposiums may cease, boards will change, but books endure. For us Cistercians, having access to our fathers in English translation was like opening the eyes of the blind. It is no exaggeration to say that those of us who entered before these works were available were blind to the richness of our spirituality. Thanks to Rozanne, a whole new world became visible to us. She and other scholars gave us a way to be formed by our heritage. We could find our experiences explained and verified in these books; it was like walking in the gardens, the meadows, and the fountains of delight. We could for once breathe in the pure air of our Cistercian heritage.

The garden of paradise is still growing; the music is still playing. New people are joining our monasteries, and they too will be taught to be humble and obedient and silent and how to be agreeable to their brothers and sisters, but their inspiration will come not from the *Spiritual Directory* or the *Book of Regulations* or Francis de Sales but instead from Saints Bernard and Aelred and William. We hope that they will be as bedazzled as many of us were on first doing *lectio* with these sacred texts and will learn humility by understanding to what a great vocation God has called us.

Thanks to Rozanne and scholars like her we can with the people in Psalm 149 "rejoice in their glory."

Fr. Luke Anderson, OCist

Faith seeking any understanding of the Cistercian charism greatly profits from serious, solid, and sustained scholarship. A mere glance at Dr. Rozanne Elder's resumé clearly manifests her tastes and talents as a fine and finished scholar. A long and faithful labor in fostering a fruitful understanding of Cistercian authors and their twelfth-century ambiance has been her inestimable scholarly benefit to many.

Three distinct audiences have profited from the scholarly prowess of Dr. Elder's industry. First, monks and nuns of the Cistercian Orders can now confirm, question, or correct their uses of their primary Latin sources. In the second place, lay men and women, some of whom are consecrated oblates in the Orders, have been given easy access to the treasures of Cistercian texts hitherto hidden from their use. Finally, academics, dedicated to teaching medieval studies, can direct students to primary sources in English translations otherwise unavailable.

Dr. Elder's initial approach to Cistercian study was her literary and theological examination of the works of William of Saint-Thierry. This led her, rather inevitably, to wider and deeper study of the Cistercian charism. In turn, she came to better understand and fondly appreciate the dogma and spirituality of this singularly vital school of twelfth-century Christianity.

With this admirable foundation, Dr. Elder became the longtime editorial director of Cistercian Publications. To this office she brought a panoply of talents: Latin competence, a discerning flair for distinguished and exact English, a keen and incisive but always kindly critical sense, and a meticulous, even scrupulous, respect for accuracy and intellectual honesty. Her vocation as an engaged professor honed her talents and fitted her well for her editorial tasks. Her intellectual gifts have brought Cistercian Studies to a high level of renewed intelligibility.

Dr. Elder has added to her mind a virtue especially dear to Cistercians, humility. Since humility is radically truth, this virtue enhances her mental acumen. On the one hand, Dr. Elder is deft to critique, to correct, or to reject scholarly foibles. On the other hand, with sensitive and gentle persuasion, she is able to inspire and encourage fledgling efforts at ever bettering mind and spirit.

Cistercian monks and nuns, devout friends of the Orders, and many medievalists have been greatly enriched by Dr. Elder's monumental labors. She fully merits our gratitude and our profound admiration.

ABBREVIATIONS

ca.	circa, about
CE	Common Era
cf.	compare
chap(s).	chapter(s)
cod.	codex
CP	Cistercian Publications
d.	died
diss.	dissertation
ed.	edited by; editor; edition
e.g.	*exempli gratia*, for example
Ep(p)	*Epistol(ae)*, Letter(s)
esp.	especially
et al.	*et alia*
fig.	figure
fol(s).	folio(s)
i.e.	*id est*, that is
Lat	Latin
MA	Master of Arts
MS	Manuscript
OCist	Cistercian Order of the Common Observance
OCSO	Cistercian Order of the Strict Observance
Pr(a)ef.	*Pr(a)efatio*, preface
Prol.	*Prologus*, prologue
r.	recto
SLG	Sisters of the Love of God

S(s)	*Sermo(nes)*, Sermon(s)
UK	United Kingdom
v.	verso
Vlg	Vulgate
WMU	Western Michigan University

The Works of William of Saint-Thierry

Editions and translations of William's works are listed in the Bibliography of William's Works, below, p. 185.

Adv Abl	*Disputatio adversus Petrum Abælardum*
Ænig	*Ænigma fidei*
Brev com	*Brevis commentatio*
Cant	*Expositio super Cantica Canticorum*
Cant Amb	*Excerpta ex libris sancti Ambrosii super Cantica Canticorum*
Cant Greg	*Excerpta ex libris sancti Gregorii super Cantica Canticorum*
Contem	*De contemplando Deo*
Ep frat	*Epistola [aurea] ad fratres de Monte Dei*
Exp ps	*Expositio psalmi*
Exp Rm	*Expositio in epistolam Pauli ad Romanos*
Med	*Meditativæ orationes*
Nat am	*De natura et dignitate amoris*
Orat	*Oratio domni Willelmi*
Sac alta	*De sacramento altari liber*
Spec fid	*Speculum fidei*
Vita Bern	*Sancti Bernardi vita prima*

Periodicals and Series

AC/ASOC	*Analecta Cisterciensia; Analecta Sacri Ordinis Cisterciensis*
CCCM	Corpus Christianorum, Continuatio Mediaevalis
CCSL	Corpus Christianorum, Series Latina

CF	Cistercian Fathers
Cîteaux	*Cîteaux: Commentarii Cistercienses; Cîteaux in de Nederlanden*
Coll	*Collectanea cisterciensia; Collectanea o.c.r.*
CS	Cistercian Studies
CSEL	Corpus Scriptorum Ecclesiasticorum Latinorum
CSQ	*Cistercian Studies / Cistercian Studies Quarterly*
NPNF	Nicene and Post-Nicene Fathers
PL	J.-P. Migne, Patrologiae cursus completus, series latina
RBen	*Revue Bénédictine*
RTAM	*Recherches de théologie ancienne et médiévale*
SBOp	Sancti Bernardi Opera
SChr	Sources Chrétiennes
S.J.	Society of Jesus
SSOC	Series Scriptorum Sacri Ordinis Cisterciensis

The Works of Augustine of Hippo

C acad	*Contra academicos*
Civ Dei	*De civitate Dei*
En in Ps	*Ennarationes in Psalmos*
Trin	*De trinitate*

The Works of Bernard of Clairvaux

Dil	*Liber de diligendo Deo*
Div	*Sermones de diversis*
SC	*Sermones super Cantica canticorum*

Introduction

When the will mounts on high, like fire going up to its place,
that is to say, when it unites with truth and tends toward
higher things, it is amor. When it is fed with the milk of grace
in order to make progress, it is dilectio; when it lays hold of
its object and keeps it in its grasp and has enjoyment of it, it
is caritas, it is unity of spirit, it is God, for God is caritas.[1]

With these words, the twelfth-century Cistercian William of
Saint-Thierry articulates a core element of his spirituality,
which has brought him increasing scholarly attention and admiration over the past forty years. Throughout his works, William
intimately links God's humanity with the development of the
human will, showing the human being finally able to approach so
closely to God as to become one with God, joined in unity of spirit.

Fifteen years have passed since the publication of the most recent
of the three previous English books centrally concerned with William, *Signy l'abbaye et Guillaume de Saint-Thierry*, and seventeen
since the colloquium that produced the papers published in that
volume. During that time, however, the international pace of William studies has increased rather than slowed. As Bernard McGinn
notes in his foreword to this volume, throughout the twentieth
century and now well into the second decade of the twenty-first,
numerous editions, translations, and studies of William and his
works have appeared, including at least eleven doctoral dissertations,
with each new publication deepening scholarly awareness and
knowledge of William's thought.

[1] William, Ep frat 235 (CCCM 88:276; CF 12:88).

A Biographical Overview

The basic chronology of what is known today of William's early life comes from the only surviving fragment of a late twelfth-century work known as the *Vita antiqua*, written by an unknown writer—probably a monk at Signy, where William spent the last thirteen years of his life—recording what he had been told by someone who knew William.[2] William's own treatises (especially his life of Bernard of Clairvaux, the first book of the *Vita prima sancti Bernardi*) provide additional information for the story. William was probably born around 1080 in the northern French town of Liège, now in Belgium.[3] After studying at Reims or perhaps, though less likely, at Laon, he became a Benedictine monk at Saint Nicaise, in Reims, sometime between 1111 and 1118. In 1118 or 1119, while returning from a trip to the south of France, William and his abbot

---

[2] For what remains of the *Vita antiqua*, see Albert Poncelet, "Vie ancienne de Saint-Thierry," in *Mélanges Godefroid Kurth* (Liège: Vaillant-Carmanne, 1908), 1:85–96. The work was edited and translated into French with helpful notes by Freddy LeBrun, "*Vita Antiqua Willelmi Sancti Theoderici* d'après le manuscrit 11782 de la Bibliothèque Nationale de Paris," in *Signy l'abbaye et Guillaume de Saint-Thierry*, ed. Nicole Boucher (Signy: Association des Amis de l'Abbaye de Signy, 2000), 437–59 (hereafter *Signy l'abbaye*). See also Paul Verdeyen, *Guillaume de Saint-Thierry, premier auteur mystique des anciens Pays-Bas* (Turnout: Brepols, 2000), 137–52 (hereafter Verdeyen, *Premier auteur*). An introduction to the work and an English translation appear in David N. Bell, "The Vita Antiqua of William of St. Thierry," CSQ 11 (1976): 246–55. For helpful reconstructions of William's early life and discussion of the sources, see Verdeyen, *Premier auteur*, 9–63, and Stanislaus Ceglar, "William of Saint Thierry: The Chronology of His Life with a Study of His Treatise *On the Nature of Love*, his Authorship of the *Brevis Commentatio*, the *In Lacu*, and the *Reply to Cardinal Matthew*," PhD dissertation, Washington, DC: The Catholic University of America, 1971; Ludo Milis, "William of Saint Thierry, His Birth, His Formation and His First Monastic Experiences," in *William, Abbot of St. Thierry: A Colloquium at the Abbey of St. Thierry*, trans. Jerry Carfantan, CS 94 (Kalamazoo, MI: Cistercian Publications, 1987), 9–33 (hereafter *William*); John Anderson, Introduction to *William of Saint Thierry, The Enigma of Faith*, CF 9 (Kalamazoo, MI, and Spencer, MA: Cistercian Publications, 1973), 1–31, here 1–7.

[3] For a brief overview of William's possible dates of birth, see Anderson, Introduction, 2; for a more detailed discussion, see Milis, "William," 16–20.

stopped over at the young Cistercian abbey of Clairvaux, where they met its abbot, Bernard.

That meeting transformed William's life. Recollecting it years later, William wrote of the immediate effect on him of Bernard's presence: "Had a choice been offered me that day, I would have wished for nothing so much as to remain there with him and serve him always."[4] Of the consequences of that encounter, Paul Verdeyen says, "The meeting of Bernard and William can be considered as the beginning of a great friendship, to which they remained faithful throughout their lives."[5] Indeed, that friendship shaped much of the rest of William's spiritual and intellectual life while pushing Bernard in new directions and helping to preserve and define his historical memory.

Although William returned to Saint Nicaise rather than staying at Clairvaux, his initial impulse remained. While obeying Bernard's refusal to let him leave the Benedictines for Clairvaux, through the remaining thirty years of his life William looked to Bernard as a model of monastic life and contemplative prayer and remained in close contact with him. In 1125, after William urged Bernard to defend Cistercian monasticism, Bernard wrote the *Apologia ad Guillelmum Sancti Theodorici*. In addition to William's occasional brief visits to Clairvaux, in the mid-1120s, when he and Bernard were both ill, the two of them spent a few months together in the infirmary at Clairvaux, with Bernard visiting William's bedside when his own illness had subsided.[6] In between such personal encoun-

---

[4] Vita Bern 33 (CCCM 89B:58–59; PL 185:246CD; William of Saint-Thierry, *Bernard of Clairvaux: Early Biographies, Vol. I by William of St. Thierry*, trans. Martinus Cawley, Centennial Edition: 1090–1990, Guadalupe Translations [Lafayette, OR: Abbey of Our Lady of Guadalupe, 1990], 44 [hereafter Cawley, *Bernard*]).

[5] Paul Verdeyen, "Guillaume de Saint-Thierry Liège (Belgique), 1075—Signy l'Abbaye (Ardennes), 1148," in *Signy l'abbaye*, 409–10, here 409.

[6] Vita Bern 1.33 (CCCM 89B:58–59); Vita Bern 1.12 (CCCM 89B:74–75). Scholars do not agree on the date of this shared convalescence; Jacques Hourlier suggests after 1124 (*Guillaume de Saint-Thierry, La contemplation de Dieu, L'Oraison de Dom Guillaume*, ed. and trans. Jacques Hourlier, SCh 61 *bis* [Paris: Les Éditions du Cerf, 1959; rev. ed., 1977; corrected ed., 1999, 2005], 18), while Ceglar settles on 1119–1120 ("William," 51–52).

ters, the two men corresponded, with William at least twice appealing to Bernard to express opposition to theological teaching that he judged dangerously unorthodox. Finally, he devoted the last two or three years of his life to memorializing Bernard in the *Vita prima Sancti Bernardi*.

In 1119 or 1120, the monks of the monastery of Saint-Thierry, on a bluff above Reims, elected William their abbot. There he remained until 1135, writing, participating in theological controversy, and working for Benedictine reform.[7] Unfortunately, none of his personal letters survive. But scholars have speculated that some of this story—specifically his longing to move to Clairvaux and Bernard's refusal—appears in his treatises. In notes to an English translation of William's *Meditationes*, Sister Penelope Lawson explicates the eleventh *Meditatio* as a transparent exploration of the conflict between William's wish and Bernard's refusal.[8] Happily, three or four letters from Bernard to William are extant, one of which supports the narrative of William's requests and Bernard's opposition to them.[9] What is particularly clear in these letters is William's growing desire to enter Clairvaux and Bernard's consistent refusal. In one letter Bernard advises, "I say hold on to what you have got, remain where you are, and try to benefit those over whom you rule. Do not try to escape the responsibility of your office while you are still able to discharge it for the benefit of your subjects. Woe

[7] For William's leading role in bringing about general chapters of Benedictine abbots, see Stanislaus Ceglar, "William of Saint Thierry and His Leading Role at the First Chapters of the Benedictine Abbots (Reims 1131, Soissons 1132)," in *William*, 34–112. This article includes critical editions of the documents from the first such chapter, including William's *Responsio Abbatum*.

[8] "On Contemplating God," in William of St. Thierry, *On Contemplating God, Prayer, Meditations*, trans. Sr. Penelope [Lawson], CF 3 (Kalamazoo, MI: Cistercian Publications, 1977), 156–66nn12, 22, 26, 27, 32, 37, 38, 55, 88, and 91. N12 reads in part, "Here begins a certain amount of autobiography which William has woven into this *Eleventh Meditation*."

[9] Epp 84 *bis*, 85, 86, and 327 in Bernard, *Epistolae*, ed. Jean Leclercq and H. M. Rochais, SBOp 7–8 (Rome: Editiones Cistercienses, 1974, 1977) (SBOp 7:219–24, 8:263; Letters 87, 88, 89, and 236 in *The Letters of St. Bernard of Clairvaux*, trans. Bruno Scott James [London: Burns and Oates, 1953], 124–29, 314–15).

to you if you rule them and do not benefit them, but far greater woe to you if you refuse to benefit them because you shirk the burdens of ruling them."[10]

In 1135 William finally achieved his wish to become a Cistercian, though not at Clairvaux. Instead, accompanied by his sub-prior from Saint-Thierry, he made simple profession at the new Cistercian abbey of Signy, thirty-one miles northeast of Saint-Thierry and one hundred eighty-five miles north of Clairvaux. Although the *Vita Antiqua* reports that the monks at Saint-Thierry, assisted by Renaud, archbishop of Reims, strenuously sought William's return, through prayer and God's grace William persevered at Signy, helping to build that young foundation by means of his own learning, experience, and appreciation for the rigorous peace of Cistercian life.[11] He spent his final years there, dying on September 8, 1148, five years before Bernard. He was buried in the monastery cloister, close to the chapter room. His reputation endured, however, and on January 12, 1215, the monks of Signy translated his relics to a shrine in an arcade cut into the wall of the cloister.[12]

William's Works

Unlike the other great Cistercian writers of the twelfth century, William left no body of sermons. Throughout his years as a monk at Saint Nicaise, Saint-Thierry, and Signy, he wrote eighteen works of spirituality, polemics, exegesis, and hagiography as well as five surviving letters. In the letter prefacing *Epistola ad fratres de Monte Dei*, he left a list of those works, with the theme of monastic life and understanding running through them.[13] He first wrote to instruct members of his community at Saint-Thierry, offering them direction

---

[10] Ep 86.2 (SBOp 7:224; #88 in James, *Letters*, 128).

[11] *Vita antiqua* 5–6 (LeBrun, "*Vita Antiqua Willelmi*," 448–51; Bell, "The Vita Antiqua," 249–50).

[12] Verdeyen, "Guillaume," 410.

[13] William, Ep frat Pref. 7–13 (CCCM 88:226–27; CF 12:5–7); the *Vita antiqua* lists most of William's works, probably, LeBrun guesses, those in the library at Signy (*Vita antiqua* 10 [LeBrun, "*Vita Antiqua*," 452–55; Bell, "The Vita Antiqua," 251–53]).

as they sought to know and love God. He continued to write for the novices there—and in part, no doubt, for himself—until the end of his abbacy, with his first two treatises, *De contemplando Deo* and *De natura et dignitate amoris*, appearing between 1119 and 1122.[14]

In the early 1120s, initially as a private response to public controversy, William turned briefly to doctrinal argumentation. One traditional view of the nature of Christ's real presence in the Eucharist explained it as union between Christ and the substance of the bread analogous to Christ's taking on human substance in the incarnation. Although this explanation was an old one, some theologians of the time saw it as a theological novelty when expressed in the *De divinis officiis* of William's compatriot and near contemporary, Benedictine theologian Rupert of Deutz (d. ca. 1129). Between 1120 and 1125, perhaps out of concern not only for Rupert's understanding but also for his reputation, William wrote Rupert a letter on the subject, explaining to him the difficulties of some aspects of his argument and specifically the misunderstandings that might result from his phrasing. As Jean Châtillon has noted, in this first instance of three theological interventions, William wrote directly and irenically to Rupert rather than either joining or initiating a public controversy.[15] At about the same time as writing the letter, however—in 1122–1123—William also wrote his formal treatise *De sacramento altaris* in opposition to Rupert's theological positions. This work provides the earliest treatise on sacramental theology by twelfth-century Cistercian writers.

---

[14] The dating of William's works in this summary depends on Paul Verdeyen's Introduction to *Expositio super epistolam ad Romanos*, CCCM 86 (Turnhout: Brepols, 1989), v–xxxi; and on *De sacramento altaris*, see John van Engen, "Rupert of Deutz and William of St. Thierry," *Revue Bénédictine* 93 (1983): 327–36. See also Jacques Hourlier, Introduction to William of Saint-Thierry, *On Contemplating God, Prayer, Meditations*, CF 3 (Spencer, MA: Cistercian Publications, 1971; Kalamazoo, MI: Cistercian Publications, 1977), 11–13; André Wilmart, "La série et la date des ouvrages de Guillaume de Saint-Thierry," *Revue Mabillon* 14 (1924): 157–67.

[15] See Jean Châtillon, "William of Saint Thierry, Monasticism, and the Schools: Rupert of Deutz, Abelard, and William of Conches," in *William*, 153–80, esp. 160–69.

As abbot of a reforming Benedictine monastery, William was instrumental in organizing the first general chapter of the Benedictine abbots in the diocese of Reims in 1131, possibly even hosting the first chapter at Saint-Thierry. The efforts of William and his colleagues were not universally appreciated, and Cardinal Matthew of Albano, papal legate in France, reacted harshly.[16] For the second general chapter at Soissons in 1132, possibly before the chapter met, William penned the *Responsio abbatum* to Cardinal Matthew.[17] The *Responsio* seems not only to have fulfilled its aim of justifying the abbots' reforms but also to have garnered even greater support.

After this brief excursion into controversy, William returned to writing on contemplation and the love of God. Probably between 1128 and 1132 he wrote what would become a series of *Meditationes*, intended for his novices. In the *Golden Epistle*, he dismissed these works ironically as *Meditative Prayers, not entirely useless for forming the minds of novices for praying.*[18] One manuscript of the *Meditationes* also includes a brief prayer generally known as the *Oratio Domni Willelmi*, which Jacques Hourlier dates to about 1122, though David N. Bell judges that date "perhaps . . . a little too specific."[19] During the same period, between 1125 and 1135, William began to explore the Song of Songs and its dramatization of the mutual love between God and the soul. Perhaps considering himself not yet prepared to explore this great work of love poems on his own, he drafted the *Brevis commentatio*, probably consisting of notes drawn from his conversations with Bernard during their shared convalescence,

---

[16] For Cardinal Matthew's letter, see "Responsio abbatum auctore Willelmo abbate sancti Theodorici," in *Guillelmi a Sancto Theodorico Opera Omnia, IV*, ed. Paul Verdeyen, CCCM 89:93–102.

[17] "Responsio abbatum auctore Willelmo abbate Sancti Theodorici," in *Guillelmi a Sancto Theodorico Opera Omnia, IV*, ed. Paul Verdeyen, CCCM 89:103–11.

[18] *Meditationes novitiis ad orandum formandis spiritibus non usquequaque inutiles* (CCCM 88:226; CF 12:6).

[19] Jacques Hourlier, Introduction to William of Saint Thierry, *On Contemplating God, Prayer, Meditations*, trans. Sr. Penelope [Lawson], CF 3 (Spencer, MA, and Kalamazoo, MI: Cistercian Publications, 1977), 77–86, here 83–86; for Bell's comment, see his chapter below (p. 22).

and then composed *florilegia* from the works of two patristic writers, Saint Ambrose of Milan (340–397) and Saint Gregory the Great (540–604).

In the first years after William entered the young abbey of Signy in 1135, he turned his thoughts for a while from contemplative prayer to theology and biblical exegesis. Thus his first two works as a Cistercian explored the relationship between human free will and God's grace. In 1137, he wrote the biblically grounded *Expositio super Epistolam ad Romanos* and later *De natura corporis et animae*, the latter work incorporating not only patristic theology but also recent Arabic studies.[20]

At about the same time, William returned to the Song of Songs, finally beginning his own commentary—*Expositio super Cantica Canticorum*—ten years after his first attempts on the subject. Although he was never to complete what he may have conceived as his grand *opus*, at his death he left four treatises devoted to this work so central to twelfth-century Cistercian spiritual thought.

But even as William was beginning to write his commentary on the Song, he became troubled by the influence of the teaching of Peter Abelard on young men entering Signy. He thus put aside the commentary for what he surely hoped would be only a time, first to read Abelard carefully and then to write to Bernard and to Geoffrey of Lèves, the bishop of Chartres, about the theological errors he had found in Abelard's works and the danger they posed to the faith. Two years later, in 1140, after writing his *Disputatio adversus Petrum Abelardum* and addressing it to Bernard, he had the satisfaction of seeing Abelard's works condemned at Sens, and then in 1142—the year in which Abelard died—seeing those works publicly burned and Abelard himself condemned.[21] A year later, still troubled

---

[20] See Bernard McGinn, Introduction to *Three Treatises on Man: A Cistercian Anthropology*, ed. Bernard McGinn, CF 24 (Kalamazoo, MI: Cistercian Publications, 1977), 1–100, here 30–47.

[21] For a brief yet substantive summary and analysis of William's involvement with Abelard's theology, see E. Rozanne Elder, Introduction to William of St. Thierry, *The Mirror of Faith*, CF 15 (Kalamazoo, MI: Cistercian Publications, 1979), xi–xxxi, here xiii–xv.

by intellectual errors threatening young monks, William wrote another cautionary letter to Bernard, now attacking the teaching of William of Conches in the *Epistola de erroribus Guillelmi de Conchis*.

That letter was William's last polemical work. In the next few years he turned from attacking theological error to writing orthodox treatises of his own. In three doctrinal works written between 1142 and 1144, he instructed the monks of Signy, first in the now-lost *Sententiae de Fide* and then in *Speculum Fidei* and *Ænigma Fidei*.

Perhaps exhausted by these intellectual endeavors just when he had expected finally to be at peace for contemplative prayer, William spent a few months at the Charterhouse of Mont-Dieu, about thirty miles southeast of Signy. When he returned home, as a gift of thanks to his Carthusian hosts, he composed one of his most powerful works, the *Epistola ad fratres de Monte Dei*, which the great monastic editor Jean Mabillon retitled *Epistola aurea*. This work, directed to the novices at Mont-Dieu, began by linking the Carthusians to the spiritual traditions of the desert fathers, in whose spiritual fervor William perceived an early Christian antecedent for the way of life being lived at Mont-Dieu.

Between 1145 and 1147, apparently at the request of Geoffrey of Auxerre, who knew of the close friendship between Bernard and William, William began to record his knowledge of the man whom he had admired for so many years and through whom he himself had come to be a Cistercian. Although Arnold of Bonneval and Geoffrey himself later supplemented William's *Vita prima* with their own narratives of Bernard's life, William's ability to provide a clear and often candid vision of Bernard in all his humanity while also conveying his clear insight that Bernard was truly a man of God makes his work the central source for knowing Bernard.[22] The *Vita prima* is not only an intimate portrait of Bernard, however, but also a source of knowledge about William's own life.

---

[22] For an analysis of William's human portrait of the saintly Bernard in *Vita prima*, see E. Rozanne Elder, "Making Virtues of Vexing Habits," in *Studiosorum Speculum: Studies in Honor of Louis J. Lekai, O. Cist*, ed. Francis Swietek and John R. Sommerfeldt, CS 141 (Kalamazoo, MI: Cistercian Publications, 1993), 75–94.

For William's lifelong friendship with Bernard affected William's life as much as his theological training in the schools. William reveals that friendship in every sentence of the *Vita prima*, and Bernard reciprocates in his letters. In fact, their mutual attachment occasionally rose to a competition, as Bernard acknowledged in a letter:

> You may be right when you say that my affection for you is less than yours is for me, but I am certainly certain that you cannot be certain. . . . But . . . although you love more than I do, you do not love more than you are able. And I too, although I love you less than I should, yet I love you as much as I can according to the power that has been given me. Draw me after you that I may reach you and with you receive more fully whence comes the power of love.[23]

Would William have been the same man had he never met Bernard? Well, no. And of course, yes. Their meeting in 1118 changed both of their lives, but probably William's more than Bernard's. In that transformative moment, William recognized the spiritual figure he was to emulate for the rest of his life, and his final coming to rest as a simple monk at Signy resulted directly from Bernard's influence. At the same time, William's sharp intellect, academic training, and profound spiritual desire—all prominent in his writings— would certainly have flourished even without Bernard's influence. William was blessed by knowing Bernard and learning from him (and vice versa), but William's theological insight and passion and his works of spiritual guidance would have been equally powerful and influential even had he been deprived of that blessing.

A Brief Historiography

The last two decades of the twentieth century saw the publication of three books in English focusing on William's life and thought.[24]

---

[23] Bernard, Ep 85:1, 4 (SBOp 7:220, 222; James, #88, *Letters*, 125, 127).

[24] These three were preceded by J. M. Déchanet's two books, which contributed significantly to bringing scholarly attention to William: *Guillaume de*

The first of these and the only monograph is David N. Bell's *The Image and Likeness: The Augustinian Spirituality of William of Saint Thierry*, published in 1984. This study, whose incisive discussion of the origins and development of William's thought make it essential for understanding William, shows not only how firmly grounded he was in Augustinian thought but also the ways in which his spiritual experience transformed what he had learned from Augustine. As Bell explains, that transformation is the core of William's spiritual understanding and helps to explain what William brought to Cistercian monasticism: "His spirituality is Augustinian in the sense that it is founded on precisely the same principles as Augustine's own spirituality—the image, likeness, love, and participation. . . . The *via mystica* of Augustine is the *via caritatis*, and the *via caritatis* is also the *via cisterciensis*."[25]

The other two books—*William, Abbot of St. Thierry* (1987) and *Signy l'abbaye et Guillaume de Saint-Thierry* (2000)—emerged from colloquia held in France and contained papers originally delivered there. Most of the contributors in both cases were European scholars. *William, Abbot of St. Thierry* contains ten chapters that offer a useful exploration of William's life and career, especially from before he entered Signy, as well as a bibliography of his works and studies of those works. It is a helpful introduction to William and to some of the most important early scholars of his thought.

Only the final third of *Signy l'abbaye* directly concerns William; the first two sections examine the monastery of Signy and its site, providing a valuable context for understanding his thirteen years as a Cistercian. The final section begins with two chapters by Paul Verdeyen, one a brief overview of William's life and career and the other a survey of the developments in William scholarship since

---

Saint-Thierry. L'homme et son oeuvre (Bruges: Editions Charles Beyaert, 1942), and *Guillaume de Saint-Thierry: Aux Sources d'une pensée*, Théologie Historique 49 (Paris: Beauchesne, 1978). The earlier book was translated into English in 1972 as *William of St. Thierry: The Man and His Work*, trans. Richard Strachan, CS 10 (Spencer, MA: Cistercian Publications, 1972).

[25] David N. Bell, *The Image and Likeness: The Augustinian Spirituality of William of Saint Thierry*, CS 78 (Kalamazoo, MI: Cistercian Publications, 1984), 254–55.

the earlier colloquium, emphasizing the proliferation of editions and translations of William's works and the predominance of studies about William's spirituality and "témoignage mystique."[26] The following seventeen chapters analyze William's works and influence. E. Rozanne Elder contributed two of those, on William's role in creating the 1131 general chapter of Benedictine abbots and on his Christology.[27] This volume too contains a lengthy bibliography of William, divided into biographical studies, editions, and translations of William's works, and studies of individual works, sources, and influence.

In the fifteen years since *Signy l'abbaye*, all of William's works have become available in critical editions and most in vernacular translations in English, French, Spanish, and Italian, stimulating scholarship in numerous languages. The notable lacuna in this bibliography is a faithful vernacular translation of the entire *Vita Sancti Bernardi*, though the 2015 English translation of a manuscript of Recension B by Fr. Hilary Costello, OCSO, helps to fill that gap.[28] More than fifty studies have appeared in English and numerous European languages, including a number of dissertations and four monographs: a 1998 German volume on the human encounter with God, a 1999 French book on William's eucharistic theology, a 2006 Italian study of William's *Exposition on the Song of Songs*, and a 2009 French consideration of what William's sapiential theology reveals about his life as a monk.[29] Other recent books have also given se-

[26] Paul Verdeyen, "En quoi la connaissance de Guillaume de Saint-Thierry a-t-elle progressé depuis le colloque de 1976?" in *Signy l'abbaye*, 411–13, here 413 (this presentation from the colloquium first appeared in *Revue de sciences religieuses* 73 [1999]: 17–20).

[27] E. Rozanne Elder, "Guillaume de Saint-Thierry et le 'Chapitre Général' bénédictin de 1131," and "Christologie de Guillaume de Saint-Thierry et vie spirituelle," in *Signy l'abbaye*, 487–503, 575–87.

[28] William of Saint-Thierry, Arnold of Bonneval, and Geoffrey of Auxerre, *The First Life of Saint Bernard of Clairvaux*, trans. Hilary Costello, CF 76 (Collegeville, MN: Cistercian Publications, 2015).

[29] Kai G. Sander, *Amplexus. Die Begegnung des Menschen mit dem dreieinen Gott in der Lehre des sel. Wilhelm von Saint Thierry*, Quellen und Studien zur Zisterzienserliteratur 2 (Langwaden [Ger]: Bernardus-Verlag, 1998); Matthieu Rougé,

rious attention to William's thought.[30] A central concern of all of them has been William's spiritual theology, specifically his teaching about *unitas spiritus*.[31]

The importance of that doctrine to William and to his twentieth- and twenty-first-century readers has led the editors of this volume to make the phrase its main title. The growing numbers of publications on William make his growing international importance clear; this book intends not only to broaden knowledge about him but also to honor a person who has contributed significantly to understanding his spiritual teaching: E. Rozanne Elder, professor of history and director of the Center for Cistercian and Monastic Studies at Western Michigan University.

Unity of Spirit: Studies on William of Saint-Thierry in Honor of E. Rozanne Elder

William wrote many of his treatises—seven of eighteen—as a Benedictine, several of them for the guidance of the other monks at Saint-Thierry. Bell emphasizes the link between William's commitment to his community and his own spiritual pilgrimage: "his prime concern was that of an abbot for his monks . . . and of a monk for his soul."[32] Indeed, William's yearning for the contemplative life characterizes most of those early works. William's spiritual and monastic journey also serendipitously mirrored that of

---

Doctrine et expérience de l'eucharistie chez Guillaume de Saint-Thierry, Théologie Historique 111 (Paris: Beauchesne, 1999); Cesare A. Montanari, *"Per figuras amatorias"*: *L'Expositio super Cantica canticorum di Guglielmo di Saint-Thierry. Esegesi et Teologia*, Analecta Gregoriana 297 (Rome: Pontificio Istituto Biblico, 2006); Denis Cazes, *La Théologie Sapientielle de Guillaume de Saint Thierry*, Studia Anselmiana 148 (Rome: Pontificio Ateneo S. Anselmo, 2009).

[30] Aage Rydstrøm-Poulsen, *The Gracious God*: Gratia *in Augustine and the Twelfth Century* (Copenhagen: Akademisk, 2002); Carmen Angela Cvetović, *Seeking the Face of God: The Reception of Augustine in the Mystical Thought of Bernard of Clairvaux and William of St. Thierry* (Turnhout: Brepols, 2012).

[31] See Aage Rydstrøm-Poulsen, "Research on William of Saint-Thierry from 1998 to 2008," *Analecta Cisterciensia* 58 (2008): 158–69, here 169.

[32] Bell, *Image*, 254.

the founders of Cîteaux. Like him, Robert, Alberic, and Stephen Harding had begun as Benedictines and then, drawn by the Spirit and by desire for a more rigorous life of adherence to the Rule of Saint Benedict, came at last to live as Cistercians.

The spiritual longing that led the Founders to the New Monastery, Bernard to Cîteaux and Clairvaux, and William to Signy appears throughout William's works. While his learning and desire for theological orthodoxy emerged in polemical works, for the most part he, like the other Cistercians of his time, sang of the Spirit in works such as *De Contemplando*, *Meditationes*, four treatises on the Song of Songs, the *Epistola Aurea*, and finally the *Vita prima*. His written legacy is thus more obviously unified than that of many other twelfth-century Cistercian writers.

The chapters in this book, arranged roughly in the order in which William wrote his works, explore his spiritual and theological teaching and provide a glimpse of his intellectual range. They also reveal Bernard's influence, with five of the nine explicitly linking the two men. The other four chapters examine specific instances of William's spiritual and theological writing without reference to Bernard. Taken together, then, they provide an overview of William's development as a monk and a writer, his concern for the spiritual and theological understanding of younger monks, the breadth of his reading, and his years of yearning for a life of contemplation.

The intellectual relationship between Bernard and William is the context for Emero Stiegman's examination of William's two earliest works, *De contemplando Deo* and *De natura et dignitate amoris*, written soon after William and Bernard met in 1118 or 1119. These works' appearance beside Bernard's *De diligendo Deo* in the twelfth-century Paris MS. Bibliothèque Mazarine 776, which attributes all three to Bernard, has caused scholars through the centuries to conflate the two men's thought, with André Wilmart only in 1924 distinguishing between their works and crediting *De contemplando Deo* and *De natura et dignitate amoris* to William.[33] At that point the perceived theological identity of the three works began to unravel, but many scholars have still perceived them as expressing essentially similar perspectives.

---

[33] André Wilmart, "La série," 157–67.

Stiegman argues here that the works of the two men reveal "sharply different points of departure" and "different perceptions of what is essential in the mind's discovery of God or in the manner of God's self-revelation, a different reception, then, of religious doctrine itself." By disambiguating the two men's understanding of how humans may know God, Stiegman offers a new insight into the difference between William's Augustinian emphasis on what the soul receives in faith and Bernard's treatment of ordinary human experience as the starting place for faith.

Between 1125 and 1138, William turned to more explicitly contemplative writing, composing his twelve meditative prayers with a compellingly intimate voice. In the Mazarine manuscript, a single leaf immediately after *De Natura et dignitate amoris* holds a brief prayer titled *Oratio Domni Willelmi*, absent from the list of William's works in *Epistola aurea*. David N. Bell identifies this prayer as "an abortive attempt at a *Meditation* that . . . needed elaboration," elaboration subsequently achieved in *Meditationes* 6 and 10. After providing the close textual and theological analysis of the *Oratio* that leads to that conclusion, Bell offers a new English translation of the work, one correcting significant errors in the earlier translation of 1977. Bell's translation is particularly valuable in allowing William's own uninterrupted voice to be heard in this volume alongside those of his explicators.

At about the same time as writing the *Meditationes*, William began to explore the Song of Songs, perhaps inspired by his conversations with Bernard and by Bernard's own sermon-commentary on the work. Mark DelCogliano here explores the prologue to William's Ambrosian *florilegium*, showing how William selected, altered, and used passages from Ambrose's works to focus on the incarnation and the human spiritual pilgrimage. Having previously examined the structure of William's Gregorian *florilegium*, DelCogliano also identifies the significant differences between the two works and examines William's reasons for shaping them so differently.[34]

---

[34] Mark DelCogliano, "The Composition of William of St. Thierry's *Excerpts from the Books of Blessed Gregory on the Song of Songs*," *Cîteaux* 58 (2007): 57–76.

DelCogliano suggests that in the case of the Gregorian *florilegium*, *Excerpta ex libris Beati Gregorii super Cantica Canticorum*, William created "a kind of running Gregorian commentary on the Song of Songs, a commentary whose thought is thoroughly and genuinely Gregorian." But in *Excerpta ex libris Beati Ambrosii super Cantica Canticorum*, DelCogliano shows, William reveals some of his own doctrine by incorporating Ambrose's words in such a way as to interpret the Song as being "principally about the mystery of the incarnation" and to explain "the stages of spiritual advancement that the Song teaches."

By the time in about 1138 that William returned to the Song of Songs and began his own independent commentary on it, he was at last a Cistercian. His friendship with Bernard had continued to grow, enhanced by their correspondence and their time of shared convalescence at Clairvaux. One of the intellectual benefits of that shared time was the opportunity it gave them to compare their readings of Scripture, including the Song of Songs, and to explain their different understandings of ideas central to the faith. Rose Marie Tillisch examines the two men's parallel treatments of Song of Songs 1:12 and two other biblical passages in William's *Expositio super Cantica Canticorum* and in Bernard's Sermon 42 on the Song of Songs.

From a close reading of the two men's explorations of humility "through the lens of their view of Christ as the humble slave, man and God," Tillisch concludes that "while William focuses on Christ as the humiliated one, Bernard focuses on Christ as humility." By comparing William's and Bernard's use of identical biblical passages and written articulation of similar ideas, she teases out the distinctive elements of each one's thought, so illuminating one aspect of their theological understanding while offering new insight into their mutual influence.

But even as William was writing his commentary on the Song of Songs, he began to hear about Abelard. When he read what he believed to be Abelard's works of systematic theology (an edition of the *Theologia scholarium*, authentically Abelard's, and the *Liber sententiarum*, compiled by a student of Abelard), he found himself so concerned about what he saw as their departure from orthodoxy that he determined to take action against them and their author. Abandoning his commentary at Song 3:4, as he explained later in his preface to *Epistola aurea*, he wrote at length to Bernard, asking him to contest Abelard's errors.[35] While the story of Bernard's struggle against Abelard's teachings is a familiar one, Tillisch and Aage Rydstrøm-Poulsen both indirectly suggest that one effect of that struggle was its causing the two Cistercians to rethink, or at least rearticulate, certain aspects of their own theology. William's argument against Abelard in particular spilled over into works conventionally seen as exemplars of spirituality. Tillisch argues that in articulating their different perspectives on humility, William and Bernard were actually protesting what they saw as the lack of humility in Abelard's emphasis on human reason: "Perhaps *humilitas* was thus a common ground, a mediator between reason and affection, a concept important for them to define in their struggle against Abelard's unorthodox thoughts."

Rydstrøm-Poulsen approaches the issue from another angle, though still through the lens of humility. He examines William's Christology as grounded in Christ's humility, explaining that the descent of Christ into human life modeled for human beings both their own descent into humility and their ascent to God, in both cases following Christ, the form of poverty. Exploring William's development of this theme in both his argument against Abelard in the *Disputatio* and the *Epistola aurea*, Rydstrøm-Poulsen makes it clear that William's orthodox Augustinianism was at the core of his opposition to what he regarded as Abelard's Pelagianism. He thus emphasizes William's insistence on the necessity of humility in the Christian life: "Christ is the Savior, and the only relevant human attitude is humility." But humility is not an end in itself, not merely a matter of moral virtue. Instead, its culmination in William's understanding, Rydstrøm-Poulsen explains, is to become like God: "he calls the highest resemblance *unitas spiritus*, which 'makes the human one spirit with God.' . . . Consequently William

---

[35] William, Ep frat Pref. 9–10 (CCCM 88:226; CF 12:6). Bernard shows his initial reluctance in Ep 327 (SBOp 8:263; James, *Letters*, #236, 314–15).

can say about the soul that it really becomes one with the triune God."[36]

The last of William's spiritual treatises, *Epistola aurea* is not only a valuable testimony to William's theological understanding, as Rydstrøm-Poulsen shows it to be, but also a witness to his deep love for solitude and simplicity of life, those things that first helped to draw him to Cistercian monasticism and then later led him to admire the new Carthusian order. After an extended visit in the mid-1140s to the nearby Charterhouse of Mont-Dieu, William wrote this work for the benefit of the novices there and to thank the community for its hospitality to him. Benedicta Ward calls attention to what he saw there as a contemporary expression of ancient monastic traditions, as he praised the Carthusians for "their poverty, solitude, and zeal for God's glory," which he described as resembling that of the Egyptian fathers of the desert. When William goes on to make a similar comparison to Clairvaux, however, he presents the Cistercians not as imitating the external behavior of the desert fathers but instead as incorporating the inner meaning of the fathers' lives in a Gospel-centered monasticism.

Examining the origins of William's interest in Egyptian desert monasticism demonstrated in *Epistola aurea*, Ward concludes that he had probably read none of the primary sources available in twelfth-century Europe but relied instead on stories he had heard from sermons and the daily monastery readings of Cassian's *Conferences* and Athanasius's *Vita Sancti Antonii*. In fact, Ward suggests that in this way William himself was participating in the oral tradition. In contrast, she notes, as Abelard had read the *apophthegmata* and found in them a love of silence and solitude, he might well be considered "the true heir to the tradition of the desert fathers."

Having completed the *Epistola aurea* and apparently being content to leave his *Expositio super Cantica Canticorum* incomplete, William set out into what was for him new territory. It is perhaps evidence of his deep humility that after a lifetime of theological and spiritual exploration and argumentation he ventured into a

---

[36] Ep frat 262: *fit homo cum Deo unus spiritus* (CCCM 88:282; CF 12:95); Ep frat 263: *quia ipsa ipse est Spiritus sanctus, Deus caritas* (CCCM 88:282; CF 12:96).

new kind of writing, composing a narrative of Bernard's early life. His statement at the beginning of the *Vita prima* that he had considered waiting to write it until after Bernard's death indicates not only his anxiety about Bernard's probable reaction to such a work but also his own long desire to write it.[37] Although he left the *Vita* unfinished at his death, it continues to be perhaps the most widely known of his treatises and is still the source for much of what is known of Bernard's early life. Indeed, as James France shows here, two medieval manuscripts of this work preserve the only surviving images of William himself, one of which appears on the cover of this book. Each manuscript portrays William with Bernard in an image that is hieratic rather than naturalistic, and in each case Bernard dominates the miniature, with William subordinated to him in position and posture.

Many of the most powerful surviving images of Bernard are based on scenes from the *Vita prima*, as France shows from two sets of sixteenth-century glass representing William's stories of Bernard's youth.[38] As he explains, the stories in these windows exemplify the way the good-looking young Bernard learned to resist the appeal of women, even those actively seeking to seduce him, while at the same time signifying aspects of his quick wit and charm. And lest the images themselves be insufficiently clear about their origin and significance, each set included the words of the *Vita prima* painted onto the glass itself. Such images make it clear that the intimate conversation that Bernard and William shared over the years bore particularly rich fruit in the *Vita prima*, enabling William to memorialize otherwise hidden details of Bernard's life and character.

As Marjory Lange explains in her chapter, William's rhetorical skills not only created insight into Bernard's life and significance but also preserved the memory of the friendship between the two men. Through an exploration of the imagistic and narrative power of this work, Lange demonstrates William's thoughtful application

[37] Vita Bern, Prologue (CCCM 89B:31; PL 185:225AB; Cawley, *Bernard*, 1).
[38] See also James France, *Medieval Images of Saint Bernard of Clairvaux*, CS 210 (Kalamazoo, MI: Cistercian Publications, 2007).

of his rhetorical skills, calling particular attention to the way he verbally shaped the work so as to reveal the meaning of Bernard's life while incorporating into that story their meeting and developing friendship. Lange's helpful discussion of medieval hagiographical conventions and the way in which William both used and departed from them makes it clear that he excelled even in this new genre, through which he bequeathed to history a portrait of a saintly man.

Having moved regularly throughout his life between teaching others and seeking personal understanding, William thus ended by stepping outside both modes of writing, or rather synthesizing the life of his spiritual model and dearest friend. Finally, of course, he wrote for himself, preserving his memories of Bernard's life while allowing others to share them and perceive their meaning.

The final chapter of this book does not adhere to the otherwise chronological format but points to the original and audacious spiritual doctrine that characterized William's thought and ran throughout his works. F. Tyler Sergent shows that William's development of the idea of human divinization, of the soul's capacity to become one with God, also led to his new use of a traditional Christian phrase to express his teaching of the unity of spirit possible between the human being and God. Sergent examines the patristic and medieval development of the phrase *unitas spiritus*, first found in the biblical letter to the Ephesians, which advises the Christians of Ephesus that they should "preserve the unity of spirit in the bond of peace" (Eph 4:3).

Fifteen authors from the fourth through the twelfth centuries use the phrase outside direct quotations of the Ephesians passage, Sergent shows, and with one exception their works always use it in reference to either the unity of the persons of the Trinity or the unity of Christian believers. In three cases William also uses it with this second meaning. But six times, in four works, William uses it to refer to the soul's union with God, first in his earliest work, *De contemplando Deo*, and finally in his last, the *Vita prima*. Thus not only did William newly define the relationship between God and humankind, but he also found a way to express that relationship with a traditional phrase newly understood.

So the body of this book ends with an examination of one of William's most distinctive contributions to Christian thought, confirming the theological, spiritual, and rhetorical gifts that the previous eight chapters showed. Coming from many different starting points, the nine contributors indicate the importance of William's role in twelfth-century Christian thought and the familiarity of his expression of Cistercian spirituality.

At the core of all that William thought and wrote stands his conviction that humans are able to become one with God through love. This insight runs like a golden thread throughout his works, leading his readers forward through reason and love, downward through humility and upward through grace and hope, finally to come to rest in God and fully one with God, "not only desiring what God desires . . . but unable to desire anything except what God desires."[39]

Like the fathers of the desert, the founders of the New Monastery, and Saint Bernard—and indeed like Cistercians from those early days until today—William throughout his life recognized and followed God's call and his own desire to know and love God more fully. And even while longing for the place in which he could yield completely to God's call, he persisted in the work he had originally taken on, to lead his monastery, teach his novices, and work with and for other Benedictine abbots. Thanks to those years of committed service to those he longed to leave, when he finally became a Cistercian, he brought with him (again like the Founders) maturity, knowledge, experience, love, and confidence in God's call.

Honoring Dr. E. Rozanne Elder

It is an honor and indeed a pleasure to offer this Festschrift to Dr. E. Rozanne Elder on the occasion of her retirement. This traditional form of academic recognition is the natural way to demonstrate the sincere gratitude of so many for her significant contributions to learning. For five decades, her distinguished scholarship on the golden age of Cistercian thought, especially on

---

[39] William, Ep frat 257 (CCCM 88:281; CF 12:94).

William of Saint-Thierry, has earned her the admiration of scholars around the world.

Dr. Elder's recognized expertise on Cistercian authors and subjects has caused her to receive many invitations to lecture and lead workshops in North American and European universities. Additionally, the respect she has earned from Cistercian monks and nuns around the world has allowed her to visit and offer conferences to monasteries from Iowa and California to England, Norway, Nigeria, and Cameroon, leading symposia for juniors, giving workshops, and lecturing. Her work has enriched monks and nuns of both Cistercian orders, giving them a fuller knowledge of their ancestral tradition.

Dr. Elder's thirty-six years as director of the Institute of Cistercian Studies and five years as director of the Center for Cistercian and Monastic Studies, both at Western Michigan University, have opened the field of monastic studies—and specifically Cistercian studies—to many superb scholars who might never otherwise have taken that path. As editorial director of Cistercian Publications, she edited and published not only many fine English translations of and introductions to works from the early Cistercian tradition but also a long list of valuable studies of Cistercian writers, of the desert fathers, and of other patristic and medieval authors. Those who have worked with her in that capacity know how painstaking have been her efforts to make each book substantive, readable, and beautiful.

Even as Dr. Elder edited and oversaw these works by other authors and so advanced their careers, she herself continued to present papers at conferences and wrote and published articles and books. She has published thirty-two articles, book chapters, encyclopedia articles, and introductions, mostly on the thought of William of Saint-Thierry, and edited no fewer than one hundred ninety-one books, including seventeen as a named editor. She is a true scholar, a woman of deep and committed learning. In recognition for her extraordinary record, in 2014 Western Michigan University honored Dr. Elder by naming her a Distinguished Faculty Scholar.

Additionally, Dr. Elder's many years as an outstanding professor and scholar in the Department of History at Western Michigan

University have opened the eyes and minds of her students to the medieval world. She has directed at least fifteen theses and dissertations as well as serving as an external reader on numerous dissertation committees. None of those who have studied closely with Dr. Elder will ever forget the firm hand with which she steered them, requiring them to work in original languages and with primary texts and thereby making them able to do so. As her students past and present report, studying with her whether in class or in a tutorial is always both challenging and rewarding. From on-the-spot parsing of compound Latin words used by medieval authors in order to understand their nuanced meanings to scouring the massive *Acta Sanctorum* volumes for hagiographical details to analyzing archaeological reports on English Cistercian abbeys, students learn both *theoria* and *praxis*. Her demands for thoroughness and rewarding of diligence reliably impart both knowledge and the skills necessary for a scholar.

Beyond teaching, Dr. Elder's range of service to her university has been extensive. She has served on numerous search and admissions committees in the Department of History and beyond and repeatedly served on the Board of Directors of the Medieval Institute. She has also arranged for Western Michigan University's hosting of numerous visiting scholars and helped build the Institute of Cistercian Studies Library, assisting in the acquisition of many volumes essential to Cistercian scholars.

As a fitting complement to her extensive work as a scholar, teacher, and participant in university governance, Dr. Elder has long been an active ecumenist, representing the Episcopal Church locally in the Episcopal Diocese of Western Michigan, as well as nationally and internationally. In addition to serving on national ecumenical boards for the Episcopal Church, she was from 1983 to 1991 a member of the Anglican-Orthodox Theological Consultation, and from 1991 to 2001, one of only two Americans on the Anglican-Roman Catholic International Consultation, drafting documents for the Commission's consideration (including the document on the Marian dogmas), and serving on a team editing the central documents from the Anglican-Roman Catholic Consultation in the United States from 1983–1985. Appropriately, in 1995 Nashotah

House Theological Seminary awarded her a Doctor of Humane Letters *honoris causa*.

The work for which Rozanne Elder is probably most widely known and appreciated is her direction of the world's annual Cistercian Studies Conference, held each May jointly with the International Congress of Medieval Studies at Western Michigan University. The Conference, largely through Rozanne's meticulous organization and intensive personal oversight, has created a worldwide community of Cistercian scholars, including both monks and laypeople. For months before each year's conference, Rozanne works to request papers, select those to be presented and inform the presenters, organize sessions and invite section chairs, arrange for a spacious, sunny room for the meetings, order flowers for that room, design and print an elegant program and mail it out, design and print distinctive nametags for participants, and plan not only for the Saturday night banquet but also for the Sunday evening collation and Monday morning Mass and breakfast, which have become expected extensions of the conference. During each conference, Rozanne introduces the first session and attends all the others, listening to the papers given and frequently raising learned and provocative questions or observations that illuminate and inform speakers and listeners alike.

In addition to organizing the conference, Rozanne also schedules priests for each morning's Roman Catholic Mass and reserves the auditorium for the Sunday morning celebration as well as making arrangements for Sunday's joint Anglican-Lutheran Eucharist, sometimes inviting diocesan bishops as celebrants. She provides the vestments, wine, wafers, and liturgical booklets for each day's worship and arrives early each morning to be sure that everything is in place. And she plans and prints the liturgy for daily Evening Prayer and makes sure that a cantor and *schola* are ready each day.

Rozanne's careful planning and oversight, as well as her gift for gracious hospitality and her generosity in exercising it so apparently effortlessly, have over the years produced not just a center for an exchange of ideas about Cistercian history, thought, authors, art, liturgy, architecture, economics, and manuscripts (and so much more) but have built a community of scholars and friends. Because of her, the papers given in Cistercian sessions are almost invariably strong, and because of her, the sessions attract people prepared to support and assist one another. Non-Cistercian scholars who drop in to hear a single paper are likely to return again and again to enjoy the supportive and well-informed company and to share in the intellectual energy in the room. Often, in time they return to offer their own papers on Cistercian subjects and to be warmly welcomed into the family.

All because of Rozanne's work. Cistercian scholars around the world owe her enduring gratitude for the community she has built and the welcome with which each year she welcomes them home again.

Because so many owe so much both professionally and personally to Rozanne Elder, the editors have created this book on their behalf. It therefore includes not only studies of William of Saint-Thierry, the twelfth-century writer who has been at the center of Rozanne's scholarly life, but also warm letters of appreciation from representatives of both Cistercian orders—Dom Brendan Freeman, OCSO, and Fr. Luke Anderson, OCist—and from lay scholars—Dr. Bernard McGinn of the University of Chicago and Dr. John R. Sommerfeldt of the University of Dallas—expressing admiration of and gratitude for Rozanne's teaching, scholarship, editorial acumen and perseverance, and gracious hospitality. They join in celebrating her contributions to Cistercian life and learning in the United States and around the world. The authors of this volume join in presenting it to her as a sign of the esteem in which so many hold her and in recognition of her immeasurable contributions to the academic world.

Unity of Spirit, this book's main title, of course expresses above all William of Saint-Thierry's central concept of the unity possible between humans and God. But it also here expresses the bond of spiritual unity between Rozanne Elder and all Cistercians, monastic or lay, wherever and however they live out the life that began in 1098 at the New Monastery.

For the most part, however, scholars will read this book to learn about William of Saint-Thierry rather than about Rozanne Elder, and that is entirely as it should be. As the first English book devoted to William's works since *Signy l'abbaye et Guillaume de Saint-Thierry*, this one aims to be useful, informative, reliable, and valuable for scholars of all stripes—Cistercians, historians, general monastic researchers, students of patristics, general medievalists, art historians, and simply *amici Guillelmi*. Otherwise it would not appropriately honor Rozanne.

Easter 2015

1

WILLIAM OF SAINT-THIERRY'S TRINITARIAN IMAGE OR SAINT BERNARD'S PRE-THEOLOGICAL SELF?

Emero Stiegman

For Dr. E. Rozanne Elder, whose devout dedication to Cistercian Studies and caring encouragement of its students have left generations in her debt.

I dentifying the starting point of spiritual awareness could affect the value given to personal experience as distinguished from religious doctrine. Here I want to call attention to a submerged and implicit disagreement on this significant issue between two highly influential twelfth-century writers whom tradition has wrongly assumed to be in full accord. The question, transcending mere adjustments of the historical record, is not antiquarian; it confronts an issue more alive today than it was in the Middle Ages.

William of Saint-Thierry and Bernard of Clairvaux, for all that they have in common, are early Cistercian contemplatives with sharply different points of departure. William's theological mastery of doctrine and Bernard's insightful grasp of the nature of experience reveal a defining contrast, i.e., different perceptions of what is essential in the mind's discovery of God or in the manner of God's self-revelation, a different reception, then, of religious doctrine itself. Even while benefiting from William's superior theological education, Bernard claims that experience precedes doctrine.

1

A brief study of these two figures, side by side at an early moment in their careers, can make the difference between them clear. It would be wrong to claim that what distinguishes one monk is simply lacking in the other. Yet a temperamental affirmation of one that suffers polite tolerance of the other would fail to put the reader or the devotee in touch with the integral Cistercian tradition. And, of broader importance, concern for the relationship of experience to doctrine or to institutional norms belongs as much to philosophical anthropology and its own demands for meaning as to the history of theology and spirituality.

William and Bernard will be found most easily and significantly separable (or better, distinguishable) precisely where they were once so fused together as to be taken as one author—i.e., in the twelfth-century *Liber de amore*.[1] As is known, that manuscript bundled two tracts by William, *De natura et dignitate amoris* and *De contemplando Deo*, with one tract by Bernard, *De diligendo Deo*, all three ascribed to Bernard.[2] Jean Marie Déchanet's suggested explanation for the omission of William's name seems most credible: Bernard's reputation would assure acceptance of William's unconventional theological views, "forestalling any suspicions of heterodoxy."[3]

For generations it seemed inevitable that Bernard's thought could be ascertained only in the context of two treatises that were not his. When William's authorship and genius were eventually recognized, it became necessary to reread the abbot of Clairvaux. I do not believe this necessity has been fully met. Experience (*experientia*)

---

[1] Jacques Hourlier describes this document, saying nothing of how the Augustinianism of William might affect a reading of Bernard ("S. Bernard et Guillaume de Saint-Thierry dans le '*Liber de amore*,'" in *Saint Bernard théologien*, ASOC 9 (1953): 223–33.

[2] William of Saint-Thierry, Nat am (CCCM 88:177–212; PL 184:379–408; M.-M. Davy, *De la nature et de la dignitate amoris*, in *Deux traités de l'amour de Dieu. De la contemplation de Dieu. De la nature et de la dignité de l'amour*, ed. M.-M. Davy [Paris: J. Vrin, 1953], 69–137 [hereafter, Davy, *Deux Traités*]; CF 30); Contem (CCCM 88:153–69; CF 3); Bernard of Clairvaux, Dil (SBOp 3:109–34; CF 13).

[3] Jean Marie Déchanet, "A Comment," in *William, Abbot of St. Thierry: A Colloquium at the Abbey of St. Thierry*, trans. Jerry Carfantan, CS 94 (Kalamazoo, MI: Cistercian Publications, 1987), 255.

as presented in Bernard's tract is not a subset of doctrines as learned and explored by William. *On Loving God* remains a casualty of the confusion. Interpreters tend to absorb its central ideas into the Augustinianism of William's work. Without such absorption, a treatise that might have been recognized as innovative thinking has, after an initial era of popularity, lain fallow in Christian tradition, frequently read as mere pious exhortation when not censured, even by friendly experts.

William of Saint-Thierry, *De natura et dignitate amoris*

Properly to understand William's treatise and to evaluate it within the body of his works, one must not lose sight of two elements that may seem peripheral, though they are not. First, this is a very early work.[4] Like all great writers, William grew.[5] Second, the degree of mistrust in the physical found here was incited to a degree by William's abhorrence of the crude sensuality of Ovid's *Ars amatoria*. In the Neoplatonic philosophical assumptions underlying Augustine's *De trinitate*, William found intellectual grounding.

William had brought with him to the Benedictine monastery of Saint-Thierry the best humanistic and theological education available, as Déchanet insists.[6] In his magisterial study of William, David N. Bell goes far beyond identifying elements that derive from or develop the Augustinian tradition. He explores the major themes

---

[4] E. Rozanne Elder argues that Nat am is William's first work ("William of Saint Thierry: Rational and Affective Spirituality," in *The Spirituality of Western Christendom*, ed. E. Rozanne Elder, CS 30 [Kalamazoo, MI: Cistercian Publications, 1976], 197–98n22). David N. Bell sees the teaching of Nat am as revealing "a nascent and formative stage of William's thinking" (Introduction to William, *The Nature and Dignity of Love*, trans. Thomas X. Davis, CF 30 [Kalamazoo, MI: Cistercian Publications, 1981], 17).

[5] For a survey of William's evolution from Benedictine abbot of Saint-Thierry to simple Cistercian monk at Signy to admirer of the Carthusians (as shown in *Epistola ad fratres de Monte Dei*), see E. Rozanne Elder, "William of St. Thierry: The Monastic Vocation as an Imitation of Christ," *Cîteaux* 26 (1975): 9–30.

[6] Jean Marie Déchanet, *William of St. Thierry: The Man and His Work*, trans. Richard Strachan, CS 10 (Spencer, MA: Cistercian Publications, 1972), 1–5.

of Augustine's metaphysics as these generate clarity and conviction in William's spirit. Readers of the devout monk quickly dismiss as implausible any suspicion of philosophy's displacing prayer.[7]

The design of William's work is to establish first what is meant by being made in God's image and then to show that the full actuation of this image, the divine likeness, must be recovered through the progress of love.[8] William offers an account of the soul's changing disposition, guided by biblical and patristic teaching—what is received in faith. Rozanne Elder, writing on William's disagreements with Abelard, identifies William's insistence on beginning in faith and describes him as "Chary of theological inquiry devoid of scriptural foundation." She goes on to say that "As William grounded the first stage [of development] in Scripture . . . , so at the second he relied more heavily on illuminating grace."[9] This account of later works of William also describes the way he traces the development of love in this tract. Would not faithful Christians seek their point of departure in faith?

Growth in love goes on: "The will, according to the development of [its] virtue, grows into love, love into charity, and charity into wisdom";[10] "Love is naturally implanted in the human soul by the author of nature."[11] However, only that which is as God creates it is natural.[12] Even as God is a Trinity, God's image in the human is

---

[7] David N. Bell, *The Image and Likeness: The Augustinian Spirituality of William of St. Thierry*, CS 78 (Kalamazoo, MI: Cistercian Publications, 1984). Bell is sensitive to nuances (and to development) in William that demonstrate more than a mere duplication of Augustine.

[8] Robert Javelet, *Image et ressemblance au XIIᵉ siècle. De saint Anselme à Alan de Lille*, 2 vols. (Paris: Letouzey et Ané, 1967), 1:188.

[9] E. Rozanne Elder, Introduction to *The Mirror of Faith*, by William of St. Thierry, trans. Thomas X. Davis, CF 15 (Kalamazoo, MI: Cistercian Publications, 1979), xviii, xix.

[10] Nat am 3 (Davy, *Deux Traités*, 74; CF 30:53).

[11] Nat am 2 (Davy, *Deux Traités*, 72; CF 30:48–49). Augustine saw love as a *naturale pondus*, a gravitational pull orienting the human to its proper "place" (Augustine of Hippo, Civ Dei 13.18; CCSL 48:400; PL 41:390). (See also Civ Dei 11.28 and Conf 13.9.)

[12] William held Ovid's *Ars amatoria* to be an example of unnatural love.

a "created trinity."[13] Most characteristic of William is the conviction that what is meant to shine through the human is not simply what is divine but (as Augustine knew) its trinitarian character. At creation (Gen 2:7) God infused into humankind "a spiritual power, that is, an intellectual power," which holds memory. This is *memoria*, an ever-available awareness of its origin in God: "memory of itself begets reason, then both memory and reason from themselves bring forth the will," reflecting the three divine Persons.[14] Love is a "vehement, well-ordered will."[15]

As William outlines the psychology of "the rational soul,"[16] he focuses on one of his most used terms, the *affectus*: "The will, in itself, is a simple *affectus* . . . filled with good when it is helped by grace, with evil when left to itself."[17] *Affectio*, on the other hand, may denote merely an inner motion of early love, where the will works "as a blind person with his hands."[18]

After long stretches of encouragement to an ascetical life, William first suggests that *affectus*, associated so insistently with the will, may have something to do with affectivity. He observes that in the satisfaction derived from the struggle for virtue, true *affectus* is not yet present. That will come only "when love has passed into charity."[19] Preparation for this moment arrives in the form of "sweet little affections" (*affectiunculas*).[20] The reader must not, then, confuse tender emotions about God with that *affectus* marking the entry of charity.

---

[13] Nat am 3 (Davy, *Deux Traités*, 76; CF 30:54). Bell points out that the idea of the soul as created trinity was the common Augustinian heritage of medieval writers (Introduction, CF 30:6–18).

[14] Nat am 3 (Davy, *Deux Traités*, 76; CF 30:54).

[15] William of Saint-Thierry, Contem 14 (CCCM 88:162–63; CF 3:54).

[16] William, Nat am 3 (Davy, *Deux Traités*, 76; CF 30:55).

[17] Nat am 4 (Davy, *Deux Traités*, 76; CF 30:56). Thomas X. Davis treats the meaning of *affectus* in William extensively in the appendix to his translation of *The Mirror of Faith*, CF 15:93–95. Bell discusses the often-confusing inconsistencies in this usage among twelfth-century writers (*Image*, 128–35).

[18] Nat am 9 (Davy, *Deux Traités*, 82; CF 30:61).

[19] Nat am 9 (Davy, *Deux Traités*, 84–85; CF 30:62).

[20] *Insolitas quasdam et dulces affectiunculas incipit colligere* (Nat am 10 [Davy, *Deux Traités*, 86–87; CF 30:64]).

William outlines the growth of love as three stages of life: youth, adulthood, and old age. He situates the use of the five spiritual senses in love's youth. Listing these five senses, he suggests that one "begin from the bottom one"—i.e., touch.[21] In its closeness to the earth, touch holds relatively little spiritual promise. Caution often dominates expectation. In his lengthy treatment of the spiritual senses,[22] William perhaps inevitably allows something of his personal needs to orchestrate the ensemble—particularly as such needs are linked to philosophical assumptions.

It is easy to fall into a simplistic anti-body interpretation of William. While avoiding that extreme, readers may also find it difficult to avoid what at times emerges as a trace of the Augustinianism that, in the words of Gilson, "falls heir first of all to the Platonic view of sensible things which, in the philosophical order, corresponds to the condemnation of the flesh in the religious order."[23] In the end, however, William's overall affirmation is that God reaches humankind through the body's animating soul. Elder offers an illuminating comment on the problem: "For William, the benedictine abbot longing to share the 'spiritual experience' of Bernard and the White Monks, being taken back to his physical being did not come easily. Paralyzed in trying to force a sense of experiential love, William very reluctantly realized that he could not skip over his physical faculties in his dash for spiritual experience."[24]

With this statement, Elder ponders lines by William himself and argues not for one human faculty over another but for respect for the integral person as subject of religious experience. In another essay, she writes of an older and more mature William as he continues to reflect on the role of the body in the life of the spirit, when

---

[21] Nat am 16 (Davy, *Deux Traités*, 96–97; CF 30:72).

[22] Nat am 15–20 (Davy, *Deux Traités*, 95–100; CF 30:72–77).

[23] Étienne Gilson, *The Christian Philosophy of Saint Augustine*, trans. L. E. M. Lynch (New York: Octagon Books, 1983), 243. Gilson makes no reference to William of Saint-Thierry here.

[24] E. Rozanne Elder, "The Christology of William of Saint Thierry," RTAM 58 (1991): 103–4, esp. n146, a reference to William, Vita Bern 12.59 (CCCM 89B:74–75; PL 185:259C). Elder adds other texts by William.

he has observed that Bernard himself struggled personally to accept that identification with the body that he eloquently argued for in *On Loving God*.[25]

William completes his presentation on love's middle phase, its growth in maturity, with remarks on the role of reason:[26] "The sight for seeing God, the natural light of the soul . . . is charity. There are, however, two eyes in this sight . . . love and reason."[27] Reason merges into the *affectus* of love.[28] However implicitly, the author distinguishes between reason and dialectics: in the school of charity, "solutions are arrived at not only by reasoning but by reason and by the very nature and truth of things and by experience."[29]

An understanding of William's spirituality as weak in affective vigor (usually placing William beside his "mellifluous" friend Bernard) risks ignoring much of the text. Elder rightly reads (among other texts) the "two eyes" of the soul—reason instructing love and love illuminating reason—as the writer's insistence on a balance between rational and affective spirituality.[30]

With this insistence, William has already moved into love's last phase, where charity becomes wisdom. One enters adulthood when "love begins to be strengthened and illumined, and to pass into

---

[25] Elder offers "an alternative reading" of that part of the Vita Bern in which William writes of Bernard's excessive and "indiscreet fervor" in ascetical attacks on the body. In William's words: "Why do we try to make excuses for what he admits. . . . He is not embarrassed to accuse himself of sacrilege" (William of Saint-Thierry, Vita Bern 1.41 [CCCM 89B:64–65; PL 185:251B; William of Saint-Thierry, *Bernard of Clairvaux: Early Biographies, Vol. I by William of St. Thierry*, trans. Martinus Cawley [Lafayette, OR: Abbey of Our Lady of Guadalupe, 1990], 54, hereafter Cawley, *Bernard*]). See E. Rozanne Elder, "Making Virtues of Vexing Habits," in *Studiosorum Speculum: Studies in Honor of Louis J. Lekai, O. Cist*, ed. Francis Swietek and John R. Sommerfeldt, CS 141 (Kalamazoo, MI: Cistercian Publications, 1993), 75–94, here 76.

[26] William, Nat am 21–23 (Davy, *Deux Traités*, 100–6; CF 30:77–82).

[27] Nat am 21 (Davy, *Deux Traités*, 100; CF 30:77).

[28] Nat am 22 (Davy, *Deux Traités*, 102–4; CF 30:78–82).

[29] Nat am 26 (Davy, *Deux Traités*, 108; CF 30:86).

[30] Nat am 21 (Davy, *Deux Traités*, 100; CF 30:90–91); Elder, "Rational and Affective Spirituality," 90.

the *affectus*"; "love enlightened is charity: a love from God, in God, for God is charity."[31] The author elaborates: "love desires to see the God of faith and hope because it loves. Charity loves because it sees. It is the eye by which God is seen."[32] "Wisdom," he writes, "is rightly placed in the mind. Since what is called mind is that which remembers or that which is eminent in the soul, . . . [we understand it as that] whereby we cleave to God and enjoy God."[33]

Before a final reflection on the beatific vision, William gives ample development to the role of Christ who is the Wisdom of God. In studying William's Christology, Elder finds in it a growing incarnational dimension that best exemplifies William's identification with Cistercian spirituality.[34] Through the redemptive mediation of Christ, humans are able even in this life to "Taste and see that the Lord is sweet" (Ps 34:8).[35] *Sapientia* is the *sapor* of God. William writes, as a good Augustinian for whom the divine image is the *mens*, "To taste is to understand."[36] He declares, preponderantly in his later years, *Amor ipse intellectus est.*[37]

To represent William's thought on divine love, it has been necessary to survey what *On the Nature and Dignity of Love* offers as his earliest version of a system—at least, to identify all the parts of the work. In all this, is there any systemic contrast to Bernard's *On Loving God*?

Saint Bernard's *On Loving God*

On Loving God is an epistolary tract responding to the question "Why and how should I love God?"[38] Bernard begins by bluntly declaring the question to represent the undeveloped religious mind

---

[31] Nat am 12 (Davy, *Deux Traités*, 88; CF 30:67).

[32] Nat am 15 (Davy, *Deux Traités*, 94; CF 30:72).

[33] Nat am 28 (Davy, *Deux Traités*, 110; CF 30:88).

[34] Elder, "Christology," 103–4.

[35] Nat am 28 (Davy, *Deux Traités*, 112; CF 30:88).

[36] Nat am 31 (Davy, *Deux Traités*, 116; CF 30:92).

[37] E.g., Ep frat 173 (CCCM 88:264; CF 12:68). Bell notes that this is "really what William's spirituality is all about" (Bell, *Image*, 221).

[38] Cardinal Haimeric, chancellor of the Roman See, was the correspondent. For details of the correspondence, see Emero Stiegman, "An Analytical Com-

of those lacking in authentic experience. These are the *insipientes*. The word is taken from Romans 1:14, where the Vulgate's *insipientes* means "unknowing people" or—in the biblical tradition of appeal to the spiritual senses—those who have no *sapor*, or taste, of the things of God, those who lack personal contact, i.e., experience. The commonly used and correct etymological sense of *insipientes*, then, refers to personal experience. The dialogue situation forces the abbot to speak to the unwise—as he will remark in a later setting—*aliter*, or in a different way.[39] Our weakened nature, he explains early, needs to "begin in the flesh."[40] He will start from every person's initial self-awareness, a state of consciousness as yet deprived of all revealed doctrine.

Bernard assumes this point of departure in his account of the first degree of love, where one loves oneself and only for oneself.[41] Only when love's growth is complete, in Bernard's fourth degree—where one loves oneself but only for God—does one (and possibly Bernard's reader as well) recognize what divine goodness and beauty lie in that work of God that is the self, formerly ignorant of

---

mentary," in *On Loving God* by Bernard of Clairvaux, CF 13B (Kalamazoo, MI: Cistercian Publications, 1995), 49–50.

[39] Bernard begins his sermons on the Song of Songs with these words: "What is said to you, brothers, must be different from what is said to people of the world, or at least said differently" (*Vobis, fratres, alia quam aliis de saeculo, aut certe aliter dicenda sunt*) (SC 1.1 [SBOp 1.3; CF 4:1]). Understanding differences between the two tracts under discussion here can be aided by attention to genre. William seems to address his monks in what was probably a series of chapter conferences (Bell, Introduction, CF 30:16–17), while Bernard, whose work was read by monks, nevertheless takes a point of view from outside the monastic world.

[40] "Since nature has become more fragile and weak, necessity obliges one to serve it first," Dil 8.23 (*Sed quoniam natura fragilior atque infirmior est ipsi primum, imperante necessitate, compellitur inservire* [SBOp 3.138.12–13; CF 13:115]).

[41] The *affectio naturalis* in Bernard's first stage of love has been often (if not generally) misunderstood, confused with William's more traditional Augustinian notion. The crux of the matter lies in how grace, in the *ordinatio caritatis*, will act on (and through) such an *affectio*—how this *eros* can be transformed by *agape* (see Stiegman, "Analytical Commentary," 105–8).

its true nature, which is now properly perceived as such. It is not belief in a doctrine that sets up this recognition.

What Bernard offers is an extended study of spiritual progress in those who have no Christian faith (or belief system) as historically revealed. He names these the *infideles*.[42] Writing a work for Christians, he nevertheless considers Christians a special case in humanity, distinguishing their consciousness only in so far as it enjoys the *memoria Christi*. (Memory in Bernard is not the Platonizing metaphysical *memoria* of William's trinitarian image.)[43] When Bernard has Christians in mind, he carefully brackets his remarks to separate them from his reflections on the *infideles*, even when they occur in the same paragraph. For Christians, he uses biblical allusions and theological language. But the category that is the ground of the tract, or its point of departure—and I think we have failed to recognize this—is *infideles*. Here Bernard consistently refrains from any theological language. In "Why should I love God?" *I* and *God* form the axis on which love's development turns. The image-and-likeness anthropology itself, prominent in William's work, is wholly absent in *On Loving God*.[44] Bernard's *I* is simply the

---

[42] In this context, the term implies an ignorance of Christian doctrine ("the faith") as such while not excluding possibilities of a saving faith.

[43] Bernard seems to go out of his way to say what he does *not* mean by memory: "memory is for the continuing ages, presence is for the kingdom of heaven" (*Memoria ergo in generatione saeculorum, praesentia in regno caelorum*) (Dil 3.10 [SBOp 3.127; CF 13:102]).

[44] A remarkable absence. Jean Leclercq noted that image and likeness is, without doubt, the most frequently studied theme in Saint Bernard, from Gilson's *Mystical Theology* (Étienne Gilson, *The Mystical Theology of St. Bernard*, trans. A. H. C. Downes, CS 120 [1940; Kalamazoo, MI: Cistercian Publications, 1990]) to the present (Jean Leclercq, Introduzzione Generale to *Opere di San Bernardo* 4, ed. Ferruccio Gastaldelli, Scriptorium Claravallense Fondazione di Studi Cistercensi [Rome: Città Nuova Editrice, 1984, 1986], 50. Bernard cites Gen 1:26 once in Dil (2.6), leaving "image and likeness" as a Hebraic parallelism, i.e., without the anthropological dynamism that demands that image be completed by likeness (SBOp 3:123; CF 13:98). Only in his *On Grace and Free Choice* (ca. 1127), written after *On Loving God*, and in his subsequent works, does the image-and-likeness anthropology flourish as the great Bernardine theme that

self as perceptible by any human, never defined except as what is not God and what "seeks its own" in the illusory *proprium*. We may suspect that the type for this self-and-God dyad is the New Testament's flesh-and-spirit, but the compulsively biblical Bernard refrains from any such allusion.

To highlight the universality of God's loving action in humanity, Bernard (who often couples *philosophi et haeretici*) plays philosopher. What guides him through the consciousness of the *infideles* is a set of clearly philosophical categories. Allow me to gather these from the entire text: we see the person of no historical faith as, first, rational, then as free, driven by desire, subject to nature, capable of discerning laws in the human condition, pressed by necessity, and aware of possibilities—all philosophical concepts. (The era, like the world in which Christianity arose, did not question the existence of God.) In such a person Bernard traces the development of love. Love's maturing is not one thing for the Christian and another for the pagan; all humans are created to love God "with all their heart, all their soul, and all their might."[45]

To be unaware of the universalizing intent of Bernard's philosophical approach would be to miss the direction of his work. He is writing about *homo rationalis* as such.[46] Modern anthropologists, archaeologists, and historians, on discovering that even our most distant human forebears were religious, tend to trace this fact to something more intrinsic to the human condition than one or another culturally inherited doctrine. Bernard's tract can offer an explanation in theology of what the anthropologist finds in science.

Leclercq observed. See Stiegman, "Analytic Commentary," 61–64. For a survey of image in Saint Bernard, see Maur Standaert, "La doctrine de l'image chez Saint Bernard," *Ephemerides Theologiae Lovanienses* 23 (1947): 118–21.

[45] *Proinde inexcusabilis est omnis etiam infidelis, si non diligit Dominum Deum suum toto corde, tota anima, tota virtute sua* (Dil 2:6 [SBOp 3:124; CF 13:98]).

[46] On reason in Dil, see Luke Anderson, "The Appeal to Reason in St. Bernard's *De Diligendo Deo* (II:2–6)," in *The Chimaera of His Age: Studies in Bernard of Clairvaux*, ed. E. Rozanne Elder and John R. Sommerfeldt, CS 63 (Kalamazoo, MI: Cistercian Publications, 1980), 132–39, esp. 135.

The discourse situation of *On Loving God* makes clear that what Bernard is saying about all humankind is addressed not to those whom he designates as *infideles*—enfolded into the rationality of humankind—but to those (represented in his questioning correspondent) whom he has called *insipientes*, those lacking in inner experience. The universal validity of his argument from experience shows the condition of those who read him to be graver than that of those whom he describes, the *infideles*. Those who have no doctrine may love God, while Christians rich in doctrine but poor in experience—lacking the *sapor* of God—may go on searching for reasons. Saint Bernard's theme is a love bound to the faith that transcends believing, a love divinely fostered in every rational creature. And the writer is rhetorician enough to leave all that quietly but powerfully implied.

Let me remark in passing that Bernard's renown for relying on experience rests on epistemological sensitivity, well exhibited in *On Loving God*. The abbot never confuses mere empirical generalization—what is learned by trial and error—with either rational certainty or the voice of God. In the secular order, modern Western thought seems to justify his view through the Enlightenment (or Kantian) notion of experience as a synthesis of the factual and its human reception—part given and part made.[47] In Bernard, what occurs in one's life becomes experience through reflections that open the soul to grace (as my conclusion claims).

The journey of experience in *On Loving God* continues: when love matures to the point of being wholly free, where one seeks not what is good for oneself but simply what is good, Bernard celebrates it in the language of Christian revelation: the lover seeks "Not what is his but what belongs to Christ, the same way Christ sought not what was his but what was ours, or, rather, ourselves."[48] Here fi-

---

[47] The philosophical and psychological literature on experience is endless, as any general work will make clear. In my view, the most relevant resource is Raimundo Panikkar, *Myth, Faith and Hermeneutics: Cross-Cultural Studies* (New York: Paulist Press, 1979), 292–308. Panikkar cites Dil 7.22 from PL 182:987 (Panikkar, *Myth*, 227n73).

[48] Dil 9.26 (SBOp 3:141; CF 13:118).

nally "love is pleasing because it is free" (*gratus quia gratuitus*).[49] The biblical reminiscence clearly does not enjoin a doctrine upon the *infideles*. Even while briefly breaking the philosophical texture of his account with a reference to the *memoria Christi*, the author maintains the coolly rational tone he has reserved for arguing the universality of God's saving action in the world.

If Bernard, explaining the universality of God's love, holds experience to be the vessel of grace at the start of loving God—"in the flesh"—he does not limit the fruit of experience to its start. When William of Saint-Thierry admires Bernard's experience, he knows it to be the full flowering of grace. But, again, what has received insufficient attention is the significance that *On Loving God* assigns to the beginning of love. Bernard writes, "The needs of the flesh are a kind of speech [*quaedam loquela*]."[50] He cites First Thessalonians 5:21 on the necessity to "test everything" and assigns this function to the mind.[51] A process of reflection is opened.

As William argues from the trinitarian image in humans and Bernard from the universality of God's loving action within all, it is also clear that the dynamism of both writers flows from what Déchanet called "an idea of man."[52] It is clear as well that both depend on doctrines. But there is a difference: Bernard sees the discovery of a loving God as starting in a consciousness deprived of all doctrine.

However valuable, these insights would add nothing essential to the comparison I am making to William of Saint-Thierry's *On the Nature and Dignity of Love*. But two motifs that loom large in Bernard's treatise can aid the comparison—his treatment of *causa* (the cause of divine love) and his attitude toward the body.

First Motif: Causa

To answer the question "Why should I love God?" Bernard begins by almost surreptitiously converting the demand for a "reason" into

---

[49] Dil 9.26 (SBOp 3:141; CF 13:118).

[50] *Est enim carnis quaedam loquela necessitas, et beneficia quae experiendo probat gestiendo renuntiat* (Dil 9.26 [SBOp 3:141; CF 13:118]).

[51] Dil 7.20 (SBOp 3:136; CF 13:113).

[52] Déchanet, "Comment," 256.

an enquiry after the "cause" of our loving God. With this maneuver he can, to brilliant effect, employ the double meaning he finds in *causa*. (The lexical ambiguity of the word is not his invention.) The *causa diligendi Deum*—its motive, or reason—will be displayed as if it were the upper side of a tapestry woven by this psychologist, though he offers no such metaphor; at the same time the *causa*— eventually to be acknowledged as love's cause rather than its motive—will form the unseen underside, kept in step-by-step coordination by this theologian. The progressive experience of God's lovableness will draw the *infideles* on—inciting conscious motives— as an exemplary cause (*causa finalis*), while God's action in the soul works, beyond human perception, as the efficient cause.[53]

Second Motif: The Body

The sheer mass of discussion on the human body in *On Loving God* commands attention.[54] The author's insistent use of *affectio*

---

[53] *Dixi supra: causa diligendi Deum, Deus est. Verum dixi, nam et efficiens, et finalis* (Dil 7.22 [SBOp 3:137; CF 13:114]). Bernard's dwelling throughout his works on God's lovableness as exemplary cause demands attention. Tomáš Špidlík observes that "the Western mind examines the efficient cause (*causa efficiens*) whereas the Eastern concentrates on the *causa exemplaris*, pondering the meaning of emerging facts" (Tomáš Špidlík, *The Spirituality of the Christian East: A Systematic Handbook*, trans. Anthony P. Gythiel, CS 79 [Kalamazoo, MI: Cistercian Publications, 1986], 55). This comment invites a scholar to enquire whether the "Maximian 'bloc'" detected by Gilson (*Mystical Theology*, 26) might be fruitfully enlarged—i.e., whether the anthropology of Maximus the Confessor (writing later than Augustine), in his difference from Augustine, may be playing a larger role in the tradition that inspires Bernard. See on the passions Andrew Louth, *Maximus the Confessor* (New York: Routledge, 1996), e.g., "The Blessed Passion of Holy Love," 40–42, and "Maximus' Correction of Origenism," 66–68, where "a fundamental rebuttal of Neoplatonism, with its ideas of emanation" seems applicable to elements of the Augustinian tradition resisted by Bernard (Louth, *Maximus*, 67). Inviting also is Bronwen Neil, "Two Views of Vice and Virtue: Augustine of Hippo and Maximus the Confessor," in *Prayer and Spirituality in the Early Church 3: Liturgy and Life*, ed. Bronwen Neil, G. Dunn, and L. Cross (Sydney: St. Paul's, 2003), 261–71.

[54] Though Bernard uses as one of his favorite biblical tags the lament from Wisdom 9:15, *Corpus quod corrumpitur aggravat animam*, rarely is a reader's

naturalis as a label for love is his way of showing love's starting point to be in the soul as the "natural" animating force of the body (given in creation). At divine love's inception, a salvific grace possesses it. Love will then mature as grace increasingly informs this soul, but, even into a blessed eternity, it will remain the love of a human—i.e., *affectio naturalis*. Bernard writes of the soul in beatitude, "The soul mixes, with the divine wine, the tenderness of that *affectio naturalis* by which it desires to have its body back as a glorified Body."[55]

There is nothing in *On Loving God* of the near-dismissive evaluation of human affections sometimes found in William of Saint-Thierry's tract, that *Antinasonem*, or refutation of Ovid. We find here no *affectiunculas*.[56] Bernard sees what is utterly human in a different light. He acknowledges that affections come "by the very law of one's desiring," *cupiditatis lege*.[57] He is not blind to risk in the will's exposure to *affectio*.[58] There is nothing lax or presumptuous

---

attention called to the fact that a mollifying reflection often accompanies this line—i.e., that it is the will and not the body that brings corruption, or that humans are often unjust to the body, or that the loss of the body in death will (in Bernard's unusual view) deprive us of our ability to love completely until the general resurrection.

[55] *Vino enim divini amoris miscet etiam tunc dulcedinem naturalis affectionis, qua resumere corpus suum, ipsumque glorificatum, desiderat* (Dil 11.32 [SBOp 3:146; CF 13:123]). Bernard dedicates five paragraphs (Dil 11.29-33) to a kind of worry that before being rejoined to the body in the general resurrection we will be, in our incompleteness, still unable completely to love God. A reader is entitled to find a theological problem in that understanding of our destiny in God, but in it the ascetical Bernard's sense of oneness with his body is extraordinary. Regarding a need to be united to the body for fully loving God, see a parallel example in Div 41.12 (SBOp 6/1:253, lines 11–12).

[56] Nat am 10 (Davy, *Deux Traités*, 13; CF 30:64: "unwonted and sweet little affections"). Elder, commenting on his distinction between *affectio* and *affectus*, writes: "This gives William an opportunity he frequently avails himself of, to contrast what is transitory and fickle (the feminine term) with what is steadfast and persevering (the masculine term)" (Elder, "Christology," 105n150).

[57] Dil 7.19 (SBOp 3:135; CF 13:112).

[58] Bernard writes, "There is an affection that the flesh begets, and one that reason controls, and one that wisdom seasons": *Sed est affectio quam caro gignit,*

in the asceticism that he holds to be necessary. Yet he depicts *affectio* as an instrument of grace. He writes, "God creates the affection";[59] "He makes you desire, he is what you desire."[60] In the Augustinian climate of William's tract there is no such assurance.[61]

Bernard's incarnational lyricism luxuriates in the whole range of sensory image—of the Beloved's garden,[62] of heaven as eternal inebriation,[63] and, in other works, of beauty in the bride of the Canticle.[64] Bernard can exclaim, "I recognize you, Lord Jesus, so beautifully formed [*formosum*] in my very form!"[65] Franz Posset recalls Luther's remark "that there is 'no friendlier word on earth' than Bernard's phrase about Christ being 'bone from my bones and flesh from my flesh'" (Gen 2:23).[66]

The William of later works will come to express longing for the kiss of the Bridegroom's lips. The William found in the *Liber de amore*, with its three confusing tracts, is not there yet.

---

et est quam ratio regit, et est quam condit sapientia (Bernard, SC 50.4 [SBOp 2:80; CF 31:32]).

[59] Dil 7.22 (SBOp 3:137; CF 13:114).

[60] Dil 7.21 (SBOp 3:137; CF 13:114).

[61] Cf. Bernard, SC 19.7 (SBOp 1:112; CF 4:144). Without mistaking William for his philosophical master and without overlooking what even an early acquaintance with Cistercian spirituality contributed to William, one tends to recall Gilson's summary remark that "it is the Christian Creator Augustine adores but the creation he thinks of as a philosopher sometimes bears the marks of Plotinus' metaphysics" (Gilson, *Christian Philosophy*, 201).

[62] Dil 3.7–10 (SBOp 3:124–27; CF 13:99–102).

[63] Dil 11.33 (SBOp 3:147; CF 13:124–25).

[64] E.g., Bernard, SC 19.7 (SBOp 1:112; CF 4:144–45).

[65] *Quam formosum et in mea forma te agnosco, Domine Iesu* (Bernard, SC 25:9 [SBOp 1:168; CF 7:57]).

[66] Franz Posset, "*Divus Bernhardus*: Saint Bernard as Spiritual and Theological Mentor of the Reformer Martin Luther," in *Bernardus Magister: Papers Presented at the Nonacentenary Celebration of the Birth of Saint Bernard of Clairvaux, Kalamazoo, Michigan*, ed. John R. Sommerfeldt, CS 135 (Kalamazoo, MI: Cistercian Publications, and *Cîteaux: Commentarii Cistercienses*, 1992), 530. The author cites Martin Luther, *D. Martin Luthers Werke; kritische Gesamtausgabe* (Weimar: Hermann Böulau, 1883, 1911), 45:304, 1–3 (stenogram), lines 9–14 (print), in reference to Bernard's SC 2.6 (SBOp 1:12; CF 4:12).

Conclusion

These texts show a rich variation in early Cistercian spirituality. William is not an intellectualized clone of Bernard, nor is Bernard a lyrical version of William. At the same time, a splendidly Cistercian dimension shared in the two tracts is the constant awareness that God works from inside the human: we encounter the human being as made in the trinitarian image, or as constant receiver of desires from the Lover whom we ultimately desire.

William the contemplative receives from Augustine the insight that the closest we can come to seeing God in human time is to see in ourselves the created trinity of the image. Throughout William's account of his prayer life, we hear an antiphon: the intellectual reiterates that the only *intellectus* reaching God is *amor*. In William we see Augustine bearing fruit at Cîteaux. By contrast, in *On Loving God* the Bernard who knows Augustine[67] initiates his search for personal identity not by contemplating the riches of a created trinity but by endlessly rediscovering the poverty and helplessness revealed in his primal self-awareness.[68]

The appreciation of Bernard as prophet of experience—William knew him this way[69]—depends on a certain construct of the

---

[67] Gilson called attention early to the importance of discerning what in Bernard is not Augustinian. The author's long endnote, a pocket lecture, is a classic, meriting to be an essential chapter of the study. While quickly recognizing William as the true disciple of Augustine and declaring that "St. Bernard [too] knew his St. Augustine admirably," Gilson expresses frequent and deep misgivings about interpreting Bernard's writings in an Augustinian manner. Regarding what had been his own assumption that the influence of Augustine on Bernard, as a writer of his era, was "preponderant," he writes: "nothing but a patient examination of facts has forced me to abandon this hypothesis, or rather this unreasoned opinion—to my great surprise, let me add" (Gilson, *Mystical Theology*, 220–21n24).

[68] My allusion is, of course, to Wordsworth's "Ode ('There was a time')": "Not in entire forgetfulness, / And not in utter nakedness, / But trailing clouds of glory do we come / From God, who is our home" (*William Wordsworth: Selected Poems*, ed. Sandra Anstey [Oxford: Oxford University Press, 2006], 91, lines 62–65).

[69] Note, for example, the admiration for the experience that William considered characteristic of Bernard (in his Vita Bern 1.59 [CCCM 89B:74–75; PL

individual as *subject* of experience—i.e., of a self initially unaware that it is "in the image," a self that is less identified by beliefs than by a call to listen. Bernard surveys the raw material of what all rational creatures undergo in the course of their lives and couples it continuously with a prevenient grace awakening them to salvific reflections—e.g., to the demand of reason that those who share the self's nature be loved[70] or to the evidence that despite its pretensions the self finds its necessities met by God alone.[71] Through such reflection the lovableness of God is gradually revealed: *paulatim sensimque Deus innotescit.*[72]

The divine giver is made known in God's gifts, discovered first as sweet (*dulcis*) and then as given. In asserting that one who feels loved "will not have trouble in fulfilling the commandment to love his neighbor,"[73] Bernard suggests that God makes the rich traditions of religious doctrine (e.g., "the commandment") accessible to those initiated in experience. "Love," he writes, "is not imposed by a precept; it is planted in nature."[74] From awareness of a helpless self, loving itself, a biblical monotheist looks for the soul's advance to what may be later articulated as doctrines regarding the *image* of God; a Christian, specifically, sees the possibility of the soul's introduction to the *memoria Christi*. On what grounds could the author change this scheme of salvation in the "law of love"[75] in regard to the existence of populations lying outside medieval Christendom's awareness?

A succinct theology of experience lies at the heart of *On Loving God*. It is the justification for Bernard's later expression, "the book of experience" (*liber experientiae*)—the abbot's bold way of approximating *experientia* to the revelation of the Scriptures (the *liber Scrip-*

185:259C; Cawley, *Bernard*, 72–73]). Elder also calls attention to this admiration in "Making Virtues," 78.

[70] Bernard, Dil 8.23 (SBOp 3:139; CF 13:116).
[71] Dil 8.24–25 (SBOp 3:139–40; CF 13:116–17).
[72] Dil 15.39 (SBOp 3:153; CF 13:131).
[73] Dil 9.26 (SBOp 3:141; CF 113:118).
[74] Dil 8.23 (SBOp 3:138; CF 13:115).
[75] Dil 12.34–35 (SBOp 3:148–50; CF 13:125–27).

turae).[76] And one searches his works in vain for what some later writers on mysticism—of great pastoral concern and an excess of caution—propose as distinctions between "religious" experience and what many thinkers in a secular mode claim for fully human experience.[77] Until events befalling the human being are met by a reflective opening onto the *sapor* of God, Bernard seems not to consider them *experientia*. Many such disjointed happenings color the lives of those whom Bernard addresses as merely *insipientes*.

How might proper attention to the principal themes of *On Loving God* affect current Christian theology? To focus on the author's insistent choice of the *infideles* as the type representing that humanity beloved of God would be to rearrange some of the furniture of current thinking on the theology of religions. And, more fundamentally, to understand his view of *experientia* as revelation, the beginning of an awareness of God, would explain his reason for so canonizing the *infideles*.

Beginnings are the subject of *On Loving God*. Bernard orients us to a destitute self rather than to a trinitarian image, not because this is of itself preferable, but because (beyond our preferences) this is where our human consciousness begins—not in a metaphysical *memoria* informing us of the divine source of our nature, but "in the flesh." He is well past the middle of his book before he starts to sketch the ascent of love through four degrees. He has laid the theological grounds for alerting us to God's loving action within us—"where it ends"—in the Beatific Vision. And at this point he announces the objective of his treatise. "Let us now see," he writes, "where our love begins."[78]

---

[76] *Hodie legimus in libro experientiae* (Bernard, SC 3.1 [SBOp 1:14; CF 4:16]). I have traced current scholarly appraisals of Bernard's *liber experientiae* in my "Bernard of Clairvaux, William of St. Thierry, the Victorines," in *The Medieval Theologians*, ed. G. R. Evans (Oxford: Blackwell Publishers, 2001), 138–39 and notes.

[77] See Johannes Schuck, *Das religiöse Erlebnis beim hl. Bernhard von Clairvaux* (Würzburg: C. J. Becker, 1922).

[78] *Dicendum iam unde inchoet amor noster, quoniam ubi consummetur dictum est* (Bernard, Dil 7.22 [SBOp 3:138; CF 13:115]).

Tracking different points of departure in the spirituality of William and Bernard can open the observer to something fundamental in the very phenomenon of religion.

2

THE PRAYER OF DOM WILLIAM
A STUDY AND NEW TRANSLATION

David N. Bell

The *Oratio Domni Willelmi*—the title was obviously not given by William—is preserved today on a single leaf, recto and verso, of a single manuscript: Paris, Bibliothèque Mazarine, MS. 776, fol. 45^{rv}. This is a fine twelfth-century volume from the Cluniac priory of Saint Peter and Saint Paul at Reuil in the diocese of Meaux,[1] and it contains three other works of William: his *Meditativae orationes* (incomplete at the end), *De contemplando Deo*, and *De natura et dignitate amoris*. The manuscript is not without faults, but it remains the most important witness to the four treatises of William that it contains, and—given that it is our only witness to the text of the *Oratio*—we may, I think, have confidence in the accuracy of the transmission. We may also state with confidence that the *Oratio* is indeed a work of William, though it does not appear in any contemporary list of his works and did not find its way into the Bernardine corpus.[2]

---

[1] For a good description of the manuscript, including transcriptions of the *ex libris* inscriptions, see Guillaume de Saint-Thierry, *Deux traités de l'amour de Dieu: De la contemplation de Dieu. De la nature et de la dignité de l'amour*, ed. M.-M. Davy (Paris: J. Vrin, 1953), 8–10. Verdeyen's description in CCCM 88:149 is less satisfactory. See also the useful note by Dom Hourlier in Guillaume de Saint Thierry, *La contemplation de Dieu; L'Oraison de Dom Guillaume*, ed. and trans. Jacques Hourlier, rev. ed., SChr 61 *bis* (Paris: Éditions du Cerf, 1968), 22n1.

[2] Presumably because the manuscript did not come from Clairvaux. It is true that there is no conceivable way that William's Latin could be mistaken for that of Bernard, but that would not have prevented the attribution.

As to the date of the work, Dom Jacques Hourlier of the abbey of Solesmes has suggested that it must have been written just a little later than the *De contemplando Deo* and *De natura et dignitate amoris* and that its position in the Reuil manuscript (it appears immediately after these two treatises) is a true indication of its place in the chronology of William's writings. It may therefore be dated, he suggests, to around 1122, when William was the Benedictine abbot of Saint-Thierry near Rheims.[3] It would be some thirteen years before he would leave Saint-Thierry and take the Cistercian habit at Signy in 1135. Dom Hourlier may well be right. The *Oratio* gives every impression of being an early work, though 1122 is, perhaps, being a little too specific. I suspect (as we shall see) that it predates the sixth and tenth *Meditations*, and the *Meditations*—or, at least, a first draft of the *Meditations*—may well have been composed some time around 1128–1132.[4]

The *Oratio* was first edited (and well edited, though with minor inaccuracies) by Dom Hourlier in 1959 in the series Sources chrétiennes (a revised edition was published in 1968).[5] It was then edited again in 1965 by Fr. Robert Thomas of Sept-Fons in the series

---

[3] William, *Contemplation*, SChr 61 *bis*:49–50; Jacques Hourlier, Introduction to *Meditations*, in William of St. Thierry, *On Contemplating God, Prayer, Meditations*, trans. Sr. Penelope [Lawson], CF 3 (Spencer, MA, and Kalamazoo, MI: Cistercian Publications, 1977), 1–35, 65–70, 75–86, 179–86, here 68.

[4] I am here following Hourlier's persuasive arguments: see Hourlier, Introduction to *Meditations*, CF 3:83–86. There can be no doubt that the *Meditations* were begun at Saint-Thierry, and there can equally be no doubt that they were composed at various times. It is possible, too, that they may have been collected together (and possibly edited) when William was at Signy (see Jean Marie Déchanet, *William of St. Thierry: The Man and His Work*, trans. Richard Strachan, CS 10 (Spencer, MA: Cistercian Publications, 1972), 41. André Wilmart ("La série et la date des ouvrages de Guillaume de Saint-Thierry," *Revue Mabillon* 14 [1924]: 157–67, here 166) includes them among works composed at Saint-Thierry (he had been anticipated by André Adam, *Guillaume de Saint-Thierry: sa vie et ses œuvres* [Bourg: Impr. du "Journal de l'Ain," 1923], 53) and implies a starting date of about 1128. I can find no clues in the sixth and tenth *Meditations* that would suggest any specific date.

[5] See William, *Contemplation*, SChr 61 *bis* (note 1, above).

Pain de Cîteaux,[6] and finally by the Jesuit Paul Verdeyen in 2003 in the series Corpus Christianorum, Continuatio Mediaevalis.[7] All three editors classicize William's medieval orthography, a practice that is as irritating as it is misleading, but Verdeyen's text is the best we have, and it is that which I have used as the basis for this present translation. Both Dom Hourlier and Fr. Thomas included very sound French translations of the *Oratio* with their editions (and Dom Hourlier very sound notes with his), but the only English translation (so far as I am aware) is that by Sister Penelope Lawson, of the Anglican Community of Saint Mary the Virgin, published in 1977 in *The Works of William of St. Thierry*, volume one, in the Cistercian Fathers Series.[8] This translation, unfortunately, has too many paraphrases and is not always quite correct. Sometimes the translator has added words that are not there, and in one place there is an egregious error in translation that wholly distorts William's actual meaning.[9] Since the *Oratio* is an important piece of work, I thought it appropriate to prepare a more accurate English translation, and it is a pleasure to dedicate it to Dr. Rozanne Elder, whose generous friendship I have enjoyed for many years and whose meticulous work at Cistercian Publications saved me from more blunders than I care to remember.

It is interesting to compare William's *Prayer* with that of Aelred of Rievaulx, of which an admirable edition, translation, and study has recently been published.[10] It is difficult to imagine two more dissimilar items. Aelred's work, as Dr. Marsha Dutton has pointed

---

[6] Guillaume de S. Thierry, *Prière de Guillaume. Contemplation de Dieu*, ed. and trans. Robert Thomas, Pain de Cîteaux 23 (Roybon [France]: Abbaye de Chambarand, 1965).

[7] See *Guillelmi a Sancto Theodorico Opera Omnia, Pars III. Opera didactica et spiritualia, De sacramento altaris, De natura corporis et animae, De contemplando Deo, De natura, et dignitate amoris, Epistola ad fratres de Monte Dei*, ed. Stanislaus Ceglar (Sac alt) and Paul Verdeyen, CCCM 88 (Turnhout: Brepols, 2003), 169–71.

[8] See William, *Contemplation*, CF 3:71–74.

[9] See n65 below: *in seipso* has been read as *in teipso*.

[10] Aelred of Rievaulx, *Oratio pastoralis* (Orat past), in *For Your Own People: Aelred of Rievaulx's Pastoral Prayer*, ed. Marsha L. Dutton, trans. Mark DelCogliano, CF 73 (Kalamazoo, MI: Cistercian Publications, 2008).

out, has as its central focus an abbot's concern for his monks. Its pervasive themes are "the relationship of the shepherd and the flock, the abbot's desire for Jesus' assistance so that he may rule his community wisely and well, and the abbot's obedience to and imitation of Jesus."[11] They are indeed laudable goals. But William's *Oratio*, from a theological point of view, is far more formidable. He begins, innocently enough, with *Domine Iesu Christe, ueritas et uita*, thus quoting the gospel of John (which he will quote four more times in the brief course of his prayer), but then plunges us straight into a discussion of the place of imagination and intention (*intentio*) in prayer and contemplation, illustrated by a complex analogy drawn from medieval theories of vision. No sooner have we made our way through this than we are subjected to an even more profound discussion of the location of the Divine Christ (not the human Jesus) in the "consubstantiality of the Trinity." Then, in a most un-Cistercian manner, William explains what he means by "spiritual prayer" (*spiritualis oratio*) and concludes with a complicated paragraph that ends with the admonition that if we do not know how to ask God for something great (namely, the vision of his face [*vultus ejus*]), then nothing great shall we receive.

We then find the blunt *Explicit*, "It ends," and end it does, though I do not believe for a moment that this is where William intended it to end. It is undoubtedly a very abrupt and peculiar ending for a prayer, and we might have expected at least an Amen, such as we find (for example) at the end of the lovely thirteenth *Meditation*.[12] Aelred's prayer has an unmistakably prayerful ending—"Grant this, our sweetest Lord, who live and reign unto ages of ages. Amen"[13]—but Aelred's prayer is unmistakably a complete prayer as well. William's whole *Oratio*, in fact, gives me the impression of being unfinished and incomplete. Some of the Latin is convoluted

[11] Dutton, Introduction to Aelred, Orat past (CF 73:15), 1–33.

[12] William, "Meditatio: Seduxisti me" (CCCM 88:171–73, immediately following Verdeyen's edition of the *Oratio*). An English translation (with Dom Déchanet's introduction) can be found in William, Contem (CF 3:179–90).

[13] *dulcissimo Domino nostro, qui uiuis et regnas per omnia secula seculorum. Amen* (Aelred, Orat past [CF 73:56]).

and cumbersome (though that, alas, is not too unusual with William[14]), and then it just stops. And if it was incomplete, this, we might suggest, was why William did not include it in his own list of his own writings, which appears at the beginning of his *Letter to the Brethren of Mont-Dieu* (the *Golden Letter*).[15] How it came to be included in the Reuil manuscript, and the Reuil manuscript alone, we cannot say.

If there is one theme that runs through the whole of (what we have of) the *Oratio*, it is the theme of spiritual idolatry. William introduces the idea (and the word *idolatria*) in the first sentence, and it continues to the end. What he means is simple, though it has profound consequences, and it is all part of his doctrine of pure or spiritual prayer: that is to say, prayer devoid of any images. At the root of this lies not some Greek pseudo-Dionysian writer but the well-known Augustinian distinction of the three visionary levels of *corporalia, spiritualia,* and *intellectualia*.[16] *Corporalia* are no more than the corporeal or physical objects of the created order, those that we see with our physical eyes, and *spiritualia* are no more than those mental objects that we see with the eyes of our imagination. They range from simple imaginary or dream images to the extraordinary visions recorded in the book of Revelation. But beyond these are the *intellectualia*, "which are separated from every bodily sense and every *significativa aenigma* of the spirit."[17] That is to say, they are wholly extraconceptual and have no form of any sort, either

---

[14] Sr. Penelope Lawson puts the matter well: it frequently happens, she writes, that William's thought "is too big for words; he tries to say too much at once, and a sentence that is overcharged in Latin is inevitably more so in our own less succinct tongue. Occasionally also William gets tied up in his self-searching and seems to lose himself in his own words" (*The Meditations of William of St. Thierry: Meditativae Orationes,* trans. A Religious of C.S.M.V. [Sr. Penelope Lawson] [London: A. R. Mowbray, 1954], 103). This is the earlier version of the translation that appeared seventeen years later in CF 3.

[15] William, Ep frat 2–13 (SChr 223:130–39; CF 12:3–7).

[16] For a full and detailed account, see Augustine of Hippo, *De Genesi ad litteram libri duodecim,* in *Sancti Aureli Augustini Opera,* ed. Joseph Zycha, CSEL 28.1 (Vienna: F. Tempsky, 1894), 12.6–37 (PL 34:458–68).

[17] Augustine, Gen ad litt 12.27.55 (CSEL 28.1:420, lines 7–8; PL 34:477).

physical or imaginary. For William, anything less than the pure experience of God at this third and highest level is idolatry, and he leaves us in no doubt on the matter in his brief *Oratio*.

Unlike Aelred or Bernard, therefore, whose devotion to the humanity and passion of Christ was so vitally important to their spirituality, William's view of the humanity and passion of Christ is that they are no more (though no less) than a stepping-stone to the extraconceptual experience of his divinity. The intellect (*intellectus*), after all, is the mark of our creation *ad imaginem Dei*, and the business of the *intellectus* is to apprehend *intellectualia*. The soul abominates as idols the "phantasms of the heart" concerning God, says William in his second *Meditation*,[18] and the same theme recurs in the *Ænigma fidei*, the commentary on the Song of Songs, the commentary on Romans, and the *Letter to the Brethren of Mont-Dieu*—in other words, all through his life.[19] We can, of course, maintain that since the humanity and divinity of Christ are an unconfused union, to grasp the one is, by definition, to grasp the other, and this is true. William says so.

But if we do "develop a certain quasi-corporeal affection for the form of his humanity, on the grounds that it is one person with the [divine] son of God, we do not err, but we do, nevertheless, retard and hinder spiritual prayer."[20] He says the same thing in the commentary on the Song of Songs.[21] It is true that prayer at the second or "spiritual" level, when it is "clothed with human affection,"[22] is often swept up into the realm of the *intellectualia* by God's superabundant grace—the soul, he says, "sometimes perceives that the effort of its intention has actually been anticipated by [God]"[23]—but,

---

[18] William, Med 2.14: *Cordis sui phantasmata de te abominatur ut idola* (CCCM 89:12, lines 139–40; CF 3:101).

[19] William, Ænig 6 (CCCM 89A:132, lines 96–98; CF 9:39–40); William, Ænig 7 (CCCM 89A:132–33, lines 107–22; CF 9:40–41); Cant 16 (SChr 82:88–91; CF 6:13); Exp Rm 5 (on Rom 8:26) (CCCM 86:122–23, lines 451–96; CF 27:172); Ep frat 173–75 (SChr 223:264–65; CF 12:68–69).

[20] William, Orat 7.

[21] William, Cant 16–18 (SChr 82:88–92; CF 6:13–14).

[22] William, Cant 16 (SChr 82:88; CF 6:13).

[23] William, Orat 2.

in general, images of any sort, whether corporeal or spiritual/imaginary, are best avoided. This is what William means when, at the very beginning of the *Oratio*, he quotes Saint John, who tells us that those who truly worship God worship him "in spirit and in truth."[24]

William says just the same thing, and quotes precisely the same verse in his tenth *Meditation*, where he elaborates on the brief discussion in the *Oratio*: "For since I have not yet progressed beyond the first stages of my sensory imagination [*sensualis imaginationis meae rudimenta*], you will allow and be pleased that my still undeveloped soul [*infirmam adhuc animam meam*] follows its natural inclination [by dwelling] on your lowly [humanity] by means of some mental imagery."[25]

What manner of "mental imagery"? William embraces the baby Jesus in the manger, he adores his sacred infancy, he clings to the feet of the Crucified,[26] he puts his hand in the prints of the nails. Indeed, says he, of all the main reasons for the incarnation, not the least was that it enabled the babes in the Church (*paruuli in Ecclesia*) to find a form with which they were familiar, since they were not sufficiently advanced spiritually "to think on you in your own way [i.e., in your divinity]" (*tuo te modo cogitantes*). Thus, in the "sacrifice of their prayer" (exactly the same expression that we find in the *Oratio*[27]), they can set this form or face before them without endangering their faith while they are still unable to gaze on "that brightness of your divine majesty" (*claritatem illam diuinae maiestatis tuae*).[28]

Yet the contemplation of Christ's passion is still only a stepping stone to something more exalted: by thinking (the verb is *cogito*) on the good that he has done for us, we may be led suddenly or unexpectedly (*repente*) to the experience of the Highest Good, which is beyond all sensory imagination. Then, as the soul is imbued with joy by a more abundant flood of the river of God's grace, "she seems

---

[24] John 4:24. See n41 below.
[25] William, Med 10.4 (CCCM 89:58, lines 32–35; CF 3:152).
[26] See William, Orat 7.
[27] William, Orat 1.
[28] William, Med 10.4–5 (CCCM 89:58, lines 35–50; CF 3:152–53). Lawson mistranslates as "the brightness of the majesty of your divinity," CF 3:153.

to see you as you are [*sicuti est*],"[29] which leads us into those glorious realms, so dear to William, that it is not our business to investigate in this brief study.[30]

This is not what we would normally think of as "Cistercian spirituality"—by which most people mean Aelredian or Bernardine spirituality—but, as I have observed elsewhere, there never was one single Cistercian spirituality,[31] and William is decidedly more apophatic than any other of the great twelfth-century saints of Cîteaux.

So where are we to find the divinity of Christ? Neither in heaven nor on earth. If God is *ubique praesens et ubique totus*—"everywhere present and everywhere whole" (as Augustine and a host of others made abundantly clear[32])—then to locate him in any place is to limit him by enclosing him in that place and excluding him from others. God's location, therefore, can have nothing to do with space or place, and William totally transcends place and space by locating his divine Lord in the Trinity itself: "Your place is your Father, and you are the Father's place. From this place, therefore, you are localized. Yet this locality of yours is far higher and more secret than any lack of locality. This locality is the very unity of Father and Son, the consubstantiality of the Trinity."[33]

With this we must compare William's very similar treatment in the sixth *Meditation*. He begins with precisely the same question, drawn from John 1:38: "Rabbi, where do you dwell?" But his answer, though similar, is subtly different from that in the *Oratio*. Here is a translation:

---

[29] William, Med 10.8–9 (CCCM 89:59–60, lines 76–88; CF 3:154–55). To see God *sicuti est* (1 John 3:2) is the ultimate goal of the Christian mystic.

[30] I have endeavored to investigate them in my *The Image and Likeness: The Augustinian Spirituality of William of St. Thierry*, CS 78 (Kalamazoo, MI: Cistercian Publications, 1984), especially chaps. 4–6, and there are a number of more recent studies; see Aage Rydstrøm-Poulsen, "Research on William of Saint-Thierry from 1998 to 2008," *Analecta Cisterciensia* 58 (2008): 158–69.

[31] See David N. Bell, "Is There Such a Thing as 'Cistercian Spirituality'?" CSQ 33 (2008): 455–71.

[32] In Augustine and William, see Bell, *Image and Likeness*, 32, 54, 101, 110, 119.

[33] William, Orat 5.

You answer swiftly and say: "I am in the Father, and the Father is in me" [John 1:38]. . . .[34] Your place [*locus*], therefore, is the Father, and you are the Father's [place]. And not only that, but we are your place, and you are ours. Since then, O Lord Jesus, you are in the Father and the Father in you, O most high and undivided Trinity, you are your own place: you are indeed your own place, you are your own heaven. For just as you do not have anything [in you] from outside [of yourself], so you need no [place] in which to dwell, save from yourself in yourself.[35]

William then goes on to expand on the idea that when the divine Son dwells in us, we are his heaven, and when we dwell in him, he is our heaven. And how is this indwelling possible? By likeness![36] Yet for Christ, the heaven of heavens is his own eternity (*eternitas*), where he is what he is in himself; and if the Father is in the Son, and the Son in the Father, it is the Holy Spirit that unites them. Thus does William introduce all three inseparable persons of the undivided Trinity and touch on that trinitarian mysticism of which he was such a master and which occupies such an important place in the pages of the *Golden Letter*.

This is not the case with the *Oratio*. William mentions only the *locus* of the Trinity as being its own consubstantiality (rather than its eternity, though they amount to precisely the same thing), and we have no discussion of the mutual indwelling of God and his human creation, and the Holy Spirit makes no appearance in the *Oratio*, save when William tells us that any form of prayer that

---

[34] Here William adds John 14:20 and John 17:23.

[35] William, Med 6.10–11 (CCCM 89:35–36, lines 77–86; CF 3:128). The last sentence reads . . . *sicut non habens ex quo, sic non indigens in quo subsistas, nisi ex teipso in teipso.* The contrast here is between *subsistere in* and *subsistere ex*: the former simply means 'to dwell, shelter, or lodge'; the latter (a philosophical usage) means 'to depend for one's existence on (or derive one's existence from) something'. God derives his existence only from himself.

[36] See Bell, *Image and Likeness*, chap. 3, and the magisterial study in two volumes by Robert Javelet, *Image et ressemblance au XIIe siècle, de saint Anselme à Alain de Lille* (Paris: Letouzey et Ané, 1967), 1:188.

contains images—idolatrous images—will hinder the coming of the Comforter.[37]

In short, it seems clear to me that the discussion in the sixth *Meditation* elaborates and concludes the truncated discussion of God's *locus* in the *Oratio*, just as the discussion in the tenth *Meditation* does the same thing for the subject of pure or spiritual prayer. My own view, therefore, is that in the *Oratio* we have an abortive attempt at a *Meditation* that never—on its own—quite worked. It needed elaboration, and it received that elaboration in *Meditations* 6 and 10. William was quite right, therefore, to omit it from his list of writings, and (as I have said) the question of how it found its way into the Reuil manuscript (some monk ransacking the garbage bucket? Some jottings at the end of a manuscript of the *De natura et dignitate amoris*?) remains a Great Unknown.

What were William's sources for the *Oratio*? At the basis of his entire discussion of spiritual prayer lies, as we have seen, the Augustinian distinction of *corporalia*, *spiritualia*, and *intellectualia*, which, by the twelfth century, had become a commonplace of medieval theology. William's biblical quotations and allusions are taken primarily from the Gospel of John (five citations), then from Genesis and Psalms (two citations each), and finally (single citations) from Deuteronomy, the Song of Songs, and the Gospel according to Saint Matthew. Dom Hourlier also points to "la finale du canon de la messe."[38] *Pace* Dom Hourlier,[39] I do not think we can see in William's discussion of the *locus* of God any direct attack on the trinitarian views of Peter Abelard.

Here, then, is a new translation of this interesting text, together with such notes as are necessary to understand William's dense Latin and not always obvious analogies.

The Prayer of Dom William

1. Lord Jesus Christ, truth and life,[40] who declared that those who, in the future, would be true worshipers of your Father would

---

[37] William, Orat 7.

[38] Hourlier, Introduction, SChr 61 *bis*:51.

[39] Hourlier, Introduction, SChr 61 *bis*:124–25n1.

[40] John 14:6: *Ego sum via, et veritas, et vita.*

be those who worshiped Him in spirit and in truth,[41] free my soul, I pray you, from idolatry. Free it, lest, in seeking you, it should fall in with its companions[42] and begin to stray after their flocks during the sacrifice of its prayer.[43] Let it rather lie down with you, and be nourished by you in the midday heat of your love.[44]

2. For by a certain natural feeling it [receives] from its source,[45] [the soul], in a certain way, dreams (as it were) of your face in whose image it was created.[46] But it has either lost, or has not developed,

---

[41] John 4:24 (Verdeyen's citation of John 4:23 is a typographical error). Worshiping God *in spiritu et ueritate* is worshiping him at the level of the *intellectualia*, free from any form or concept, including Christ's humanity. We may compare William, Med 10.3 (CCCM 89:58, line 28; CF 3:152), and William, Cant 17–20 (SChr 82:90–94; CF 6:14–15), where William uses the same Johannine verse to introduce a much longer discussion of precisely the same theme. Since we cannot attain to the full knowledge of God in this life, says William, God entrusts to the soul "a certain semblance of the knowledge of himself, not in an imaginary mental image, but in a certain devout affection" [*aliquam cognitionis suae effigiem, non praesumpti phantasmatis, sed piae cujusdam affectionis*] (William, Cant 20 [SChr 82:94; CF 6:15]). Theologically, William is treading on dangerous ground here, and those familiar with the Eastern Orthodox tradition will detect a foretaste of what, a century later, would be Barlaam's arguments in the Hesychast controversy.

[42] Reading *suos* with Verdeyen and Thomas. Hourlier reads *tuos*. The soul's companions and flocks are the products of the imagination, i.e., the *spiritualia* of Augustine's threefold visionary scheme. Falling in with these companions and straying after their flocks is idolatry.

[43] *Sacrificium orationis* is an expression that occurs at least four times in William: see n27 above (Med 10.5 [CCCM 89:58, line 48; CF 3:152]; Exp Rm 5 [on Rom 8:26] [CCCM 86:122, lines 456–57; CF 27:172]; and Ep frat 173 [SChr 223:282; CF 12:68]). Ep frat 4 (SChr 223:194; CF 12:9–10) has *sacrificium devotionis*. William did not invent the phrase; it appears (for example) in the fifth-century *Homiliary* of Eusebius Gallicanus, and also in Augustine, Gregory the Great, and Aelred of Rievaulx. *Pace* Sister Penelope, we cannot say that William uses it "frequently" (William, *Contemplating*, CF 3:71n4).

[44] Cf. Song 1:6.

[45] Sister Penelope's translation of *principium* as "First Cause," CF 3:72, is misleading here: it implies that William has been reading Aristotle, which he certainly had not. The *principium*—source or origin—of the soul is God, who (as William is about to say) created the soul in his own image.

[46] Gen 1:27, but the addition of *facies* is William's own. *Facies* may also mean "form, appearance, nature," or "character."

the habit of not agreeing to replace this [image] with another when many [other images] present themselves [to it] at the time of its prayer.[47] But when it struggles to direct the gaze[48] of its intention onto this [face], yet not seeing it, [the soul] sometimes perceives that the effort of its intention has actually been anticipated by it. Often, however, it is only in the heavy sweat of its brow that it can eat its bread, in punishment from the ancient curse.[49] And often, too, neither the latter way nor the former applies,[50] but [the soul] is forced to return to the house of its poverty[51] poor and hungry.[52] For it either makes speedy progress or speedily falls short.

3. Just as with the eye, the pupil will not project its vision merely because it sends forth from itself a natural beam of light, or because it finds that the path [this beam] takes through the air is pure and clear.[53] [The beam it emits] must also strike the object at which it is

[47] The cumbersome English here intentionally reflects William's cumbersome Latin (Sister Penelope and the French translators paraphrase the sentence). What William means is that the soul, being created *ad imaginem Dei*, has a natural tendency to seek the Face of God at the extraconceptual level of the *intellectualia*, but (because of its lack of progress) it finds that, when praying, it is confronted with a host of conceptual or imaginary images at the level of *spiritualia*. These tend to replace the extraconceptual image of God's Face, and, since the soul has either lost or not acquired the habit of refusing to allow this to happen, the imaginary images take over.

[48] *Acies*: "gaze, glance, keenness of vision, mental effort."

[49] See Gen 3:17-19.

[50] William is terse: *Saepe uero nec sic, nec sic.*

[51] *Domus paupertatis*: William uses the same expression in Nat am 10 (CCCM 88:185, lines 295–96; CF 30:64) and Cant 146 (SChr 223:310; CF 6:119). He probably took it from Augustine, En in Ps 84.7 (PL 37:1072).

[52] In these three sentences William suggests three possible outcomes for the soul's attempts at experiencing the Face of God extraconceptually. Sometimes, when the soul is striving unsuccessfully to achieve its goal, God comes to its aid and, by a superabundance of grace, anticipates (*praeuenire*) its efforts and precipitates the soul into the experience it seeks (see Bell, *Image and Likeness*, 33, 207–11). At other times, however, this is not the case, and the soul achieves its goal only after long and arduous effort. And sometimes, alas, it has no success at all and is forced to return to its *domus paupertatis* wholly unsatisfied.

[53] To appreciate William's rather complicated analogy, we have to understand the medieval theory of vision. For the vast majority of medieval scientists

aimed and in which it ends as quickly as possible, for if it continues further it exhausts itself and does not accomplish its proper intention.[54] [Instead], it splits up into [many] parts, and, being divided, perishes. It is the same with [the soul's] intention in contemplation or prayer. If the understanding of reason or of love[55] does not receive something definite from you, something placed before it very quickly, where its impulse[56] can rest and its intention find an end, and [where it can] offer and lay down the fruit of its devotion, then contemplation is dulled, prayer becomes lukewarm, one's intention

---

(following Augustine), vision was not a passive but an active phenomenon. That is to say, they did not think in terms of light rays from an illuminated object being received by the eye and processed by the brain. Instead, the eye itself was thought to emit a beam of light, rather like a minute searchlight, which would fall upon an illuminated object (one cannot see in the dark), establish contact with it, produce an image inside the eye, and thus render the object visible. This also requires that the air between the eye and the object be clear. If, for example, it is full of fog or smoke, the beam emitted cannot find its object and does not see it. But if there is no object there at all, then the beam finds nothing on which it can fall, and it wanders off into the distance, fragments, and vanishes away. Nothing whatever is seen. Furthermore, says William, this act of vision must occur rapidly. If the eye is looking for something and does not find it, it soon gives up. Baldwin of Forde uses the same analogy in an even more complicated way and (rightly) warns his listeners that they will need to pay the closest attention to what he is saying (see Baldwin of Forde, Tractate 13, in *Spiritual Tractates*, 2 vols., trans. David N. Bell, CF 41 [Kalamazoo, MI: Cistercian Publications, 1986], 2:134–35, 139).

[54] Or its "true goal," but we need to keep the parallelism between the *intentio* of the eye in vision and the *intentio* of the soul in contemplation.

[55] *Intellectus rationis aut amoris.* This is pure William, and much has been written on the subject. See, for example, E. Rozanne Elder, "William of Saint Thierry: Rational and Affective Spirituality," in *The Spirituality of Western Christendom*, ed. E. Rozanne Elder, CS 30 (Kalamazoo, MI: Cistercian Publications, 1976), 85–105, 197–200, here 85–105; and Bell, *Image and Likeness*, 217–49 (chap. 6).

[56] *Affectus*, which is a word of wide meaning in William. See, for example, W. Zwingmann, "*Ex affectu mentis*: Über die Vollkommenheit menschlichen Handelns un menschlicher Hingabe nach Wilhelm von St. Thierry," *Cîteaux* 18 (1967): 5–37; this is an excerpt from Zwingmann's thesis, "Der Begriff *Affectus* bei Wilhelm von St.-Thierry," PhD dissertation, Rome: Gregorian University, 1964.

becomes exhausted, understanding is weakened, and reason can do nothing.

4. But what have I in Heaven, and what do I desire on earth apart from you?[57] For if, in praying, I seek you in that heaven I see above me—beautiful, certainly, yet corporeal—I make just the same mistake as if I sought you in the earth on which I tread. If [I seek you] in any place whatever, or outside of place, I either enclose you in a place which you have created, or exclude you from it! And if I visualize for you, my God, any form or anything formed,[58] I am become an idolater.[59]

5. O Truth, answer me, I beg you! "Rabbi, where do you dwell?" "Come," he said, "and see."[60] "Do you not believe that I am in the Father, and the Father is in me?"[61] Thanks be to you, O Lord: we have made no small progress—we have found your place![62] Your place is your Father, and you are the Father's place. From this place, therefore, you are localized. Yet this locality of yours is far higher and more secret than any lack of locality. This locality is the very unity of Father and Son, the consubstantiality[63] of the Trinity.

6. What then? Surely we have not found a place for the Lord in one way alone? No indeed! Shine forth, O soul, as much as you can, not so much by the [logical] activity of reason, as by the affective [understanding] of love.[64] And if God's place is God, and if this locality of the Trinity is its consubstantiality, then, having done away with all the usual conceptions of place and location, understand that you have found God in himself.[65] He himself shows this

---

[57] Ps 72:25.

[58] See Deut 4:12.

[59] *Idolatra fio*: William here returns to the theme of his first sentence.

[60] John 1:38-39.

[61] John 14:10; see John 10:38.

[62] See Ps 131:5.

[63] *Consubstantialitas*. So far as I am aware, the word first appears in Hilary of Poitiers and Ambrosiaster. Bernard of Clairvaux uses it twice, and it also appears in William's Ænig 90 (CCCM 89A:185, line 1840; CF 9:116–17).

[64] *Non tam rationis effectu, sed quam amoris affectu*. This, too, is typical William.

[65] There is here a grave error of translation in Sister Penelope's text. She translates *in seipso* as if it were *in teipso*: "you have found God in yourself."

to be so, he who is so much more true and certain as he is what he is from himself, in himself, and through himself. And as those ancient philosophers defined it with regard to truth, "He possesses being from what he is in such a way that nothing can be from which his being can be not being."[66] What is there more certain, what more firmly based, to which our intention may be directed [and] which our affection may grasp?

7. But if we sometimes clasp the feet of Jesus[67] in our prayer, and develop a certain quasi-corporeal affection for the form of his humanity, on the grounds that it is one person with the [divine] son of God, we do not err, but we do, nevertheless, retard and hinder spiritual prayer, as he himself tells us: "It is expedient for you that I depart. Unless I go away, the Paraclete will not come to you."[68]

This, indeed, is (effectively) what William does say in his discussion of the same question in the sixth *Meditation*, but it is not what he says here. God's place is God, and when you find him, you find him *in himself*.

[66] *Sic habet esse unde est, ut nichil possit esse, unde ei esse possit non esse.* This is a nightmare to translate. Sister Penelope paraphrases: "He has being by such right that nothing exists which could possibly challenge his right to be" (CF 3:73). Dom Hourlier is a little closer to the Latin: "il possède l'être à tel titre, qu'il n'existe rien qui puisse être pour lui un titre à ne pas être" (*Contemplation*, SChr 61 *bis*:127). Both convey the sense, but what is the source? Who are these "ancient philosophers" whom William cites? The sentence, as it appears in William, appears nowhere in the pages of the Migne Patrology, nor in any of that large repository of writings included in the Library of Latin Texts database published by Brepols. Dom Hourlier, *Contemplation*, SChr 61 *bis*:126, to whom we are indebted, suggests that at the basis of the *dictum* is Zeno as quoted by Augustine in his C acad 2.5.11 (PL 32:925)—*Id verum percipi posse, quod ita esset animo impressum ex eo unde esset, ut esse non posset ex eo unde non esset*—and he is probably right. The electronic databases offer no help, and I suspect that the form of the quotation as it appears in the *Oratio* is William's own—hence his attributing it to *antiqui illi philosophi* in the plural.

[67] See Matt 28:9 (Verdeyen's citation of Matt 25:9 is a typographical error).

[68] John 16:7. William means that Jesus' physical form—the corporeal imagination—must be put aside if one is to pray to him truly in the Spirit/Paraclete. Spiritual prayer, as we have seen, is beyond all images. He quotes the same verse in Cant 17 (SChr 223:90; CF 6:14) and explains there what he means: "'It is expedient for you that I depart'—that is, that I remove from your sight the

8. If, however, we give ourselves up wholly to idleness and sloth, yet call on God out of the depths of our ignorance,[69] as though from a prison cell, and if we really wish to be heard, but have no interest in the grace of the face of him to whom we cry, and if we do not care whether he gives what we ask in anger or pleasure, so long as we get it, then people like this must be content with what they receive from God. For since they do not know how to ask for something great from God, what they receive is not great either.

It ends.

---

mask [*persona*] of my humanity—'for unless I go away, the Paraclete will not come to you,' for as long as someone praying thinks of anything corporeal in him to whom he prays, he prays devoutly [*pie*], but not wholly spiritually [*non omnino spiritualiter*]."

[69] See Ps 129:1.

3

A Fresh Look at William
of Saint-Thierry's
Excerpts from the Books of Blessed Ambrose
on the Song of Songs

Mark DelCogliano

Like many monks of his era, William of Saint-Thierry had a passionate interest in the Song of Songs. He left us no fewer than four works that deal with this biblical book.[1] Perhaps the earliest is the so-called *Brief Commentary*, which is thought to be a reworked version of notes made of conversations on the biblical book that William and Bernard had while convalescing in the infirmary at Clairvaux sometime after 1118.[2] During his tenure as abbot of Saint-Thierry (1121–1135), William composed two *florilegia* of patristic interpretations of the Song, one drawn from the works of Ambrose of Milan (Cant Amb) and the other from the works of Gregory the Great (Cant Greg).[3] His own commentary on the Song

---

[1] William, *Expositio super Cantica canticorum* (Cant), *Brevis commentatio* (Brev com); *Excerpta de libris beati Ambrosii super Cantica canticorum* (Cant Amb); *Excerpta ex libris beati Gregorii super Cantica canticorum* (Cant Greg), ed. Paul Verdeyen, et al., CCCM 87 (Turnhout: Brepols, 1997), 205–384, 385–444.

[2] See William, Vita Bern 1.32–34 (CCCM 89B:58–60; PL 185:246B–247D; William, *Bernard of Clairvaux: Early Biographies, Vol. I by William of St. Thierry*, trans. Martinus Cawley [Lafayette, OR: Abbey of Our Lady of Guadalupe, 1990], 44).

[3] On the date of the *florilegia*, see William, Brev com (CCCM 87:387) and Paul Verdeyen, Introduction to *Expositio super Epistolam ad Romanos*, CCCM 86 (Turnhout: Brepols, 1989), xxvii.

of Songs was written in his earliest years as a Cistercian monk at Signy (1135–1138).[4]

There has been some debate over the purpose and significance of the two patristic *florilegia*. Hermann Kutter and André Wilmart considered them part of William's arsenal against Peter Abelard, a judgment that turns out to be untenable given their date.[5] André Adam and Jean Marie Déchanet viewed them as examples of William's industrious research into what the fathers said about the Song.[6] Déchanet went so far as to dismiss them as simple compilations of patristic texts that offered little insight into William beyond his dedication to the thought of the church fathers and presumed that they were conceived as source material for William's or another's (possibly Bernard's) commentary on the biblical book.[7] Louis Bouyer shared Déchanet's view that William produced these *florilegia* as "patristic dossiers" for those planning to comment on the Song of Songs and endorsed Déchanet's suggestion that William possibly compiled them at the request of and for the use of Bernard.[8] In the estimation of these scholars, these two patristic *florilegia* are of little or no significance for understanding William.

William's Gregorian *florilegium* has attracted more attention recently. Paul Verdeyen, the text's most recent editor, suggested that William hid a personal message in the collection by employing a unique method of excerption whereby he did not simply copy blocks of texts from his source but produced a careful pastiche of Gregory's

---

[4] William himself tells us that he ended his commentary abruptly (at Song 3:4) when he took up his pen against Peter Abelard; see William, Ep frat Praef. 9–10 (CCCM 88:226; CF 12:6).

[5] Hermann Kutter, *Wilhelm von St. Thierry: ein Repräsentant der mittelalterlichen Frömmigkeit* (Giessen [Ger]: Ricker, 1898), 49, 64–65; André Wilmart, "La série et la date des ouvrages de Guillaume de Saint-Thierry," *Revue Mabillon* 14 (1924): 157–67, here 165.

[6] André Adam, *Guillaume de Saint-Thierry: sa vie et ses œuvres* (Bourg: Impr. du "Journal de l'Ain," 1923), 51–52; Jean Marie Déchanet, *William of St Thierry: The Man and His Work*, trans. Richard Strachan, CS 10 (Kalamazoo, MI: Cistercian Publications, 1972), 35.

[7] Déchanet, *William of St Thierry*, 35.

[8] Louis Bouyer, *The Cistercian Heritage* (London: Mowbray, 1958), 79–80.

texts.[9] Hence Verdeyen was the first to propose that one of William's *florilegia* might add something to our knowledge of William's doctrine. Verdeyen's suggestion is attractive, given William's remarks at the beginning of his commentary on Romans, where he says that he has woven together the opinions and statements of the fathers in order to avoid the appearance of novelty by appeal to their authority.[10] But on further analysis, Verdeyen's hypothesis has been revealed as without merit. Elsewhere I have argued that William's Gregorian *florilegium* was not conceived as a mere preparation for a commentary on the Song of Songs (*pace* Déchanet and Bouyer) or a compilation of patristic *auctoritates* (*pace* Kutter and Wilmart), but rather that William composed it by a unique method of excerption in order to produce a kind of running Gregorian commentary on the Song of Songs, a commentary whose thought is thoroughly and genuinely Gregorian and which, as such, contains nothing of William's own original ideas (*pace* Verdeyen).[11]

In the following remarks, I turn my attention to William's Ambrosian *florilegium*, titled *Excerpts from the Books of Blessed Ambrose on the Song of Songs*. Considerably longer than the Gregorian *florilegium*, it is a massive work that William himself called "large and remarkable."[12] I will demonstrate that the character of the Ambrosian *florilegium* is fundamentally different from that of the Gregorian *florilegium*: William's method of excerption is traditional and does not present itself as a running Ambrosian commentary on the Song.[13] But one of the striking differences between the two *florilegia*

---

[9] Verdeyen, Introduction to Cant Amb (CCCM 87:392).

[10] William, Exp Rm Praef 1–19 (CF 27: 15–16).

[11] Mark DelCogliano, "The Composition of William of St. Thierry's *Excerpts from the Books of Blessed Gregory on the Song of Songs*," *Cîteaux* 58 (2007): 57–76.

[12] William, Ep frat Praef. 11: *Excerpsi enim ex libris sancti Ambrosii quicquid in eis disseruit super Cantica canticorum, opus grande et inclytum* (CCCM 88:226–27; SChr 223:138; CF 12:6).

[13] *Contra* Thomas Falmagne, who suggests that both the Gregorian and the Ambrosian *florilegia* tend to present a complete commentary on the biblical book (Thomas Falmagne, *Un texte en contexte. Les Flores paradisi et le milieu culturel de Villers-en-Brabant dans la première moitié du 13ᵉ siécle* [Turnhout: Brepols, 2001], 379).

is that the Ambrosian includes a prologue that has no parallel in the Gregorian. I argue that in this prologue William does in fact reveal some of his own ideas about the Song of Songs. Hence this study of the prologue of the Ambrosian *florilegium* allows new vistas on the doctrine of William from an unexpected and untapped source.

General Description of the Ambrosian *Florilegium*

William organized his book of excerpts from Ambrose into one hundred forty-five chapters and presented each as a single excerpt from a single work. But on further analysis, the composition of the *florilegium* is more complicated than William would have us believe. Antonius Van Burink, the text's editor, noted the presence of two hundred forty-six distinct excerpts, though he could not identify the provenance of twenty-three of them. But I have identified the source of two of these twenty-three.[14] The two hundred forty-six excerpts derive from fifteen treatises and seven letters of Ambrose. In the following table, the number in the right-hand column indicates the number of excerpts from the work in the left-hand column:

Expositio psalmi CXVIII	100
Isaac vel anima	40
De virginitate	27
De virginibus (ad sororem)	13
De bono mortis	6
Expositio evangeli secundum Lucam	5
De sacramentis	4
De apologia David altera	4
De mysteriis	3
De spiritu sancto	2
De Iacob	2

[14] Cant Amb 1, lines 3–4 (*Apologia David altera* 8.43), and Cant Amb 2, lines 11–16 (*De paenitentia* 2.6).

De officiis	2
De Nabuthae historia	1
De paenitentia	1
Epistola 11 *Irenaeo*	4
Epistola 12 *Irenaeo*	2
Epistola 31 *Orontiano*	1
Epistola 34 *Sabino*	1
Epistola 39 *Sabino*	2
Epistola 52 *Anysio*	1
Epistola 54 *Irenaeo*	2

In most cases, William correctly identifies the source of his excerpt, but sometimes he is mistaken. For example, he mistakenly attributes two of the excerpts from *Epistola* 11 *Irenaeo*, one to the letter *Ad Simplicianum* (Cant Amb 16) and the other to *Expositio psalmi CXVIII* (Cant Amb 17).[15]

Of the one hundred forty-five chapters in the *florilegium*, ninety-four contain a single excerpt from a single work. Forty-nine chapters contain multiple excerpts. Of these, twenty contain more than one excerpt from the same work,[16] fifteen contain more than one excerpt from different works,[17] and fourteen contain at least one excerpt from a known work and at least one excerpt of unknown provenance.[18] Finally, the remaining two chapters each contain what is presumably a single excerpt of unknown provenance.[19] Hence, though William presents each chapter as a single

[15] See also William, Cant Amb 40, 59, 81, 105, 133, and 139 for other examples of William's mistakes in attribution.

[16] From the Exp ps 118: Cant Amb 6, 22, 27, 29, 39, 72, 74, 92, 96, 101, 106, 127, and 134; from the *De virginibus*: Cant Amb 3; from the *Isaac*: Cant Amb 78, 114, and 119; from the *De virginitate*: Cant Amb 98 and 100; from Ep 39 *Sabino*: Cant Amb 113.

[17] William, Cant Amb 2, 14, 20, 31, 57, 61, 64, 68, 70, 73, 77, 83, 94, 107, and 145.

[18] William, Cant Amb 1, 19, 53, 60, 62, 63, 65, 67, 97, 102, 108, 112, 115, and 123.

[19] William Cant Amb 109 and 111.

excerpt from a single work, only a little fewer than two-thirds of the chapters actually fit that pattern.

The titles that William uses to refer to the works from which he has excerpted sometimes differ from the standard titles assigned to them. For example, he uses the title *Super beati immaculati* to refer to the *Expositio psalmi CXVIII*. He derives this title from the first words of Psalm 118:1 (*beati immaculati*). Similarly, he calls *De mysteriis* by the name *De sacramentis*, which is confusing because Ambrose wrote two treatises, one called *De mysteriis* and the other *De sacramentis*, and William quotes from both. In a similar vein, William uses the title *De patriarchis* for three separate treatises: (1) *Isaac vel anima*, (2) *De Iacob*, and (3) *De patriarchis*.[20] Likewise, he refers to both *De virginitate* and *De virginibus* as *Ad sororem*, even though Ambrose wrote only the latter to his sister Marcellina. Finally, William refers to two separate letters written to Sabinus as *Ad Sabinum*[21] and three separate letters written to Irenaeus as *Ad Irenaeum*.[22]

Both the manner in which William organizes his excerpts and the inclusion of the titles of the works from which the excerpts are taken constitute major differences between the Gregorian and Ambrosian *florilegia*. He presents the excerpts in the Gregorian *florilegium* not as coming from a particular source but as commenting on a particular verse of the Song. Though he orders the Ambrosian excerpts more or less according to the sequence of the verses of the Song on which they comment, he presents each chapter as an extract from a particular work, not as a comment on a particular verse. In the Gregorian *florilegium* he does not even list his sources. Rather, he begins each chapter with the citation of the relevant verse of the Song as the lemma, and the excerpt from Gregory follows. As a result, the Gregorian *florilegium* reads like a self-contained Gregorian commentary on the Song of Songs. In contrast, the Ambrose *florilegium* does not mask the fact that it is a collection of excerpts.

---

[20] Note that William quotes from *De patriarchis* only twice. In Cant Amb 62, he refers to it as *De patriarchis*, but in Cant Amb 105 as *De benedictionibus patriarchae*.

[21] William, Cant Amb 77 and 113 (CCCM 87:301–4, 347–48).

[22] William, Cant Amb 117, 129, 124, and 126 (CCCM 87:352, 364, 359, 362).

The differences outlined in the previous paragraph are due to the fact that William employs quite different methods of excerption in each *florilegium*. In the Ambrosian *florilegium*, William's method is analogous to cutting and pasting in a word processor. He excerpts blocks of text from Ambrose and places them one after the other. His method here is quite traditional, found in many other medieval texts.[23] In the Gregorian *florilegium*, William uses a unique method of excerption. When there are several Gregorian passages on a particular verse of the Song, he carefully weaves them together to produce a single logical unit of Gregorian commentary. As a result of this weaving together, William frequently rearranges the order of Gregory's lines. In contrast, in the Ambrosian *florilegium* he usually preserves the lines of Ambrosian texts in their pristine order. Although William's interweaving and rearrangement necessitate a host of minor changes in the Gregorian *florilegium*, he never compromises the *thought* of Gregory. The modification of the Gregorian texts is *structural*, and it leaves Gregory's *doctrine* intact.[24] Because William employs a much more straightforward method of excerption for the Ambrosian *florilegium*, it does not contain the same kinds of textual changes as does the Gregorian *florilegium*. In consequence of this difference, the changes that William does make to the Ambrosian texts may be more telling of his own ideas.

The Prologue of the Ambrosian *Florilegium*

The Ambrosian *florilegium* also includes a prologue, which has no parallel in the Gregorian *florilegium*. The Gregorian begins by citing Song 1:1 as the lemma and follows that immediately with commentary drawn from the works of Gregory. In contrast, the Ambrosian *florilegium* begins with five chapters of prologue that

---

[23] The same traditional method is used in the Gregorian *florilegia* on the Song of Songs that were compiled by Paterius and Bede; see DelCogliano, "Composition," 64–66. For further comments on medieval collections of excerpts, see DelCogliano, "Composition," 74–75.

[24] For a more detailed treatment of the method of excerption in the Gregorian *florilegium*, with examples, see DelCogliano, "Composition," 64–74.

are preceded in the two best manuscripts by *prologus* or *incipit prologus* and followed by *explicit prologus*.[25] Hence the prologue of the Ambrosian *florilegium* probably stems from William himself, not a copyist. This prologue constitutes another of the major differences between the Gregorian and Ambrosian *florilegia*. It is here that William expresses his own thoughts about reading the Song of Songs using the words of the Milanese bishop. The prologue thus constitutes the major site in the *florilegium* for recovering William's own ideas.

The five chapters of the Ambrosian prologue comprise eight distinct excerpts, only four of which come from passages in which Ambrose comments on the Song. In the following list, these four excerpts are marked with an asterisk:

Cant Amb 1, lines 3–4	*Apologia David altera* 8.43
Cant Amb 1, lines 4–6	(of unknown provenance)
Cant Amb 2, lines 2–10	*Expositio psalmi CXVIII* 12.2
Cant Amb 2, lines 11–16	*De paenitentia* 2.6
Cant Amb 3, lines 2–19	**De virginibus* 2.42–43
Cant Amb 3, lines 20–30	**De virginibus* 2.40–41
Cant Amb 4, lines 2–5	*Expositio psalmi CXVIII* 4.12
Cant Amb 5, lines 2–9	**De virginibus* 2.39–40[26]

[25] The two best manuscripts, both from the twelfth century, contain both *florilegia* and are connected with the Abbey of Saint-Thierry: (1) Reims, Bibliothèque municipale, MS. 142, twelfth century, originally from the Abbey of Saint-Thierry [=R]; (2) Valenciennes, Bibliothèque municipale, MS. 50, twelfth century, originally from the Abbey of Saint-Amand [=V]. William's successor at Saint-Thierry was Hellinus, the prior of Saint-Amand. Verdeyen surmises that Hellinus had copies made of both *florilegia* for his original monastery when he became abbot of Saint-Thierry; see CCCM 87:387.

[26] Ambrose of Milan, "De paenitentia" in *Sancti Ambrosii Opera*, ed. Carolus Schenkl, CSEL 32 (Vienna: F. Tempsky, 1897), 117–206; Ambrose of Milan, *Ambrosius pars V: Expositio psalmi CXVIII*, ed. Michael Petschenig and Michaela Zelzer, CSEL 62 (Vienna: Verlag des Österreichischen Akademie de Wissenschaften, 1996); Ambrose of Milan, *La pénitence*, ed. Roger Gryson, SChr 179 (Paris: Les Éditiones du Cerf, 1971); and Ambrose of Milan, *De virginibus, libri tres*, ed. Egnatius Cazzaniga (Turin: Paravia, 1948) (hereafter Cazzaniga).

The prologue does not comment on specific verses of the Song but provides guidelines for reading the Song of Songs. In other words, William has assembled eight excerpts from Ambrose that he believes are useful as an introduction to reading the Song, regardless of whether the excerpts were originally from contexts that discussed the Song. I suggest that the prologue of the Ambrosian *florilegium* provides insight into William's own approach to the Song. He uses the words of Ambrose to express his own doctrine. In what follows, I examine each chapter of the prologue in detail to see what ideas of William they reveal.

Prologue, Chapter 1

The first chapter of the prologue is quite brief. Though it begins with a citation of Song 1:1, William uses it not to comment on this verse but as a point of departure for speaking about the subject of the Song of Songs as a whole:

> *Let him kiss me with the kiss of his mouth* [Song 1:1]. Here there is a celebration of the mysteries of purity, not the impulses of filthy behavior. They are performed spiritually through affective contemplation of the marriage and union of Christ and the church, of the uncreated and created spirit, of the flesh and spirit.[27]

Thus the prologue begins with an apology for the blatantly sexual language of the biblical book. The Song, William says, does not exalt carnal desires but celebrates the pure mysteries of the incarnation. These mysteries are celebrated not in a physical way but spiritually through contemplation. Hence this chapter clarifies not only the true subject of the Song of Songs but also the appropriate response to it. Like many commentators on the Song before him, William begins his Ambrosian *florilegium* by explaining its genre and the proper approach to it.

Even though William cites *De apologia David* as his source for this chapter, Van Burink could not identify its provenance. It seems, however, to be a combination of Ambrosian phraseology and William's

---

[27] William, Cant Amb 1 (CCCM 87:206).

own words. This fact is clearest in the first line after the scriptural citation, which is loosely based on Ambrose's *Apologia David altera*.[28]

Ambrose, *Apologia David altera* 8.43	William, Cant Amb 1
(CSEL 32.2:387, lines 8–9)	(CCCM 87:207, lines 3–4)
Non hic **adulterii obprobria**, sed	Non hic **foeditatis incentiva** sed
mysteria castitatis **sunt**.	castitatis **celebrantur** mysteria.
Here **there are** the mysteries of	Here **there is a celebration** of the
purity, not **shameful acts of**	mysteries of purity, not **the**
debauchery.	**impulses of filthy behavior.**

The Ambrosian passage comes at the end of a comment on Song 1:5–6, not Song 1:1.[29] Ambrose states here that Christ desires to see his beloved church denuded of all coverings, so that he may scrutinize the hidden depths of the human heart. In the passage cited here, Ambrose reminds his readers of the deeper significance of this sexual language. Immediately after this passage, he quotes several other verses from the Song and comments on them; William excerpts these elsewhere.[30] Therefore, William has viewed this comment of Ambrose on a specific verse of the Song as helpful for reading the Song of Songs as a whole.

William makes three significant alterations to his Ambrosian source. First, by replacing *obprobria* ("shameful acts") with *incentiva* ("impulses"), he shifts the focus from deeds to intentions. Hence he implies that while the Song is not about carnal deeds, it is even more not about carnal desire. Note that while William often uses the word *incentiva* in a positive sense, as *incentiva amoris*, here it

[28] In this and the following tables, words in boldface signal differences between Ambrose and William.

[29] Ambrose, *Apologia David altera* 43, in *Sancti Ambrosii Opera Pars 2*, ed. Carolus Schenkl, CSEL 32.2 [Vienna: F. Tempsky, 1897], 357–408, here 387).

[30] William, Cant Amb 48 (=*Apologia David altera* 43–44), 94.3 (*Apologia David altera* 45–46), and 102.1 (=*Apologia David altera* 47).

has a negative connotation, a usage that is frequent in Ambrose.[31] Therefore, William's use of this word seems to be influenced by Ambrose rather than by his customary usage. Second, William replaces *adulterii* ("debauchery") with *foeditatis* ("filthy behavior"), a word that is rare in Ambrose but used four additional times by William.[32] So in this case William prefers his own terminology to Ambrose's. Third, William speaks of the Song as a celebration, adding a whole new dimension to Ambrose's interpretation.

The remainder of the chapter is a tissue of Ambrosian and Guillelmian phrases. The adverb *spiritualiter* ("spiritually") is not found in Ambrose but is frequent in William. Ambrose himself speaks of "the marriage of Christ and the church, or of spirit, flesh, and soul."[33] This line of Ambrose lacks the phrase "of the uncreated and created spirit," which William added. This phrase is not Ambrosian, but a similar phrase shows up elsewhere in William, once in the *Brief Commentary* and once in his proper *Commentary on the Song of Songs*.[34]

Therefore, in this first chapter of the prologue, by way of introduction, William discloses the spiritual content of the Song of Songs and how one should approach it. It is a celebration of the mystery of the incarnation, in which there is a marriage and union of Christ and the church, of uncreated and created spirit, of flesh and spirit. The Song is to be approached spiritually through affective contemplation. William intertwines Ambrose's words with his own to express what he thinks are the most important things to know when reading the Song of Songs.

---

[31] See William, Cant Amb 46, 55, and 63 (CCCM 87:256–59, 271–74, 282).

[32] William, Contem 8 (CCCM 88:160; CF 3:49); William, Ep frat 222 (CCCM 88:274; CF 12:85); William, Exp Rm 3, 6:2 (CCCM 86:77; CF 27:111); Nat am 2 (CCCM 88:178; CF 30:49).

[33] William, Cant Amb 8 (CCCM 87:213).

[34] The phrase is *creati spiritus ad increatum*; see William, Brev com 4 (CCCM 87:159; CF 6:78); Cant 20 [91] (CCCM 87:70; CF 6:78).

Prologue, Chapter 2

The second chapter of the prologue is considerably longer than the first. It consists of two distinct excerpts. The first comes from Ambrose's *Expositio psalmi CXVIII*:

> So we should circumcise our heart. We should seek nothing contemptible, nothing bodily. Now every earthly thing is contemptible. So we should suppose that there is nothing earthly, nothing carnal, nothing worldly, nothing bodily, nothing unstable and mutable in these heavenly words—for "the words of the Lord are pure words" [Ps 11:7]. Only in this way can a spiritual interpretation reveal the immaculate and chaste purity in these words of heavenly mysteries. Divine thoughts should not be mixed with our debased, earthly ideas. And that inviolable sacrament of prophetic insight and everlasting heavenly speech should not be violated by the musings of our nature.[35]

Here William continues the theme of the first chapter. Though the Song of Songs uses overtly carnal language, there is actually nothing carnal in it. For it is a collection of heavenly, pure words. Only by putting aside earthly and bodily interpretations of the Song, by circumcising our heart, by refusing to tarnish the divine sentiments of the Song with lowly thoughts, will we have access to the heavenly mysteries that the Song reveals. Note that William again emphasizes that the Song contains a divine mystery.

In its original context, this Ambrosian excerpt is in a passage commenting on Psalm 118:89 and the meaning of the twelfth letter of the Hebrew alphabet, *lamed*.[36] Ambrose notes that this letter can be interpreted as either *cor* ("heart") or *servo* ("I preserve"). He interprets this fact as meaning that the verse admonishes the reader to have prudent understanding and to keep the commands carefully. He observes that these are the traits of a pure heart, which is not hindered by the delights of this world, and adds that Mary

---

[35] William, Cant Amb 2 (CCCM 87:207).
[36] Ambrose, Exp ps CXVIII 12.1 (CSEL 62:252–53).

had such a heart. The passage that William excerpts immediately follows.

In this excerpt, William has hardly altered his Ambrosian source. He insignificantly reverses the order of the words *mysteriorum caelestium*.[37] He also inserts *nihil carnale* ("nothing carnal") within a list of more or less synonymous phrases, a change that adds nothing to Ambrose's thought.[38] Except for these minor alterations, William preserves Ambrose's text intact. Note that there is nothing in the original context about the Song of Songs. William must have excerpted this text because it was a good summary of how he thought the Song should be approached.

The second excerpt of the second chapter of the prologue is from Ambrose's *De paenitentia*:

> For everything is fitting, whether it be kisses or similar things, when it is transferred to religion. So we need not be ashamed of any religious act that is conducive to the worship and honoring of Christ, as in the dancing of David before the ark. For that dancing was not associated with pleasure and wantonness, but it is that by which each one raises up an energetic body and does not permit the limbs to lie listlessly on the ground or to grow sluggish with slow steps.[39]

William continues with the same theme but now explains why the explicitly carnal language of the Song of Songs is fitting. Anything, even if carnal, done for religious reasons that promote the worship of Christ has a value. He uses the example of David's dancing before the ark of the covenant (2 Sam 6:14).

William alters his Ambrosian source in several ways:

---

[37] William, Cant Amb 2 (CCCM 87:207).

[38] William, Cant Amb 2 (CCCM 87:207). William also added superfluous synonyms in the Gregorian *florilegium*; see DelCogliano, "Composition," 72.

[39] William, Cant Amb 2 (CCCM 87:207); Ambrose, *De paenitentia* 2.6 (SChr 79:260).

Ambrose, *De paenitentia* 2.6 [42–43] (SChr 179:260, lines 26–33)	William, Cant Amb 2 (CCCM 87:207, lines 11–16)
Sed saltationem eam mandavit quam saltavit David ante arcam **Domini**. Totum enim decet quidquid defertur religioni, ut nullum obsequium quod proficiat ad cultum et observantiam Christi, erubescamus. Non **ergo** illa deliciarum comes atque luxuriae saltatio **praedicatur**, sed qua unusquisque corpus adtollat inpigrum, nec humi pigra iacere membra vel tardis sinat torpere vestigiis.	**Sive enim de osculis sive de talibus** totum enim decet quidquid defertur religioni, ut nullum obsequium quod proficiat ad cultum et observantiam Christi, erubescamus **sicut in illa saltatione** David ante arcam. Non **enim** illa deliciarum comes **fuit** atque luxuriae saltatio, sed qua[40] unusquisque corpus adtollat inpigrum, nec humi pigra iacere membra vel tardis sinat torpere vestigiis.
But that dancing is commended, which David danced before the ark **of the Lord**. For everything is fitting when it is transferred to religion. So we need not be ashamed of any religious act that is conducive to the worship and honoring of Christ. **Therefore,** that dancing is not **said to be** associated with pleasure and wantonness, but it is that by which each one raises up an energetic body and does not permit the limbs to lie listlessly on the ground or to grow sluggish with slow steps.	For everything is fitting, **whether it be kisses or similar things,** when it is transferred to religion. So we need not be ashamed of any religious act that is conducive to the worship and honoring of Christ, **as in the dancing of David before the ark. For** that dancing **was** not associated with pleasure and wantonness, but it is that by which each one raises up an energetic body and does not permit the limbs to lie listlessly on the ground or to grow sluggish with slow steps.

This excerpt in its original context comments on Luke 2:32: "We sang to you and you did not dance."[41] Ambrose begins by noting that while such language may be contemptible, there is nothing contemptible about the mystery it reveals.[42] He then warns against

---

[40] I emend *quia* to *qua.*

[41] Ambrose, *De paenitentia* 2.6 [41].

[42] Ambrose, *De paenitentia* 2.6 [42].

a vulgar interpretation of this passage: "Do not be deceived by the vulgarity of this language and think that we are commanded to engage in the theatrical motions of wiggly dancing and the nonsense of the stage. Such things are contemptible even in youth."[43] Ambrose then brings in the example of David's dancing before the ark, which William excerpts. Following this passage, Ambrose turns to the example of Paul and creatively compares the motions required of those being baptized to dancing.[44] After this, he returns to the Lukan verse and concludes his exegesis, saying that the song that was sung was the New Testament and the Jews did not dance to it insofar as they did not raise their souls to spiritual grace.[45] Once again, the Song of Songs is not mentioned at all in the original context.

William entirely reworks the passage. Note that he inserts "whether it be kisses or similar things" to show that the general principle is applicable to the Song of Songs, too. In addition, he shifts the passage about David's dancing before the ark from the beginning of the passage to its middle. And so the passage, rather than being an explanation of David's dancing before the ark, is now a general statement of how physical actions can have an appropriate religious dimension, an example of which is David's dancing.

Prologue, Chapter 3

The third chapter of the prologue consists of two long excerpts from Ambrose's *De virginibus*. Both concern themselves with the stages of spiritual progress as taught by the Song of Songs. The first reads:

---

[43] Ambrose, *De paenitentia* 2.6 [42]: *Et ideo cavendum ne qui vulgari quadam sermonis huius deceptus interpretatione putet nobis saltationis lubricae histrionicos motus et scenae deliramenta mandari; haec etiam in adulescentula aetate vitiosa sunt* (SChr 179:260).

[44] Ambrose, *De paenitentia* 2.6 [43].

[45] Ambrose, *De paenitentia* 2.6 [44].

For this is not a teaching that we have invented but one that
we have received. The heavenly doctrine of the mystical song
has instituted the following: "Let him kiss me with the kisses
of his mouth! For your breasts are better than wine and the
odor of your ointments surpasses all perfumes. Your name is
ointment poured out" [Song 1:1-2]. The whole of this passage
speaks of delights: it buzzes with amusement, it rings with
merriment, it thrills with love. "Therefore," it continues, "the
young girls have loved you and been drawn to you. After the
odor of your ointments we shall run. The king has brought
me into his bedchamber" [Song 1:2-3]. She begins with kisses
so as to arrive at the bedchamber. And she is moved to be
impatient with the hard toil and practice of virtue so that she
opens the gate with her hand [see Song 5:6], goes out into the
field, stays in the villages [see Song 7:11]. Yet in the beginning
she ran after the odor of his ointment. When she arrives at the
bedchamber, the ointment will be changed. See then where
she will go from the villages: "If there is a wall," it says, "we
shall build silver towers upon it" [Song 8:9]. She who once
amused herself with playful kisses now builds towers, so that
fortified with the inestimable lofty towers of the saints, she
will not only ward off hostile attacks but also be protected by
the bulwark of their good merits.[46]

According to Ambrose there is an order to the spiritual progress
that the Song of Songs teaches. The journey begins with kisses and
the subsequent bliss of the bedchamber. The next stage is the toil
of the practice of virtue, which enables the bride to open the gate,
go into the field, and remain in the villages. Finally, after remaining
in the villages, the bride builds towers of holiness. And so the Song
of Songs charts a spiritual journey of three stages: (1) the initial
delight in God, (2) the hard work of growth in virtue, and (3) the
consolidation of holiness.

Once again, William has hardly altered his Ambrosian source.
The addition of *enim* at the beginning of the excerpt is typical of
the kind of alterations that William makes in the Gregorian *florile-*

---

[46] William, Cant Amb 3 (CCCM 87:208).

gium when recontextualizing passages.[47] The change from the plural *propugnacula* to the singular *propugnaculum* ("bulwarks" vs. "bulwark") is also probably insignificant, unless William is intentionally stressing the unity of the holiness of the saints in a way that Ambrose does not.[48] William's omission of *mox* ("soon") in the line "soon when she arrives at the bedchamber," if not accidental, may indicate less optimism than Ambrose concerning the swift attainment of the bedchamber of the king.

Finally, William has *atque illa impatiens duri laboris exercitataeque virtutis agitur* ("And she is moved to be impatient with the hard toil and practice of virtue") instead of Ambrose's *Atque illa tam patiens duri laboris exercitataeque virtutis* ("And she is so patient with the hard toil").[49] This alternate reading does not appear to be an intentional change on the part of William himself but rather is the manuscript reading of the text of Ambrose that he had available to him. One family of Ambrosian manuscripts reads *impatiens*, but the editor does not indicate whether the *tam* was also omitted in this case. I suspect that *tam patiens* was corrupted into *impatiens*, which then necessitated the addition of *agitur* to make sense of it. William's text contains this corruption and correction. Interestingly, the original Ambrosian text has almost the opposite meaning of the Guillelmian text and admittedly makes more sense than William's. The bride patiently practices virtues in order to pass to the more advanced stages of the spiritual journey. William's text thus suggests that the bride is frustrated by the practice of virtue and for this reason is eager to pass onto the next stages.

The second excerpt of the third chapter of the prologue continues with the same theme of the stages of spiritual progress:

> Even in these temporal unions the woman getting married is given a time of merriment before she is issued commands, in case harsh commands give offense before love has grown through caresses and fawning. Heifers are taught to love the

---

[47] DelCogliano, "Composition," 67–68.
[48] William, Cant Amb 3 (CCCM 87:208).
[49] William, Cant Amb 3 (CCCM 87:208).

sounds of merriment so that they will not refuse the yoke on their neck. Then they are trained by playful words rather than by the blows of discipline. But once their neck has been submitted to the yoke, they are checked by the rein, urged by the prod, pulled by their yokemates, and compelled by the team. In the same way our virgin ought first to amuse herself with pious love, wonder at the golden posts of the heavenly marriage bed, and on the verge of marriage look upon the doorposts garlanded with wreaths of leaves and drink the delights echoing from the chorus within, lest she withdraw because she is intimidated by the Lord's yoke before yielding when called.[50]

Here the stages of the bride's relationship with the Lord are explained by analogy with two mundane examples. An earthly bride's relationship with her husband begins with merriment, caresses, and fawning, which lay the foundation for a love that will later require submission to harsh commands. Heifers are coaxed into the yoke by soothing words, but once the yoke is on their neck, they must submit to the steering of their yoke masters. Similarly, the bride is called to the Lord by being enticed to the marriage bed through the delights of love lest the harshness of the Lord's yoke intimidate her. Hence two stages of the journey are envisioned here: (1) the delights that entice and lay the foundation, and (2) the hard work that an ongoing relation with the Lord entails.

Once again, William has hardly altered his Ambrosian source. He replaces *Eculeorum vis plausae* with *Bucula plausus cuiusdam* ("heifers . . .").[51] The phrase *Eculeorum vis* ("the strength of ponies") is actually Ciceronian, found in one of the fragments of the lost *Hortensius*.[52] Perhaps the expression sounded archaic to William, prompting him to change it. But for some reason William chose to replace it with *bucula* ("heifers, young oxen"). Nonetheless, the analogy remains intact, whether it is ponies or heifers.

[50] William, Cant Amb 3 (CCCM 87:208).

[51] William, Cant Amb 3 (CCCM 87:208).

[52] Marcus Tullius Cicero, *Hortensius, Lucullus, Academici libri*, ed. and trans. Laila Straume-Zimmerman, et al. (Munich: Artemis and Winkler, 1990), 78 Bait.

Prologue, Chapter 4

The fourth chapter of the prologue continues the theme of the steps of spiritual advancement:

> For it is fitting that we should know the steps by which we advance and their order, which ought to be first, which second. After all, knowing what you should do and not knowing the order in which you should do it is a sign of imperfect knowledge. In general, doing things out of order leads to stumbling about.[53]

Here William offers a general rationale for stages of advancement. We need to know not only the stages but also the sequence of the stages. Performing the steps out of order results in failure to attain the goal.

William has modified his Ambrosian source so as to obscure its original context. The excerpt comes from a passage wherein Ambrose interprets Psalm 118:27: "Instruct me in the way of your righteous precepts, and I shall be exercised in your wondrous works." After citing this verse, Ambrose comments: "See the order. First is that we learn the precepts of the Lord, then that we know the steps in which we fulfill the righteous precepts and their order." The first sentence of William's excerpt begins in the middle of this sentence from Ambrose:

Ambrose, *Expositio psalmi CXVIII* 4.12 (CSEL 62:73, lines 23–26)	William, Cant Amb 4 (CCSL 87:209, lines 2–5)
deinde ut gradus quosdam **iustificationum** et ordinem noverimus, quid prius, quid consequens esse debeat.	**Oportet enim** ut gradus quosdam **profectuum** et ordinem noverimus, quid prius, quid consequens esse debeat.

By a few careful alterations, William transforms Ambrose's comments on Psalm 118:27 into a general rationale for order in the spiritual journey. First, he deletes Ambrose's *deinde*, thereby concealing

---

[53] William, Cant Amb 4 (CCCM 87:209).

the fact that he has borrowed only part of Ambrose's two-step interpretation of the verse. He adds *oportet enim*, so generalizing Ambrose's statement. Next, he replaces *iustificationum* with *profectuum*, thereby obscuring the fact that Ambrose's comment was originally about the "righteous precepts" mentioned in Psalm 118:27 and emphasizing his theme of advancement. The remainder of the Ambrosian passage, which William does not cite, discusses what it means for someone to be righteous. Once again the Ambrosian passage does not deal with the Song of Songs in any way. William has recontextualized it for his own purposes.

Prologue, Chapter 5

The fifth chapter of the prologue constitutes its conclusion. William quotes from Ambrose, exhorting his readers to use the *florilegium* he has compiled to the extent that it is spiritually beneficial to them:

> And so "there are as many opinions as there are people."[54] If there is anything clarified in our speech, all should read it. If there is anything advanced, the more mature should approve of it. If there is anything pure, your hearts should cling to it and your cheeks take on its hue. If there is anything fragrant, the fragrant age of youth should not disapprove of it. We ought to stir up a bride's love, for it is written: "You shall love the Lord your God" [Deut 6:5]. At the marriage, we ought to adorn a bride's hair with the curls of prayer, for it is written: "Clap your hands and stamp your feet" [Ezek 6:11]. We ought to strew roses upon everlasting marriage beds.[55]

William's excerpt differs in minor ways from his Ambrosian source. First, William has replaced *Et quoniam* ("and because") with *Itaque* ("and so").[56] This replacement has changed Ambrose's mean-

[54] Terence, *The Phormio of Terence*, ed. John Bond and Arthur Sumner Walpole (London: Macmillan, 1884), 3.3.14 (30, line 484).
[55] William, Cant Amb 5 (CCCM 87:209).
[56] William, Cant Amb 5 (CCCM 87:209).

ing slightly. Second, he has changed *calamistris quibusdam crines saltim orationis ornare* ("to adorn her hair at least with the curls of prayer") to *crines sponsae calamistris quibusdam orationis ornare* ("to adorn a bride's hair with the curls of prayer").[57] It is admittedly difficult to determine why he might have made this alteration.[58] In this conclusion to the prologue, William has recontextualized Ambrose's exhortatory words so that they commend the *florilegium* to its readers.

William's Use of Ambrose's *De virginibus* in the Prologue

Three of the eight excerpts in the prologue are taken from the conclusion of the second book of Ambrose's *De virginibus*. Notably, William does not present them in their original order:

> *De virginibus* 2.39–40 (Cazzaniga, 53, lines 18–54, line 4) = Cant Amb 5
>
> *De virginibus* 2.40–41 (Cazzaniga, 54, lines 4–16) = Cant Amb 3.2
>
> *De virginibus* 2.42–43 (Cazzaniga, 55, lines 1–56, line 6) = Cant Amb 3.1

The second book of *De virginibus* is devoted to models of virginity. At *De virginibus* 2.39, Ambrose begins his conclusion to this book. He notes that even though he has only been a bishop less than three years, he has learned from the virginal way of life. He then asks his readers to use whatever is useful in this book, noting that he has not given precepts but examples. He has tried to show the virgins the virtue they already possess, to reflect it back to them. Therefore his book is like a mirror. Indeed the virgins to whom he is writing are the inspiration for his work.

[57] William, Cant Amb 5 (CCCM 87:209).

[58] The reversal of the phrases *calamistris quibusdam* and *crines sponsae/saltim* may have been the result of a copying error. In other words, William might have skipped over *calamistris* to *crines* because these words started with the same letter. Then, realizing his mistake, he added *calamistris quibusdam* as a correction. But this explanation does not explain replacing *saltim* with *sponsae*, which seems to be the result of nothing more than carelessness.

Until this point William does not excerpt from the conclusion of *De virginibus*. But he excerpts from what immediately follows as the conclusion to his prologue (Cant Amb 5). Immediately following this passage in the original text is what appears in William as Cant Amb 3, lines 20–30. Then for some reason William skips a few lines. Here Ambrose first cites Song 4:8 and then says, "For we ought to recite this verse often, so that she who has been called may follow the Lord's works, even if she does not trust human words."[59] Then William uses what follows through to the end of the second book of *De virginibus* as Cant Amb 3, lines 2–19. So William has redeployed the conclusion to the second book of Ambrose's *De virginibus*, which is itself heavily indebted to the Song of Songs, as the chief source for a prologue to Ambrose's exegesis of the same biblical book.

Conclusion

The vastly different character of William's Gregorian and Ambrosian *florilegia* is puzzling. One can only guess why William employed such different methods of excerption in the two cases. My own suspicion is that for the most part, the manner in which each of the Latin fathers used the Song dictated William's methodology. Gregory tended to repeat his comments on specific verses of the Song, even verbatim, in several different places; at any rate, his interpretations of specific verses were highly consistent with each other. As a result, William could weave them together into a unified whole, forming self-contained units of Gregorian commentary on specific verses. Ambrose's comments on verses of the Song were less self-consistent and did not easily lend themselves to weaving together. Accordingly, William compiled the Ambrosian *florilegium* in the traditional manner, but in the Gregorian *florilegium* he could be innovative.[60]

---

[59] *Saepius enim nobis iste versiculus recantandus est, ut vel dominicis vocata verbis sequatur, si qua non credit humanis* (Cazzaniga, De virginibus, 54).

[60] DelCogliano, "Composition," 74–75.

But the manner in which Ambrose used the Song of Songs does not explain why William chose to begin the Ambrosian *florilegium* with a prologue that the Gregorian *florilegium* lacks. William assembled eight texts from Ambrose into a prologue. Only four of these texts came from contexts that discussed the Song of Songs. But even in these four cases William excerpted them not as comments on particular verses of the Song but as introductory material. Therefore he used the words of Ambrose, regardless of whether they originally commented on the Song, and with minor alterations, to construct a preface that expressed his own ideas—not Ambrose's—on how the Song of Songs should be approached. It is the most remarkable feature of the Ambrosian *florilegium* and affords us a peek into William's thinking that the Gregorian *florilegium* does not.

Two main themes emerge from the Ambrosian prologue. The first is the necessity of properly interpreting the explicitly sexual language of the Song. Above all, William uses Ambrose's words—peppered with his own—to teach that the Song is about heavenly mysteries, principally about the mystery of the incarnation, which through affective contemplation is recognized as the marriage and union of Christ and the church, of the uncreated and created spirit, of the spirit and the flesh. The second theme is the emphasis on the stages of spiritual advancement that the Song teaches. The Ambrosian passages that William excerpts speak of both a two-stage and a three-stage progression. But the point is that the initial approach to God is animated by a strong, deeply felt attraction to God, which is characterized by delight and desire. This desire lays the foundation for a relationship of love on which the Christian may then undertake the sometimes arduous task of growth in virtue and holiness. And so, despite the denigration of the Ambrosian *florilegium* by scholars such as Déchanet, a careful analysis of how William arranged his source texts into a prologue does in fact provide insight into William's thought.

4

HUMILITY AND HUMILIATION
IN WILLIAM OF SAINT-THIERRY'S EXPOSITIO
AND BERNARD OF CLAIRVAUX'S
SERMONS ON THE SONG OF SONGS

Rose Marie Tillisch

William of Saint-Thierry (ca. 1080–1148) and Bernard of Clairvaux (1090–1153), contemporaries, theologians, and friends,
were both masters of allegorical and mystical interpretations of the
Song of Songs. William gave his interpretation in *Expositio super
Cantica Canticorum* (Cant), begun in 1138, and Bernard gave his in
eighty-six *Sermones super Cantica Canticorum* (SC), written from
1135 through 1153. Both men read the dialogue between the bride
and bridegroom of the Song of Songs as the individual soul's spiritual dialogue with Christ (with Bernard sometimes allowing for
an understanding of the soul as represented by the church), a dialogue that would eventually bring the soul and/or the church and
Christ together into the bridal chamber.[1]

Thus William and Bernard read the Song of Songs as an allegory
of the soul's longing and seeking for God, God's longing and seek-

---

[1] For a valuable overview of the reception of the Song of Songs over the last
two millennia, see Ludger Schwienhorst-Schönberger, "Die Hoheliedsauslegung Bernhards von Clairvaux im Gespräch mit neueren Entwicklungen in
der Bibelwissenschaft," in *Von der Freude, sich Gott zu nähern: Beiträge zur cisterciensischen Spiritualität*, ed. Wolfgang Buchmüller (Heiligenkreuz [Austria]:
Be&Be-Verlag, 2010), 77–107.

ing for the soul, and the eventual union of these two. As a *terminus technicus*, this unity is by a later tradition called *unio mystica*, the mystical union of God and humankind. How is that union achieved? Is it through love, through faith, through grace, or through them all, depending on the point of view from which the union is experienced? And is it a total union? Do humankind and God become one, as William claims, or do they unite as two incompatibles, like oil and water, as Bernard argues? As Aage Rydstrøm-Poulsen has already answered these questions not only for William of Saint-Thierry and Bernard of Clairvaux but also for many of their contemporaries in *The Gracious God:* Gratia *in Augustine and the Twelfth Century*, this chapter does not attempt to elaborate them fully.[2]

Rather, this chapter examines and compares the Christologies of the two masters through the lens of their view of Christ as the humble slave, man and God, as Paul describes him in the hymn in his second letter to the Philippians. Through an examination of William's and Bernard's explications of the hymn from Philippians 2:7-8 and of their reading of Song 1:12, this chapter describes the two theologians' differing but also harmonizing views on the concepts of humility and being humbled, as their different approaches illuminate their different Christologies. While William focuses on Christ as the humiliated one, Bernard focuses on Christ as humility itself. But finally their differences complement rather than contradicting one another.

The Link

As often happens in academic work, the inspiration for the following pages comes from another scholar's work. In a footnote to his edition of William's Cant 108, Jean Marie Déchanet links William to Bernard, the Song of Songs to the hymn in the second chapter of Paul's letter to the Philippians, and William's views on humility and humiliation to Bernard's: "*Phil.* 2, 8. Ces remarques de Guillaume, à propos de l'humilité du Christ, ont leur pendant

[2] Aage Rydstrøm-Poulsen, *The Gracious God:* Gratia *in Augustine and the Twelfth Century* (Copenhagen: Akademisk, 2002).

chez S. Bernard, *Serm. super Cant.*, XLII, 7–8."[3] That is, what William
writes in Cant 108 has its counterpart in Bernard of Clairvaux's
Sermon on the Song of Songs 42.7-8. Now is that so? Do these texts
in fact reveal a dialogue between William and Bernard concerning
their differences—or similarities—on significant theological issues?
It may be so. To find an answer it is necessary to consider William's
words in Cant 108 and Bernard's in Sermon 42.7–8.

As Déchanet suggests, both William and Bernard use the hymn
from Philippians 2:8 to refer to Christ in his humility. In Cant 108,
William quotes this passage as he describes the great differences
among the flowers of the fields and the lilies of the valleys. The
flowers are all humility, William says, but of different kinds. Christians cannot excuse themselves from participating in this variety.
The condition for humans according to the simple judgment of
reason is to submit to one's superior and not to oppress one's equal.

But see, there is another flower here, more subtle than all the
others, a lily of the valley wearing the gown of perfection. This
flower, in order to show its love for God, submits to both its equal
and its inferior, and it does so not by reason alone but by a movement of affection in its soul. So here it is, the flower of the valley
that blossoms amid profound hearts, saintly souls, perfect men and
women who hold one another as superiors. The neighboring mountains are divided by the heights of the valleys and united by their
depth. For these souls the apostle says, "There are different kinds
of gifts, but the same Spirit" (1 Cor 12:4). And for the same souls
the psalmist says, "The valleys are abundant with grain" (Ps 64:14).

These perfected ones—and here William is most certainly thinking of both himself and his brothers—distinguish themselves by the
quality of their different merits and their sanctity in various degrees.
But what unites them in the depths of their conscience, given them
through humility, is the pious judgment of *caritas*, of love and affection. In them the peak of sanctity is the higher as the valley of
humility is the more profound. William continues by distinguishing
between human humility and Christ's humiliation:

[3] William, *Exposé sur Le Cantique des Cantiques*, ed. Jean Marie Déchanet, trans.
M. Dumontier, SCh 82 (Paris: Les Éditions du Cerf, 1962), 242n1.

And this is where the lily resembles the lily; this is where the copy is conformed to and made just like the deified condition of humility in Christ. Otherwise indeed it is the humility of a simple man, who through his condition and self-knowledge is conditioned to revile himself before God and neighbor; that is different from the humility of a God-man who, in order to lift man up from below, of his own free will places himself in the most extreme human condition. In the Mediator between God and humankind, this act of descending from God to humankind, which has its unique source in pure goodness, should be called humiliation rather than humility. That is why the apostle says: "He humbled himself" [Phil 2:8]. In humankind, on the other hand, self-knowledge is always humility. Even if it is an unavoidable confusion for the unwilling, for the willing it is a desire of virtue.[4]

Thus William interprets the Lord's humble gesture, the deified humility that derives from the unique source of goodness, to be humiliation rather than humility. At the same time he stresses that the union between humankind and God is total: "this is where the copy is conformed to and made just like the deified condition of humility in Christ."

In SC 42, Bernard uses the same letter to the Philippians, though a different verse, to discuss humility, not humiliation. His starting point is Philippians 2:7—"He emptied himself, accepting the form of a slave"—and he concludes by saying that Christ was thereby giving humankind the form or condition of humility.[5] The truly

---

[4] *Et ibi est lilium sicut lilium, hoc est ad deificae in Christo humilitatis exemplar conformatum et coaptatum exemplum. Alia siquidem est humilitas simplicis hominis, cum ex conditione et cognitione sui, coram Deo vel proximo ipse vilescit sibi; alia Dei et hominis ad sublevandum hominem in ultima conditionis humanae semetipsum sponte deponentis. In Mediatore etenim Dei et hominis, ex solo bonitatis fonte prodiens Dei ad homines condescensio, humiliatio potius quam humilitas est; unde dicit Apostolus: Humiliavit semetipsum; in homine vero cognitio sui humilitas est semper; et est seu in nolente confusio necessitates, seu in volente affectus virtutis* (William of Saint-Thierry, Cant 108 [SChr 82:242; CF 7:88]). Partially my translation.

[5] *Semetipsum exinanivit, inquit, formam servi accipiens, et formam humilitatis tradens* (Bernard of Clairvaux, SC 42.7 [SBOp 2:37; SChr 452:216; CF 7:37]).

humble, he says, is humble in heart, humble with that humility
that springs from the heart's love.

Bernard's eloquent Latin in this sermon, reusing the *formam* of
the *servi* for the *humilitatis* and using the two participles to link the
words, generates an imagery of order as well as of both difference
and solidarity in the mind of the listener. Christ's accepting of the
form or condition (*formam*) of a slave transforms itself into the
example or condition (*formam*) of humility. The process beginning
in Christ's accepting servitude—Christ who is God and man—
opens the way for humanity to receive the condition of humility
through him. It is important for Bernard to insist on "the difference
between the Trinitarian unity in God and the unity between God
and humankind."[6]

Humility in the Song of Songs
and in the Woman Anointing Jesus

Just as William and Bernard both use the passage from Philippians 2 to explore humility as manifested by Christ, they also interpret a single image from the Song of Songs to signify the virtue
of humility and connect that image to the Lukan woman who
anointed Jesus. William uses nard to explain Christ as being true
humiliation, meeting the Bride as an equal in her humiliation and
making her one with him in this humble but terrifying resemblance
and equality. In Cant 77 he introduces humility as nard: "My nard
gave forth its fragrance. Nard is an insignificant [*humilis*] herb,
having abundant leaves and thorns; it symbolizes humility rich in
virtues. It is warm, signifying the heat of holy desire."[7]

William then explains that the nard is a miracle of fragrance turned
into perfume, its fragrance distinguishing it from all other herbs. He
goes on to say that without the virtue of humility, one would have

---

[6] Rydstrøm-Poulsen, *Gracious God*, 269.

[7] *Nardus mea dedit odorem suum. Nardus humilis herba est, comas vel spices habens uberes; per quam significatur humilitas fecunda virtutibus. Calida est, aestum sancti desiderii designans* (William of Saint-Thierry, Cant 77 [SChr 82:190; CF 6:65]). My translation.

no devotion before God. In its humility, he says, it also designates the confession of sins (*confessio peccatorum*) and may be seen in the alabaster jar filled with a perfume of purest nard with which the devoted woman anointed Jesus (Luke 7:36), anticipating his burial.

Bernard also treats nard as an image of glowing, holy love when he says in SC 42, "Nard is an insignificant [*humilis*] herb, said by those who specialize in the study of plants to be of a warm nature. Hence it seems to be fittingly taken in this place for the virtue of humility, but aglow with the warmth of holy love."[8] Thus whereas William uses the warmth of nard to designate the confession of sins, Bernard uses its warm nature to distinguish between two kinds of humility. Warm humility, Bernard says, has *caritas*, love, as its source and affection as its key, while cold humility has truth as its source and knowledge as its key: "I say this because there is a humility inspired and inflamed by charity and a humility begotten in us by truth but devoid of warmth. This latter depends on knowledge, the former on affection."[9]

Bernard describes the humility that lacks warmth by explaining that people who examine their inner dispositions in the light of truth will judge them as unworthy. Being utterly humiliated by what this true knowledge reveals about them, they will find it hard to allow others to see their own true reflection, their image. If one is bound to truth without love, Bernard says, at the end one finds oneself bound to necessity. As long as only truth compels one's humility, that humility remains untouched by any infusion of love, because this kind of true knowledge makes it all too often inexpedient to reveal to others what we know about ourselves: "But if under the impulse of self-love you inwardly conceal the true judgment you

---

[8] *Est nardus humilis herba, quam et calidae ferunt esse naturae hi, qui herbarum vires curiosius explorarunt. Et ideo per hanc videor mihi non inconvenienter hoc loco virtutem humilitatis accipere, sed quae sancti amoris vaporibus flagret* (Bernard, SC 42.6 [SBOp 2:36; SChr 452:214; CF 7:214]).

[9] *Quod propterea sane dico, quoniam est humilitas quam caritas format, et inflammat; et est humilitas, quam nobis veritas parit, et non habet calorem. Atque haec quidem in cognitione, illa consistit in affectu* (Bernard, SC 42.6 [SBOp 2:36; SChr 452:214; CF 7:214]).

have formed of yourself, who can doubt that you lack a love for truth, since you show preference for your own interest and reputation?"[10] In this humility devoid of warmth, people somehow by their own effort and by cold knowledge turn humility into an inner humiliation and despair—and into an outward pride.

In an earlier sermon, SC 23, Bernard introduces humility as closely related to the mother of virtues, *discretio*, discernment, or the capacity to distinguish. There he explains that the person of perfect discernment is so drunk with the wine of *caritas*, of love, as to have contempt even for his or her own good name. Without love, he says, discernment is lifeless.[11] The perfect and most admirable person—that is, the humble person—is obedient to superiors and obliging to companions and attends with kindness to the needs of subjects. Bernard assigns all of these attributes to the bride, identifying her with both the repentant woman at Jesus' feet and the woman who anointed those feet, as he says in SC 23:10: "the first woman took her rest on the secure ground of humility, the second on the seat of hope."[12]

Bernard returns to his exploration of humility in SC 34, reaching the climax of his discussion in SC 42. In SC 34.3 he elaborates on his definition of humility, distinguishing between humiliation and humility. He judges the experience of humiliation as common to all people but says that not all grasp that experience with true humility: "Do you see how humility justifies us? Yes, I said humility, not humiliation. When humiliated, many are not humble! Some take humiliation with bitterness, others with patience, and others again with gladness."[13]

Those who become bitter are to be judged, Bernard continues. Those who patiently tolerate humiliation are innocent but not jus-

---

[10] *Alioquin si privato amore tui tentus, detines pariter intra te iudicium veritatis inclusum, cui dubium est minus te veritatem diligere, cui proprium praefers vel commodum, vel honorem?* (Bernard, SC 42.6 [SBOp 2:37; SChr 452:216; CF 7:215]).

[11] Bernard, SC 23.8 (SBOp 1:44; SChr 431:216; CF 7:32).

[12] Bernard, SC 23.10 (SBOp 1:145; SChr 431:220; CF 7:34). Matt 26:7 (synoptic parallels: Mark 14:3, Luke 7:37; possible Johannine parallel: John 12:3).

[13] Bernard, SC 34.3 (SBOp 1:247; SChr 452:76; CF 7:162).

tified. Only the few who are glad in being humbled are justified and filled with grace; they are the truly humble, as Christ's power, his humility, rests on them, Bernard says, quoting 2 Corinthians 12:9. What is needed in the search for true humility, Bernard says in the following sermons, is a double knowledge: self-knowledge and knowledge of God, which are actually two sides of the same thing. For knowing oneself is giving oneself up, letting God infuse himself. To gain this double knowledge, one must dig one's way through a double ignorance: ignorance of self and of God. This double ignorance is pride and arrogance combined with something less than animal behavior, as animals do not know that they could know better, but humans do.

In SC 42.6–8 Bernard distinguishes between the true humility that is Christ and humility based on truth.[14] The first is inspired and inflamed by charity; the other is begotten in humans by truth but is devoid of warmth. The former depends on affection, the latter on reasoning and knowledge. Describing the free choice that emerges from the will liberated by grace, Bernard concludes: "Because the light of truth is convicting you, you can see that not holding a high estimate of yourself is far from the equivalent of a voluntary association with the lowly that springs from the gift of love. Necessity compels the former; the latter is of free choice."[15]

How can a person arrive at this point of voluntariness, this glad humility? Through Christ. After having described Christ's emptying himself, taking the form or condition of a slave, Bernard continues elaborating on the issue of free will. Christ emptied himself not out of necessity but out of love, *caritas*. Because he knew himself, he became humble voluntarily, not through any truthful judgment. What he did came from his heart, not from obligation but because his heart felt love, *caritas*. He did what he did because he was humble at heart, that is, humble with the kind of humility

---

[14] Bernard, SC 42.6–8 (SBOp 2:37–38; SChr 452:214–20; CF 7:215–17).

[15] *Vides igitur non esse idipsum, hominem de seipso non altum iam sapere, veritatis lumine redargutum, et humilibus sponte consentire, munere caritatis adiutum. Illud enim necessitatis est, hoc voluntatis* (Bernard, SC 42.7 [SBOp 2:37; SChr 452:216; CF 7:215]). Partially my translation.

inspired by affection in the heart, not by the humility that he could have achieved through the judgment of truth.

The Lily of the Valley and the Bride

In Cant 111 William returns to his earlier discussion of the variety of flowers in the valley. All are varieties of humility, but the only one perfect and sublime is the lily of the valley. He is Christ; he is the Bridegroom. The unity of God and the perfected person takes place in Christ, him who humbles himself. But what about the perfected ones who through grace are in Christ? Having begun in Cant 108 to compare the bride to the lily, in Cant 111 William goes further, now insisting that embracing humility does not transform the bride into humility. Although she resembles humility, she is a barren fruit, unlike the bridegroom, who is a fruit-bearing apple tree. The bride is barren, *infecundi*.[16] Barren! A remarkable characteristic for a bride. One might wonder if it might mean that the soul is merely able to receive the fruit of humility but cannot pass it on.

In Cant 112 William continues, explaining that nothing whatever makes it possible to compare human beings with God, not even this resemblance in humility. Just as the power of the omnipotent Divinity is incomparable, his Majesty inscrutable, his Virtue invaluable, his Wisdom incomprehensible, so "as the weakness of God is stronger, the foolishness of God is wiser" (1 Cor 1:25), and the way God humbled himself is more sublime than the humility found in any human being. Even the humility of John the Baptist is surpassed, because he who appeared showed himself as the lowest of the low, the least of the least. William says: "In the Kingdom of Heaven, that is, in the Church, the greatness of John the Baptist's humility indeed radiated; however, there appeared in this Church the one who, greater than John, greater than all, showed himself as the least. As greatly as he descended from the higher to our lowland, just so much he appeared in the world more humble than all the humble."[17]

[16] William, Cant 111 (SChr 82:246; CF 6:90).

[17] *Magna quippe in regno coelorum, hoc est in Ecclesia, effulsit Johannis humilitas, in qua tamen major eo apparuit qui major omnibus se minimum exhibuit. Qui quanto*

He who descended from high above to our lowlands is Christ, the Bridegroom. That is why the bride—instructed by the bridegroom, formed through temptation, devoted to imitation of the bridegroom (*devota ad imitationem*), and terrified by equality (*pavida ad parilitatem*) with him—calls to mind in the image of the apple tree, with its nobly lifted branches, how the Lord and his disciples lay side by side in the house of the Pharisee, and how she herself arrived as the sinful woman whom the Lord justified (Luke 7:36-50).[18]

In this gospel of tenderness, as William calls it, the bride transforms everything to her own favor:

> Just as the fruit-bearing apple tree among the barren trees of the woods embellishes them with its loveliness, delights them with its perfumes, and honors them with its fruits, so my beloved lies among the sons of tender affection and masculine virtue, that is, the apostles, and there he enlightens them with his virtues, strengthens them by his example, confirms them through his works, and delights them with his teaching. In the shade of his defense while the Pharisee condemned me, I anxiously wished to be protected and hidden. But listening to the judgment that came from his mouth reserved for those who love the name of the Lord, I sat down safely. For he said, "Her sins, which are many, are forgiven, for she loved much." (Luke 7:47)[19]

This is the moment when the bride gives herself up totally, pouring out her abundant love, a love that comes from God; it is at the same time the moment of faith, as it is provided by true humility

---

de altiori ad nostra infima descendit, tanto omnibus humilibus humilior in mundo apparuit (William, Cant 112 [SChr 82:246; CF 6:90]).

[18] William, Cant 112 (SChr 82:248; CF 6:90–91).

[19] *Sicut malus fructifera, inter sterilia ligna silvarum, suo ea decore venustans, laetificans odore, fructu honorans; sic dilectus meus inter filios dulcis affectionis et masculae virtutis, apostolos scilicet, accumbens, quos virtutibus illustrat, confortat exemplis, confirmat operibus, et doctrina laetificat. Sub umbra vero defensionis ejus condemnante Pharisaeo, protegi et abscondi desideravi anxia; audiens vero judicium diligentium nomen Domini ex ore ejus, sedi secura. Dixit enim: "Dimissa sunt ei peccata multa, quoniam dilexit multum"* (William, Cant 112 [SChr 82:248; CF 6:91]). Partially my translation.

infused through the love of God. This is the moment when she who has loved much is forgiven because of her faith. She—the lowliest soul—can pour the nard over God himself because God as the lowliest of the lowliest has infused himself into her. In that moment God and human beings resemble one another, but only because of God's infusion. In that moment they are equals. And this equality is terrifying. The only remedy is staying humble. In Cant 113 William's bride exclaims:

> And his fruit was sweet to my taste, that is, the taste of his love filling my desire with good things, when the abundance of his indulgence made my conscience rejoice as he said, "Your faith has saved you. Go in peace" [Luke 7:50]. I desired when I walked by faith and hope; I sat when by the love of the spirit I rested in him. His fruit was sweet to my taste when by the virtue of enlightened love I began to taste the sweet experiences of his sweetness.[20]

Enlightened love gives true knowledge. William mediates affection and reason, spiritual love and knowledge with humility, and all is given through the movement of the heart implemented through grace: faith and forgiveness of sins. It all depends on the movement of the heart, the heart combined with truthful reasoning.

At the beginning of Cant 112, William writes, "one cannot compare a man in any way with God, not even in this likeness in humility."[21] So he qualifies his exclamation in Cant 108 that through Christ's humiliation the perfected person and God become totally

---

[20] *Et fructus ejus dulcis gutturi meo, scilicet sapor amoris ejus replens in bonis desiderium meum, cum laetificat conscientiam meam plenitudo indulgentiae ejus, ipso dicente: "Vade in pace, fides tua te salvam fecit." Desideravi autem, cum per fidem et spem ambivi; sedi, cum per amorem spiritus in ipsum acquievi; et fructus ejus dulcis gutturi meo, cum per illuminati virtutem amoris suavitatis ejus suaves experientias degustare coepi* (William, Cant 113 [SChr 82:248; CF 6:91]). Translation by Marsha Dutton.

[21] *Nusquam enim hominis ad Deum comparatio, nec in ipsa similitudine humilitatis* (William, Cant 112 [SChr 82:246; CF 6:90]). My translation. See William, Cant 110 (SChr 82:244; CF 6:89).

united, become one. But how can the person and God be one when there is no resemblance whatever? The answer is that becoming one with God is not the same thing as resembling God.[22] Every unity with God happens only through Christ's humiliation and the faith that saves.

The Humility of the Woman Who Anoints Jesus

Do William's discussions of humility bear any resemblance to Bernard's description? A brief detour to the tender gospel itself may help to answer that question. In Luke 7, the sinful woman comes of her own free choice, uninvited, giving Jesus an astonishing gift. She strikingly resembles the bride of both William and Bernard.

The Gospel of Luke 7:36-50 might be read as a continuation of objections to the Son of Man for having come eating and drinking (Luke 7:34). The objection is placed in a kind of pre-eucharistic setting, with Jesus eating at the table in the house of Simon the Pharisee. The issue is faith. The setting of the scene might serve as a counter image to the Last Supper, where Judas Iscariot of his free choice leaves Jesus and receives a measurable and poisonous gift from his new employers for his betrayal. In that case the issue is betrayal.

In Luke 7, however, the opposite happens, as an unnamed sinful woman comes of free choice, uninvited, to give Jesus an extravagant gift. Does this woman give so superfluously, emptying her jar of oil, because she has already received grace in abundance? In other words, is Luke's sinful woman forgiven because she loves much, or does she love much because she is already forgiven? Either meaning or both would fit the teaching of God's forgiveness in Christ and her loving response.[23]

---

[22] *Sponsus ergo flos campi et lilium convallium; Sponsa vero sicut lilium. Sed Sponsa humilitatem amplectens imitationis, et devotae similitudinis, sed altitudinem expavescens parilitatis, humilis quidem lilii, sed infecundi* (William, Cant 111 [SChr 82:246; CF 6:90]).

[23] See Raymond E. Brown, *An Introduction to the New Testament* (New York: Doubleday, 1997), 240–41.

How does this solution fit William or Bernard? Their responses are similar. William stresses God's loving response to human sin, whereas Bernard focuses on God's forgiveness and action through Christ. Both say that true humility is formed by faith and hope: "I desired when I walked by faith and hope," says William's humble and barren bride (Cant 113). Bernard's bride also sits on the secure ground of humility at the feet of the Lord (SC 23), and on the seat of hope as well.

At times, however, William and Bernard differ regarding the experience of humility. William's bride incorporates humility into her actions and reactions and has the power to confess. Her action is a confession, and her confession is her faith. Writing of the person's relation to God, William describes the woman of Luke 7 and the other Synoptic Gospels as giving what she has herself received in abundance, weeping over Jesus and/or anointing his feet or head with nard. She is the New Testament bride, the soul, the transformed church, the Sulamite, the bride of the Old Testament Song of Songs. For Bernard, on the other hand, humility and hope are the foundations upon which the bride already sits. Thus she is able to look around among her companions and to forget herself. Both William and Bernard use Paul's letter to the Philippians to write of humility and the perception of the Trinity, showing the intratrinitarian relationship in the graciousness of Christ, of him who emptied himself and took on the form of a slave, even unto death on a cross. He is the Bridegroom.

For both William and Bernard these two New Testament figures—the woman who anoints Jesus and Christ, who emptied himself—thus meet and merge in the Old Testament figures of the bride and the bridegroom. The emptying of the fragrant oil in the alabaster flask over Jesus as a preparation for his burial resembles Jesus' emptying of himself when, inspired by love, he took the form or condition of a slave. To William the woman's pouring of the nard signifies confession of sins, *confessio peccatorum*.[24] To Bernard, however, the emptying of the fragrant oil points to justification, because

---

[24] William, Cant 77 (SChr 82:190; CF 6:65).

Jesus never rejects anyone seeking him: "But it was in the fragrance of justice that Mary Magdalene ran, whose many sins had been forgiven because she loved much. Yes, she was just and holy, and no longer a sinner, although the Pharisee upbraided her as one, not knowing that justice and holiness are gifts of God, not the work of humans."[25] For Bernard, humility is all about justification and forgiveness of sins, *remissio peccatorum*, as Christ already has forgiven the woman many sins.[26]

In other terms, William distinguishes between the humiliation of Christ and the God-given humility of humans, but Bernard distinguishes between humiliation and humility in another way. He sees humiliation as a general experience, a condition for all people, including Christ, whereas he presents the humility of Christ as a parallel to the humility infused by God into humankind. For him the voluntary debasement of Christ shows his immense humility, not his immense humiliation.[27]

Finally, although William and Bernard express their ideas differently, they agree on the soul's liberated willingness, helped by the grace of God, stressed in the action of William's bride. And the condition of humility in Bernard's version is to give oneself up freely, cheerfully inspired by love, and to open oneself up to pass this love on to others. The condition is an ever-ongoing process written in the heart as awareness—awareness of one's knowledge of self and of God, as well as of one's ignorance of self and of God. For Bernard, those who constitute the social context, who live in the monastery, have a responsibility to mirror the love of God infused by grace into humanity. He is interested in describing how true humility creates relationships as it is infused by grace. One gets the impression that the condition of humility is recreated in

---

[25] *Verum in odore iustitiae cucurrit Maria Magdalene, cui dimissa sunt peccata multa, quoniam dilexit multum. Iusta profecto et sancta, et iam non peccatrix, quemadmodum Pharisaeus exprobrabat, nesciens iustitiam seu sanctitatem Dei esse munus, non opus hominis* (Bernard, SC 22.9 [SBOp 1:135–36; SChr 431:190; CF 7:21–22]).

[26] Bernard, SC 22.9 (SBOp 1:135; SChr 431:190; CF 7:22).

[27] Bernard, SC 42.6–9 (SBOp 2:36–30; SChr 452:214–22; CF 7:214–18).

the heart of every brother listening to or reading with faith the example given in the perfect humility of Christ.

At first glance, the end of William's version of the condition of humility in the individual seems to be barren and sterile, but can that really be so? No. The infusion of God's love causes William's bride to act. Although the bride is barren, her humility is rich and fruitful because it is given by Christ. Her actions are fruits of the humility infused by the most humble of the humble. Bernard's Christ, however, is himself true humility: he is the nard that is poured out. At the same time he is the Bridegroom who is anointed and is in the heart of the bride. He is everywhere, never one with the bride but always creating space for new meeting points of wholeness for the one whose heart through grace is willing.

The differences between William and Bernard occur in their differing perspectives rather than in their insight and experience. Whereas Déchanet suggests that William's commentary in Cant 108 is the counterpart of Bernard's in SC 42.7–8, a comparison of the passages from William's Cant 77, 108, and 111–13 with Bernard's SC 34–42 suggests that the two men had already thoroughly discussed the matter with one another before writing about it.[28] They seem to have enabled one another to reach wider perspectives of understanding and therefore to provide more exact imagery and formulations in their works.

Describing the same experience must inevitably vary according to whether one uses the Song of Songs as a didactic tool to lift the awareness of the brothers in a monastery or intends it as an intellectual means of expounding the idea, the meaning of the Song of Songs. Thus rather than focusing on what divides William and Bernard in their discussions of humility, I suggest that they inspired each other in their complementary insights on Christ's humility and humiliation.

Some of the variations and differences between the two theologians might be due to the different genres in which they wrote rather than to their different Christologies. In writing his treatise William sees occasions for unity between God and humankind, with Christ's voluntary self-humbling as the mediating factor, whereas Bernard focuses on God's solidarity with humankind through Christ's humility. William and Bernard were friends, but they had different opinions concerning the human relationship to God. According to Rydstrøm-Poulsen, William argues that it "is in the conscience that the junction of God and man 'takes place.'"[29] Perhaps it is because for William the junction occurs in the conscience that he stresses the conscious *confessio* instead of the voluntary *remissio* connected to Bernard's bride. William's Christology might then be called a theology from below and Bernard's Christology a theology from above. Bernard emphasizes the difference between the trinitarian unity in God and the solidarity expressed through "the unity between God and humanity."[30] In Bernard's universe, the reason the bride can do anything at all is that she is already forgiven.

But given these differences in perspective, why was it so important to William and Bernard to describe the virtue of humility as precisely as possible?

A Dialogue of Love

The answer to that question—the source of William's and Bernard's concern—might be a third person, whom they discuss between the lines of their works, Peter Abelard. William, fearing that Abelard's dialectical logic was turning God into a mere rational necessity, passed the problem on to Bernard. According to Henry Adams, Bernard wrote of Abelard, "he sees nothing as an enigma, nothing as in a mirror, but looks on everything face to face" (see 1 Cor 13:12). Adams further explained Bernard's concern about Abelard: "Pure logic admitted no contingency; it was bound to be necessitarian or ceased to be logical; but the result, as Bernard understood it, was that Abelard's world, being the best and only possible, need trouble itself no more about God, or Church, or man."[31] Abelard's logic, Bernard and William feared, removed spirituality from religion.

---

[29] Rydstrøm-Poulsen, *Gracious God*, 278.

[30] Rydstrøm-Poulsen, *Gracious God*, 269.

[31] Henry Adams, *Mont-Saint-Michel and Chartres* (Boston and New York: Houghton Mifflin Company, 1913; Garden City, NY: Doubleday, 1959), 349, 350.

Marie-Dominique Chenu phrased this concern of Bernard's differently: "It was not Abelard's mistakes concerning appropriation within the Trinity or concerning the absolution of penitents that St. Bernard combatted; it was the proud pretension that divine mystery can be penetrated by dialectical procedures."[32] If Chenu is right, William and Bernard were fighting Abelard's pride. The vice of *superbia*, pride, has its opposite in the virtue of *humilitas*, humility. In "William of Saint Thierry: Rational and Affective Spirituality," E. Rozanne Elder expands on Chenu's insight:

> Reason posed no problem for Bernard, who did not emphasize it in his works. It was, however, a problem for William, or rather it became a problem after he encountered and reacted to the dialectical theology of Pierre Abelard. More than his contemporaries and confreres, William deliberately tried to bridge the gap which was developing between traditional monastic theology and the newer theology of the schools. . . . In the persons of William (and Bernard) and Abelard, the dialectic between them was focused in a confrontation which symbolically sundered in the west *the integrity of man's response to God*. Affect and rationality went separate ways, and western man divided love from reason, action from thought, being from doing.[33]

In his Introduction to *The Spirituality of Western Christendom*, Jean Leclercq writes, "There is in any theology worthy of the name a meeting and a dialogue of love."[34] The dilemma of Western humanity in the twelfth century was the respective places of love and

---

[32] M.-D. Chenu, *Nature, Man, and Society in the Twelfth Century: Essays on New Theological Perspectives in the Latin West*, ed. and trans. Jerome Taylor and Lester K. Little (Toronto: University of Toronto Press, 1997), xvii.

[33] E. Rozanne Elder, "William of Saint Thierry: Rational and Affective Spirituality," in *The Spirituality of Western Christendom*, ed. E. Rozanne Elder, CS 30 (Kalamazoo, MI: Cistercian Publications, 1976), 85–105, 197–200, here 86–87, emphasis mine.

[34] Jean Leclercq, Introduction to *The Spirituality of Western Christendom*, ed. E. Rozanne Elder, CS 30 (Kalamazoo, MI: Cistercian Publications, 1976), xi–xxxv, here xii.

reason. In "William of Saint Thierry: Rational and Affective Spirituality," Elder explains William's understanding of the difference between reason and rationality:

> In his physiology, William made a distinction between *reason,* a part of the brain, and *rationality,* the ability to use reason. Just as vision (the ability to see) is one thing and the eye another, so rationality differs from reason. Reason is one of three faculties of the brain; rationality is one of three powers of the soul. As reason is located between imagination and memory, so rationality mediates between concupiscence (the ability to desire) and irascibility (the ability to be angry). Rationality moderates. . . . Because of reason's mediation we can speak of charity as being grounded in irascibility: if the soul is to love good, it must be angry at iniquity. . . . Reason and rationality direct man naturally toward God.[35]

Conclusion

Though the theologies of William and Bernard differ concerning their perception of the Trinity and the person's relation to God, I find no serious differences in their view on the basic virtue of *humilitas.* They are not really opposed, though their perspectives differ. Rather, they complement and inspire each other with an inbuilt dynamic deriving from their different Christologies. William tends to discuss humility as *confessio peccatorum,* linked to his understanding of *ratio,* and distinguishes between *humiliatio* and *humilitas* differently than Bernard does. Bernard interprets *humilitas* in its sense of *remissio peccatorum,* connected to the voluntariness that lies in a will liberated by grace. Perhaps *humilitas* was thus a common ground, a mediator between reason and affection, a concept important for them to define in their struggle against Abelard's unorthodox thoughts. For the two friends personally, this concept may have mediated acceptance of one another's christological position, as they both described the same perfect flower and its sublime fragrance.

[35] Elder, "William . . . Rational and Affective," 88.

5

THE WAY OF DESCENT
THE CHRISTOLOGY OF WILLIAM OF SAINT-THIERRY[1]

Aage Rydstrøm-Poulsen

The Way of Ascent

Ascent is a well-known theme in William of Saint-Thierry's writings. Odo Brooke's articles from 1963 and 1966, "William of St. Thierry's Doctrine of the Ascent to God by Faith," are also clear in pointing out what Brooke calls "the dynamism of faith" in William's thought.[2] He concludes his investigation of William's *Speculum fidei* and *Aenigma fidei* with the statement that William "always sees faith dynamically as an ascent to God"[3] and distinguishes between faith as a spiritual ascent and faith as an intellectual ascent; he continues by saying that both lead "us beyond every limited insight into the depths of the trinitarian life and ultimately into the

---

[1] This article is a revised edition of a presentation for the Cistercian Studies Conference in honor of E. Rozanne Elder during the forty-fourth International Congress on Medieval Studies, May 7–10, 2009, Western Michigan University, Kalamazoo, Michigan.

[2] Odo Brooke, "William of St. Thierry's Doctrine of the Ascent to God by Faith" [Doctrine 1963], RTAM 30 (1963): 181–204, and "William of St. Thierry's Doctrine of the Ascent to God by Faith" [Doctrine 1966], RTAM 33 (1966): 282–318, here 318. See also Brooke's earlier "The Trinitarian Aspect of the Ascent of the Soul to God in the Theology of William of St. Thierry," RTAM 26 (1959): 85–127.

[3] Brooke, Doctrine 1966, 316.

vision when God is no longer seen 'per speculum' and 'in aenig-mate' but 'facie ad faciem.'"[4]

Accordingly, in William's concluding spiritual and theological treatise, *Epistola ad fratres de Monte Dei*, there is plenty of evidence that William speaks about the situation of the human person in relationship to God as that of a pilgrim following the leadership of Christ on the way to God and as that of a climber who ascends step by step as on a ladder up to heaven. As William writes in *Epistola*: "By all means then allow the wise men of this world, puffed up as they are with its spirit, caught up in lofty thoughts while they lick the dust, allow them to go down with their wisdom into hell. But do you, while a pit is being dug for the sinner, continue as you began: "fools for God's sake, through God's folly which is wiser than that of all humans," following Christ's leadership, make your own the humble art of ascending to heaven."[5] And "The servant of God must always either make progress or go back; either he struggles upwards or he is driven down into the depths."[6]

The monastic "geography" seems thus unmistakable according to William, and the *Epistola* is also composed following the three stages of this journey: the beginner is on the animal level, the proficient is on the rational level, and the perfect has reached the spiritual level.[7] In William's words, "there are beginners, those who are making progress, and the perfect. The state of beginners may be called 'animal,' the state of those who are making progress 'rational,' and the state of the perfect 'spiritual.'"[8] William also makes the observation that the relationship among these steps, and thus among the groups belonging to the different stages, is much more complex than it sounds: "It should be noted that when we speak of carnal or animal perception, of rational knowledge, or of spiritual

---

[4] Brooke, Doctrine 1966, 317.
[5] William, Ep frat 8 (CCCM 88:229; CF 12:10).
[6] Ep frat 38 (CCCM 88:236; CF 12:23).
[7] On the animal person and advice for novices, see Ep frat 41–139, on the rational person, see Ep frat 195–248, and on the spiritual person, see Ep frat 249–300.
[8] Ep frat 41 (CCCM 88:236; CF 12:25).

wisdom, we have in mind both a single person, in whom according to various degrees of progress and advancement and differing intensities of fervor, all these can be found at one time or another, and three kinds of persons, each of whom engages in the combat of the religious life in the cell in accord with the characteristics of one of these states."[9] This instructive observation, however, does not change William's view of the basic structure of Christian life, namely, that it is about progress, development, or ascent to God.

Just as William points to Christ as the leader of this journey, he writes in his characteristic way in the *Epistola* about the general human situation in relationship to Christ as the example or "form"— *forma*—to be followed. Christ is the example of *poverty*. And with this image, William also gives an impression of the Christian's journey that seems to point in another direction from that of the image of the ladder of ascent: "We are . . . earthly animals, clinging to the earth and to the senses of our flesh, living according to the dictates of the flesh, depending on others for our livelihood. As regards that, however, we can find some slight consolation in the example of him who although he was rich became poor for our sakes and laid down the commandment of voluntary poverty, while he himself deigned to show us an example of the same poverty in his own life."[10]

Christ as the Teacher

In the years leading up to 1972, E. Rozanne Elder, then a student at the University of Toronto's School of Graduate Studies, had already conducted a comprehensive investigation and description of William's Christology. The result was a 513-page PhD dissertation titled "The Image of Invisible God: The Evolving Christology of William of Saint Thierry." Unfortunately, this work was never published. A microfilm of the typed manuscript can be obtained, however, from the University of Toronto library. Later, in 1991, Elder published a

---

[9] Ep frat 140 (CCCM 88:257; CF 12:57).

[10] Ep frat 159–60 (CCCM 88:261; CF 12:63). See also William's words in Nat am 45: *Scire autem debet omnis sapiens ascensor, non sic esse gradus huius ascensionis, sicut gradus scalae* (CCCM 88:212; CF 30:109).

comprehensive article on "The Christology of William of Saint Thierry" in *Recherches de théologie ancienne et médiévale,* and again in 2000—this time in *Signy l'abbaye,* the collection of contributions to an international colloquium that took place in 1998—an article entitled "Christologie de Guillaume de Saint-Thierry et vie spirituelle."[11]

Elder's dissertation has two parts. Part one explores William's theology of Christ, and part two considers Christ in the spiritual life. The main section of the second part is titled "Christ and the Ways of Ascent."[12] The 123 pages in this chapter thoroughly prove what has been mentioned already about William's view in the *Epistola* of Christ as the example—or the teacher—to be followed in the spiritual life.[13] The first part of the dissertation, however, also examines the Christology of William as the keen theologian, and it devotes a special section to one of William's deeply theological writings, maybe one of his clearest ones conceptually, namely, his *Disputatio adversus Petrum Abaelardum.*[14]

The Christology of the *Disputatio adversus Petrum Abaelardum*

As Elder points out, the *Disputatio* leaves no doubt about William's orthodox Augustinian Christology as part of the Augustinian

---

[11] E. Rozanne Elder, "The Christology of William of Saint Thierry," RTAM 58 (1991): 79–112, and "Christologie de Guillaume de Saint-Thierry et vie spirituelle," in *Signy l'abbaye et Guillaume de Saint-Thierry. Actes du Colloque international d'Études cisterciennes 9, 10, 11 septembre 1998, Les Vieilles Forges (Ardennes),* ed. Nicole Boucher (Signy l'abbaye: Association des amis de l'abbaye de Signy, 2000), 575–87.

[12] E. Rozanne Elder, "The Image of Invisible God: The Evolving Christology of William of Saint Thierry," PhD dissertation, University of Toronto, Canada, 1972, 254–377. In 1962 Elder had already published an article with the emblematic title "The Way of Ascent: The Meaning of Love in the Thought of William of St. Thierry," in *Studies in Medieval Culture 1,* ed. John R. Sommerfeldt (Kalamazoo, MI: Medieval Institute Publications, 1964), 39–47.

[13] "Created in the image of God, man fell through proud and wilful sin. Cut off from the vision of God, unable to see and therefore unable to love God, man needed a teacher" (Elder, "Image of Invisible God," 489).

[14] Elder, "Image of Invisible God," 93–135; William, Adv Abl (CCCM 89A:17–59; PL 180:249–82).

theological universe.[15] Therefore, to William it is a problem in itself that Peter Abelard says something new.[16] True theology is a tradition to be received and taken over, William maintains.[17] And what we may call Abelard's introduction of philosophy into theology can for William only lead to mistakes, as it did for Abelard, since—in William's words—"This our theologian manifestly professes, a wisdom of the flesh rather than of the spirit, a wisdom of humans rather than of God."[18]

In chapter 3, William accuses Abelard of Sabellianism for destroying the persons in the Trinity, and of Arianism for maintaining the dissimilarity and inequality of the hypostases.[19] More interestingly, however, in chapter 6 William accuses Abelard of Pelagianism, a charge that not only shows William's Augustinian view of predestination and inherited sin but also gives a clear impression of his Christology.

Abelard had asked whether all humans are saved by divine mercy in such a way that there is no one who could have a good will except by God's prevenient grace, which moves the heart and

---

[15] See Elder's conclusion just before: "All in all William seems to stand firmly in the tradition of Augustine and the Benedictines" (Elder, "Image of Invisible God," 92). She also refers to Augustine as "The authoritative bishop of Hippo—from whom William borrowed his arguments" (Elder, "Image of Invisible God," 111).

[16] Adv Abl 1: *Petrus enim Abaelardus iterum noua docet, noua scribit* (CCCM 89A:13; PL 182:531B); see Elder, "Image of Invisible God," 93–94.

[17] See, e.g., Elder, "Image of Invisible God," 99.

[18] Adv Abl 4: *Hic theologus noster palam omnibus est quomodo carnem potius sapiat quam spiritum, hominem quam Deum* (CCCM 89A:31; PL 180:260C); Elder, "Image of Invisible God," 103, and "His [Abelard's] basic fault William seems to have considered his preference for worldly knowledge over spiritual wisdom" (Elder, "Image of Invisible God," 103). See also Ep frat 7, *Vbi sapiens inter uos? Vbi scriba? Vbi conquisitor huius saeculi?* (CCCM 88:228; CF 12:10), and Ep frat 8 on *sapientes saeculi* (CCCM 88:229; CF 12:10; see n5 above).

[19] Adv Abl 3: *quantum ad destructionem personarum Sabellianum est; quantum ad dissimilitudinem et imparilitatem, hoc in sententiam Arii pedibus ire est* (CCCM 89A:26; PL 180:257B). See also Adv Abl 3: *Etenim destructio personarum destruit in Deo Trinitatem; dissimilitudo maioris et minoris unitatem* (CCCM 89A:26; PL 180:257C).

inspires good will. If this is so, Abelard writes, a human can actually do nothing good alone, and if the free will cannot receive divine grace without the help of grace, there will be no real reason for punishing someone who sins.[20]

Against this view, William quotes Christ's laconic words from the Gospel of John, "Without me you can do nothing."[21] And he quotes Augustine's words that human nature is so fallen and corrupt that the human will is only free to sin. Only if liberated by grace can it do good, William says, echoing Augustine.[22] This liberation is to be found in only one place, namely, in the Savior's grace, he continues. This happens in baptism, but the liberation is still necessary since the concupiscence of the flesh remains for the punishment of sin, and no one can be free from this concupiscence unless liberated by undeserved grace, he concludes.[23] Accordingly, in chapter 7, William summarizes the history of salvation:

> Created and placed in Paradise, Adam sinned, and God became angry with him, and enmity occurred between God and

[20] Adv Abl 6: *"Quaeritur etiam," inquit, "utrum omnes homines ita sola misericordia Dei saluentur, ut nullus sit qui bonam uoluntatem habere possit nisi gratia praeueniente Dei, quae cor moueat, et bonam uoluntatem inspiret, et inspiratam multiplicet, et multiplicatam conseruet. Quod si ita est, scilicet ut homo nichil ex se boni operari possit, ut aliquo modo ad diuinam gratiam suscipiendam per liberum arbitrium sine auxilio gratiae, prout dictum est, se erigere non possit, non uidetur ratio quare, si peccauerit, puniatur"* (CCCM 89A:39; PL 180:266D–267A).

[21] Adv Abl 6: *Haec plane Pelagiana haeresis est. . . . Contra quod Dominus dicit: "Sine me nihil potestis facere* [John 15:5]." *Augustinus: "Qui nichil dixit, nichil excepit." Et Paulus: "Deus est qui operator in uobis et uelle et perficere pro bona uoluntate* [Phil 2:13]" (CCCM 89A:39–40; PL 180:267CD).

[22] Adv Abl 6: *Sed in hoc per peccatum [humana natura] est corrupta et deiecta, ut hominis arbitrium ad malum tantummodo liberum sit; ad nullum uero bonum sit, nisi liberante gratia* (CCCM 89A:40; PL 180:268A).

[23] Adv Abl 6: *"Justo enim iudicio alieno omnes peccato tenemur, a quo aliena in fide in baptismo liberamur per gratiam saluatoris, quamuis in poenam peccati maneat concupiscentia carnis in qua crudiamur. A qua nemo potest esse liber, nisi ab indebita gratia liberatus; contra quod nemo murmurat, nisi ad mortem praedestinatus." Haec omnia quae praemisimus, beati Augustini uerba sunt, ex libro De libero arbitrio ad Bonifacium papam* (CCCM 89A:40; PL 180:268AB).

humanity. . . . The enmity between God and humanity is the same as that between justice and sin. But when the time to be merciful came, God sent his Son in order to save the world, and he made him a human so that he could save humans. He who predestined the Savior of the world knew also beforehand that he would be killed in the world, and he had predestined what his death would bring about, namely the salvation of the world.[24]

A little later in the same chapter, William quotes the letter to the Hebrews: "God was in Christ reconciling the world to himself";[25] he concludes that Christians will therefore "live by a foreign justice as sons of grace, just as they have died by a foreign sin as sons of anger."[26]

These few quotations from the *Disputatio* may suffice to show how traditional William was in his understanding of Christ. According to this view, Christ is first of all the Savior, and his salvation is indispensable, since humans cannot do anything by themselves to reestablish the right relationship to God.

As Elder also points out, William does not simply repeat Anselm's objective understanding of redemption, but he is not in doubt that Christ has redeemed the human person by his death; by an unjust death he bought the human person freedom.[27] Clearly,

---

[24] Adv Abl 7: *Factus Adam et positus in paradiso peccauit, et iratus est ei Deus, et factae sunt inimicitiae inter Deum et hominem. . . . inimicitiae inter Deum et hominem non aliae quam quae esse solent inter iustitiam et peccatum. Cum autem uenit tempus miserendi, ad saluandum mundum misit Deus Filium suum, faciens eum hominem propter saluandum hominem. Quem cum saluatorem mundu praedestinasset, praesciuit etiam quod in mundo occideretur, et praedestinauit, quid de ipsa morte eius ageretur, scilicet salus mundi* (CCCM 89A:47–48; PL 180:273D–274A). See also Adv Abl 7 (CCCM 89A:49; PL 180:275AB).

[25] Adv Abl 7: *Deus erat in Christo mundum reconcilians sibi . . .* [Heb 9:14] (CCCM 89A:48; PL 180:274D).

[26] Adv Abl 7: *ut uiuerent aliena iustitia filii gratiae, sicut alieno moriebantur peccato filii irae* (CCCM 89A:48; PL 180:274B).

[27] See Elder, "Image of Invisible God," 131, also 127–31. See Adv Abl 7: *Cui perfecte affectus homo Christus, nouam per eam obtinuit iustitiam patiendo poenam peccati sine peccato* (CCCM 89A:49; PL 180:275A).

therefore, William has to reject Abelard's interpretation that the meaning of the incarnation and the passion is first of all to provoke human love of neighbor.[28] Elder concludes regarding Abelard's interpretation: "Christ loved man even to the point of dying for him. His love must find echo within the human breast and enkindle a responsive love which can alone obliterate the contempt for God, which in Abelardian terms is sin, inherent in fallen man. Man is justified by the love of Christ in His passion and by the love which that passion evokes within himself. Redemption becomes a subjective response more than an objective gift. By the example of love supreme, Christ commended His love to men."[29] It seems a little surprising, then, to interpret William's view of Christ as an example of humility as "overlapping" with Abelard's as proposed by Elder:

> After condemning Abelard for interpreting Christ's passion almost exclusively as a divine exhortation to inflamed devotion, William tended predictably to emphasize the objective value of the crucifixion. Christ redeemed man and loosed his sins, William insisted. At the same time he continued to repeat with dogged insistence his earlier assertion that Christ in his incarnate life and by His willing death had given man an example of humility and a provocation of love, and provided the means for man's eventual elevation to the likeness of God. These latter opinions remained basically unchanged throughout William's life and they overlap with Abelard's.[30]

---

[28] Adv Abl 7: *Cum enim in dispensatione mediatoris tria praecipue intelligenda sint fidelibus, scilicet sacramentum redemptionis et reconciliationis omnium, et ad eos qui maxime per superbiam peribant, exemplum humilitatis, et ad eos quorum amor in terrenis computruerat, prouocatio caritatis, primo leuiter perstricto, secundo penitus neglecto, tertio totus incumbit, dicens hoc fuisse consilium, et hanc esse causam incarnationis et passionis Domini, ut luce sapientiae suae mundum illuminaret, et ad amorem suum accenderet, tamquam posset prouocari homo superbus ad amorem Dei, nisi primo humiliaretur ab amore sui, et nisi prius sacramento redemptionis solueretur ligatus a conditione et uinculo peccati* (CCCM 89A:50; PL 180:276AB).

[29] Elder, "Image of Invisible God," 132.

[30] Elder, "Image of Invisible God," 198.

Actually, to William, Abelard's interpretation meant that if this had been the purpose of the incarnation, Christ would have died for nothing.[31] And thus, as Elder also concludes, William stresses "that the passion of Christ had first [of all] a real objective meaning for mankind."[32]

Christ and Humility

Elder is undoubtedly right in observing that William's theology was secondary to his Christian life.[33] He was concerned about the Christian human life, and, as has already been mentioned, his late work the *Epistola* is first of all about what we call his spirituality. Nevertheless, his theological principles, in this case the understanding of Christ, show up again and again in his reflections on his experiences.[34] It would be surprising if they did not.

For instance, in his praise of the solitary monk seeking God in his cell, William warns strongly against any elitist pride by pointing to the meaning of Christ. William urges his audience to humble themselves: "Think of yourselves rather as wild beasts shut up in

---

[31] Adv Abl 7: *Deinde ingreditur causam cum Deo homo ingratus, et astruere uelle uidetur quod Christus gratis mortuus sit. Quod et scholares eius quasi ex sententiae eius submurmurant, ex propositis quaestionum calumniis dicentes, si auderent, non fuisse necessarium in mundo Christi aduentum* (CCCM 89A:42; PL 180:269C); see Elder, "Image of Invisible God," 118.

[32] Elder, "Image of Invisible God," 133.

[33] "We, like other students of William, have repeatedly asserted that William of Saint Thierry's theology must be taken as secondary to his application of that theology to the individual Christian life"; "More than a theologian, he was a practical man who aimed at the practical goal of living the Christian life as perfectly as possible and of being able to contemplate God fleetingly in this life and eternally in the next" (Elder, "Image of Invisible God," 219).

[34] See also Elder's observations: "In almost every one of his works, he envisaged the spiritual life as a dynamic progression toward God and he carefully constructed an ascending pathway from man's fallen state to God's very presence" ("Image of Invisible God," 224); "Only by seeing the patterns of ascent in their entirety can we appreciate the places at which William most clearly saw the activity of Christ" ("Image of Invisible God," 225).

cages."[35] And again, "Take care . . . , servant of God, not to seem to condemn any of those whom you do not wish to imitate. I would have you act while you are still sick the way he did in the best of health who said: 'Christ Jesus came to save sinners, of whom I am the first'" (1 Tim 1:15).[36] He asks: "Does God belong to solitaries alone? Rather he belongs to all humans [Rom 3:29]. For God takes pity on all humans."[37]

Thus, according to William, Christ is the Savior, and the only relevant human attitude is humility. It is equally clear to William that the Christian person only owns his life in Christ. Again he writes about the solitary monk, "in recalling to mind what he did when he suffered for you, you eat his body and drink his blood. As long as you remain in him through love and he in you through the sanctity and justice he works in you, you are reckoned as belonging to his body and counted as one of his members."[38]

Later, William again brings together this unity of love with Christ. First, after quoting Romans 4:5, "The man who does not work but believes in him who justifies the impious has his faith reckoned as justice according to God's gracious plan," he goes on to recall "that sinful woman who was forgiven much because she loved much."[39] Then he concludes, "so that without any justice deriving from works or any confidence based on merits . . . [the soul] may be justified by the sole fact that it has loved much."[40]

But still, William thinks from within the Augustinian worldview and points out that this love of God in the human person is a gift from God through the Spirit of the Father and the Son. The human spirit was created, William says, in the image of the Creator, but it

---

[35] Ep frat 18: *Feras uos potius indomitas et incaueatas, et bestias* (CCCM 88:231; CF 12:15).

[36] Ep frat 19 (CCCM 88:232; CF 12:16).

[37] Ep frat 20: *An solitariorum Deus tantum? Immo et omnium communium. Miseretur enim omnium Deus* (CCCM 88:232; CF 12:16).

[38] Ep frat 119 (CCCM 88:253; CF 12:31).

[39] Ep frat 167 (CCCM 88:263; CF 12:66).

[40] Ep frat 167 (CCCM 88:263; CF 12:66).

lost its natural freedom to will and to act.[41] He continues, however, that it did not lose its power of choice, but the choice became captive, and the will is set free only when it becomes love, when the love of God is poured into the human heart by the Spirit.[42]

Nevertheless, in his praise of virtue William can talk about virtues as a certain force of nature. But in the same sentence he writes that it is only as the result of grace that this force becomes a virtue,[43] and we may add that "by grace" again means because of Christ.

In the same way, when William continues to talk—almost like Abelard—about Christ's passion as going to the limit of love so that humans should love him without limits and keep his commandments,[44] it is still evident that he thinks from within a theological worldview in which this love is actually not a natural quality in the human but belongs to the human being "in Christ" and is thus a divine gift. William continues along the same line when he talks about the spiritual person's knowledge of God or—as he writes—"true experience of the Lord."[45] He says, "this way of thinking about God does not lie at the disposal of the thinker. It is a gift of grace, bestowed by the Holy Spirit."[46]

---

[41] Ep frat 199: *Spiritus enim hominis, in appetitu boni, subtilis et efficacis naturae conditus . . . ; uitio tamen carnalis originis implicitus, peccati seruus effectus est, et captiuatus in legem peccati quae est in membris* (CCCM 88:270; CF 12:79).

[42] Ep frat 200: *Nam in poenam peccati, et testimonium amissae dignitatis naturalis, positum est ei in signum arbitrium, sed captiuum* (CCCM 88:270; CF 12:80); Ep frat 201: *Liberatur uero uoluntas quando efficitur caritas, cum caritas Dei diffunditur in cordibus nostris per Spiritum sanctum qui datur nobis* (CCCM 88:271; CF 12:80). See also Ep frat 265: *Ipse est enim omnipotens artifex, creans hominis ad Deum bonam uoluntatem* (CCCM 88:282; CF 12:96).

[43] Ep frat 227: *Sed redeamus ad laudem uirtutis. Quid est uirtus?. . . Vis enim quaedam est ex natura; ut autem uirtus sit habet ex gratia* (CCCM 88:275; CF 12:86).

[44] Ep frat 230: *In dilectione quippe Dei, non alia ratio, non alia discretio est, nisi ut sicut ille cum dilexisset nos, in finem dilexit nos, sic, si fieri potest, in infinitum diligamus eum nos, sicut beatus uir qui in mandatis eius cupit nimis* (CCCM 88:276; CF 12:86).

[45] Ep frat 250: *uere sentitur de Domino* (CCCM 88:279; CF 12:92).

[46] Ep frat 251: *Sed modus hic cogitandi de Deo, non est in arbitrio cogitantis, sed in gratia donantis* (CCCM 88:279; CF 12:93).

The Conclusion of *Epistola ad Fratres de Monte Dei*:
The Way of Descent

Perhaps the most emblematic example of William's both practical and theological Christology appears on the last pages of the *Epistola*. Here William talks about the ultimate goal of salvation, namely, that the human become like God. As he writes: "Resemblance to God is the perfection of the human."[47] And he calls the highest resemblance *unitas spiritus*, which "makes the human one spirit with God . . . , it is the Holy Spirit himself, the God who is Love."[48] Consequently, William can say about the soul that it really becomes one with the triune God: "The soul in its happiness finds itself standing midway in the kiss and the embrace of the Father and the Son. In a manner that exceeds description and thought, the person of God is found worthy to become not God but what God is, that is to say that the human becomes by grace what God is by nature."[49]

But just after this famous summit of William's thought, in which he points to Christ by using the christological keyword *gratia*, he actually returns to his Christology and his understanding of the human life and the knowledge of God in Christ. This existence of love must, he writes, "to a certain extent" be "like that love which made God like to humans by accepting the humiliation of our human lot in order that the human might be made like God."[50] And William concludes: "Then it is sweet for one to be abased together with supreme majesty, to become poor together with the Son of

[47] Ep frat 259: *Et haec hominis perfectio est, similitudo Dei* (CCCM 88:281; CF 12:95).

[48] Ep frat 262: *fit homo cum Deo unus spiritus* (CCCM 88:282; CF 12:95); Ep frat 263: *quia ipsa ipse est Spiritus sanctus, Deus caritas* (CCCM 88:282; CF 12:96).

[49] Ep frat 263: *Cum in osculo et amplexu Patris et Filii mediam quodammodo se inuenit beata conscientia; cum modo ineffabili et incogitabili, fieri meretur homo Dei, non Deus, sed tamen quod Deus est: homo ex gratia quod Deus est ex natura* (CCCM 88:282; CF 12:96).

[50] Ep frat 272: *Quousque amor proficiat in aliquam similitudinem amoris illius, qui Deum similem fecit homini, per humiliationem humanae conditionis, ut hominem similem Deo constituat* (CCCM 88:284; CF 12:98).

God,[51] to become conformed to divine wisdom, and to sense in oneself that which is in Christ Jesus our Lord" (Phil 2:5).[52] By this it appears that William understands the divine love as being the reason for the descent of God in Christ, just as it is in itself a descent to humankind. Thus it seems more precise to say that according to William the gift of divine love and knowledge of God to humans also means a descent or a humbling of the human.

Thus the human situation is to be receptive; just as any seeking and understanding of God is a gift, William says, "the things of God . . . [the soul] can seek or expect to understand only by God's gift."[53] Accordingly, when William in the same place chooses his words about the human life in relationship to God, he writes of humility. God can only be perceived—William says in the concluding pages of the *Epistola*—by "humble and enlightened love,"[54] "only by humble love from a clean heart."[55] It seems appropriate to say, then, that William thinks in this way about salvation, namely, that divine love descended to—and into—humans in Christ and still does so in the Spirit of the Father and the Son.

Likewise, William's understanding of the human life in Christ and the journey to the likeness of God should be described more adequately as a descent, namely, as the process of annihilation of the human person in the midst, as it were, of the filling up of divine love in the human person. Accordingly, for the human situation in this relationship, among the words William chooses for the final lines of the *Epistola* are *humiliare* and *uilescere*. About this christological understanding of human existence, William concludes in the last paragraph of his letter, in words that can also appropriately conclude the

---

[51] See also the Cistercian ideal of poverty in *Exordium parvum* 15, as Theodore Berkeley notes in his translation of Ep frat (CF 12:98n26).

[52] Ep frat 272: *Et tunc dulce est homini cohumiliari summae maiestati; compauperari Filio Dei; diuinae sapientiae conformari, hoc sentienti in seipso quod et in Christo Iesu Domino nostro* (CCCM 88:284; CF 12:98).

[53] Ep frat 292: *Quae uero Dei sunt, nonnisi a Deo quaerat uel expectet intellectum* (CCCM 88:288; CF 12:103).

[54] Ep frat 294: *sensu humilis et illuminati amoris* (CCCM 88:288; CF 12:104).

[55] Ep frat 296: *nisi mundo corde humiliter amantis* (CCCM 88:289; CF 12:104).

present chapter, "It is for one who entertains such thoughts to abase oneself in everything and to glorify in oneself the Lord his God, to become of no worth in one's own eyes as one contemplates God, to subject oneself to every human being for the love of one's Creator, to offer up one's body as a holy victim, living, pleasing to God, the worship due from one as a rational creature."[56] In accordance with this conclusion, even though Elder emphasizes William's understanding of the spiritual life as an ascent, she is clearly aware of Christ as the teacher of humility in William's thought:

> Throughout his works, despite changes in emphasis, he maintained that pride must learn humility from the humble Christ. Love must come through the example of Christ's love to focus on God rather than on self.[57]

---

[56] Ep frat 300: *Cogitantis ergo est in omnibus humiliare seipsum et glorificare in seipso Dominum Deum suum; in contemplatione Dei, uilescere se sibi; in amore Creatoris subiectum esse omni humanae creaturae; exhibere corpus suum hostiam sanctam, uiuentem, Deo placentem, rationabile obsequium suum* (CCCM 88:289; CF 12:103).

[57] Elder, "Image of Invisible God," 490.

6

WESTERN DARKNESS / EASTERN LIGHT
WILLIAM OF SAINT-THIERRY
AND THE TRADITIONS OF EGYPT

Benedicta Ward

It is often said that the new orders of the twelfth century drew on the traditions of the monks of Egypt, and William of Saint-Thierry is assumed to be someone particularly influenced by their stories in his praise of the Carthusians and of the Cistercians. Indeed, William began his *Golden Letter* to the monks of Mont-Dieu by linking them specially with Egypt, seeing them as a new expression of the earlier tradition: "The brethren of Mont-Dieu introduce to our Western darkness and French cold the light of the East and that ancient fervor of Egypt for religious observance—the pattern of solitary life and the model of heavenly conduct."[1]

William then praises the monks for their poverty, solitude, and zeal for God's glory.[2] He refers to earlier "deserts filled with men who had taken up this life of individual solitude," citing Paul, Macarius, Antony, and Arsenius.[3] Again, he praises "our fathers in Egypt and the Thebaid," whose cells were self-built, and he asserts that by their work they fed the poor with their own hands.[4] William was suggesting that the same fervor that animated the fourth-

---

[1] William, Ep frat 1 (CCCM 88:228; CF 12:9).
[2] William, Ep frat 9 (CCCM 88:229; CF 12:10–11).
[3] William, Ep frat 13 (CCCM 88:230; CF 12:13).
[4] William, Ep frat 157–58 (CCCM 88:260–61; CF 12:62).

century Christian monks was alive and flourishing under the totally different conditions of twelfth-century France. Like Cassian, he noted the differences in climate, but he was sure that the mainstream way of life was similar, according to the Gospel: "suddenly we found it in the depths of a wood, on God's mountain, on the fertile mountain, where the fair places of the desert [*deserti*] now wax fat on its richness and the hills are girt with exultation."[5]

In the individual style of hermit life at Mont-Dieu, William claimed that he could see the traditions of the solitaries of Egypt. When he wrote about the Cistercian monks, however, he was less explicit. In his famous description of Clairvaux, he did not see the new order as a repeat of fourth-century desert ways but as a new form of Gospel living, analogous to but not copying that found in Egypt. He does not describe a barren desert of harsh solitude and extreme asceticism among rocks and waterless wastes. He is well aware that the new desert has buildings in valleys, among trees, with liturgy in common and manual work together in rich fields:

> At the first glance as you entered Clairvaux by descending the hill you could see that it was a temple of God; and the still, silent valley spoke, in the modest simplicity of its buildings, of the genuine humility of Christ's poor. Moreover, in this valley full of men, where no one was permitted to be idle, where all were occupied with their allotted tasks, a silence deep as that of night prevailed. The sounds of labour, or the chants of the brethren in the choral service, were the only exceptions. The orderliness of this silence, and the report that went forth concerning it struck such a reverence even in secular persons that they dreaded breaking it, I will not say by idle or wicked conversation, but even by suitable remarks.[6]

Here William saw brothers living together and working in the fields. They were not the *fellahin* of Egypt, unlearned individuals,

---

[5] William, Ep frat 3 (CCCM 88:228; CF 12:9).
[6] William, Vita Bern 1.35 (CCCM 89B:60; PL 185:247D–248B; *St. Bernard of Clairvaux: The Story of his Life*, trans. Geoffrey Webb and Adrian Walker [London: A. R. Mowbray, 1960], 59, hereafter Webb and Walker, *St. Bernard*).

from a mixed background of crime and poverty, but middle-class young men from a society long Christianized, capable of singing the office and speaking about the Scriptures.

His next section continues this present-day focus with reference to both inner poverty and an inner richness, with a basis of Gospel teaching:

> The loneliness of this place, hidden among the woods and closed in by the surrounding hills, was comparable to the cave where the shepherds found our holy father Saint Benedict, so closely did the monks of Clairvaux follow his form of life and style of dwelling. Although they all lived together, it may truthfully be said that they were all solitaries, for although the valley was full of men the harmony and charity that reigned there were such that each monk seemed to be there all by himself. We all know well that an unstable man is never alone even when he is by himself, and in the same way among men whose lives are under the stabilizing influence of the rule in silence and unity of purpose, the way of life itself helps to establish an inner solitude in the depths of the heart.[7]

William was presenting a picture of a Gospel-centered life (perhaps with a defense against criticism of the new orders in mind), not suggesting that they were imitating the practical lifestyle of Egypt but seeing their ways as caused by a similar ideal. Having in mind the value placed in Christian contexts on community life, love of the brothers, and charity toward all, he described the Cistercians at Clairvaux as a community in which solitude was practiced only as a group, not individually as in Egypt.[8] William's reference is to Benedict in the sixth century, not Antony in the fourth.

Here it was not the individual continuous recitation of psalms alone as in the solitary tradition of Egypt but the corporate office in choir that William praised. He had more to say about the monks' corporate

---

[7] William, Vita Bern 1.35 (CCCM 89B:60–61; PL 185:248B; Webb and Walker, *St. Bernard*, 60).

[8] William, Vita Bern 1.35 (CCCM 89B:60; PL 185:247D–248B; Webb and Walker, *St. Bernard*, 59).

work, which seems to have impressed him especially, just as much as if not more than their singing together, since they were of good birth and education and were now doing manual labor together:

> This was indeed the golden age of Clairvaux. Virtuous men, who had once held honours and riches in the world, lovingly embraced a life of poverty in Christ. And thus they helped to plant the Church of God by giving their lives in toil and hardship, in hunger and thirst, in cold and exposure, in insults and persecutions and many difficulties, just like the Apostle Paul. These were the men who made it possible for Clairvaux to enjoy the peace and sufficiency which it has to-day, for they did not regard their lives as being lived only on their own account, but for Christ's sake and for the benefit of the brethren who would serve God in the monastery in years to come. They did not think selfishly of their own poverty and lack of even the necessities of life, and it is through the hardships and efforts faced by them that there is now enough to supply the monastery with all that is needed without dulling the realization that a monk's life is one of voluntary poverty for Christ's sake.[9]

William suggests that the way of Gospel living once seen among the hermits of Egypt has here taken on a modern dress. It was not the outer trappings of the desert that he saw but its inner meaning that was being reenacted by example and by words. His own friends and many who had held high position in church and state were alongside in manual work. This is not at all the picture given of the monks of Egypt, where most of the monks were used to hard manual labor and had no thought of position within the church; they were astonished when a patrician, Arsenius, lived with them.[10]

However clear the ideal urged by William was, it could suggest to others later that it was the practical details in the accounts of

---

[9] William, Vita Bern 1.35 (CCCM 89B:60; PL 185:247C–248A; Webb and Walker, *St. Bernard*, 59).

[10] *The Sayings of the Desert Fathers: The Alphabetical Collection*, trans. Benedicta Ward, CS 59 (London and Oxford: A. R. Mowbray; Kalamazoo, MI: Cistercian Publications, 1975), 9–19.

monks in fourth-century Egypt that were central to the reform of Cîteaux. It is a myth that persisted, though with concentration on the life in Egyptian monasteries rather than the solitary way of the hermits. When Conrad of Eberbach wrote his account of the Cistercian order in Germany in the thirteenth century, he included a chapter on the origins of monasticism in general. It had a section on the monks of the deserts of Egypt in the fourth century. He named Macarius, Paphnutius, Pambo, and Isidore, but he devoted most of this section not to the hermits but to practical details of the communities of Pachomius and Basil, the masters of the cenobitic life, making use of Cassian and of Palladius rather than the *apophthegmata*.[11] It was the fact that their lives of prayer and austerity caused them sometimes to give practical service to the poor and needy that inspired William; he was interested not in personal silence and solitude but in the concept of groups who lived together in solitude and charity according to the Gospel as an integral part of the church.

How did William know anything about the monks of Egypt? He would certainly have relied, as he says, on "word of mouth." This would mean mention of stories from the desert that he had heard in sermons but also, and predominantly, the daily readings aloud in Chapter of the writings of John Cassian. But Europeans of the time also had contacts with the Eastern tradition itself. The extent of the influence of learning by hearing and by imitation cannot be too strongly stressed. As Dr. Bernard Hamilton showed in his seminal paper *"Orientale lumen et magistra latinitas,"* it was not writings but living contact with exiled Eastern monks, many of them solitaries, that inspired the monastic revival in the West, and William may have encountered them.[12]

---

[11] Conrad of Eberbach, *Exordium Magnum cisterciense sive Narratio de initio Cisterciensis ordinis* 1.3, ed. Bruno Griesser, CCCM 138 (Turnholt: Brepols, 1994), 8–9; *The Great Beginning of Cîteaux: A Narrative of the Beginning of the Cistercian Order*, trans. Benedicta Ward and Paul Savage, ed. E. Rozanne Elder, CF 72 (Collegeville, MN: Cistercian Publications, 2012), 51–53.

[12] Bernard Hamilton with P. A. McNulty, *"Orientale lumen et magistra latinitas*: Greek Influences on Western Monasticism (900–1100)," in *Monastic Reform,*

William says he also read "in books" about the early monks. What were the written texts available to him? In the West in the twelfth century there were certainly some written accounts in Latin, for example the *Life of Saint Antony* by Athanasius and the *Life of Paul* by Jerome, as well as Sulpicius Severus's *Life of Martin of Tours* and *Dialogues*, the first of which concerns a supposed visit to the Desert Fathers of Egypt by someone called Postumianus.[13] Also Augustine of Hippo, in his account of his conversion, mentioned a "little book," a copy of the *Life of Saint Antony*, which had greatly influenced friends of Pontricianus near Trier, presumably the Latin version by Evagrius. Augustine himself was not converted by reading this book but by hearing of the response to it by these "poor in spirit."[14] This dependence on oral tradition continued in other writings by sophisticated writers; for instance, in the letter to Principia, Jerome says that Marcella learned first about Antony in Rome "from some priests of Alexandria and from Pope Athanasius and from Peter afterwards," not from Athanasius's book.[15]

John Cassian's works, as has been said, were also available as written texts, as was of course the Rule of Saint Benedict, but mostly these were known in memory and by public exposition rather than by personal reading. To say that written texts were available means of course just that: there were a very few copies, usually in monastic or cathedral libraries, which could be referred to by a few, not that they could be read or owned by the many. William was therefore among the few who actually read some of the texts. What he read about Egypt he found in books by well-known authors, not in the anonymous collections of *Sayings*.

Catharism and the Crusades (900–1300), ed. Bernard Hamilton (London: Variorum Reprints, 1979), 181–216.

[13] Sulpitius Severus, *The Works of Sulpitius Severus*, trans. Alexander Roberts, ed. Philip Schaff and Henry Wace, Nicene and Post-Nicene Fathers, 2nd series (New York: Christian Literature Publishing Company, 1894), 11:1–122, here 24.

[14] Augustine, *Confessions* 8.6; ed. Lucas Verheijen, CCSL 27 (Turnhout: Brepolis, 1990), 122.

[15] Jerome, "Letter CXXVII, to Principia," in *Select Letters of St. Jerome*, trans. F. A. Wright, Loeb Classical Library 262 (Cambridge, MA: Harvard University Press, 1933), 439–67, here 449.

It should be remembered that the earliest Christian monastic set-
tlements were nonliterate. The majority of Desert Fathers themselves
wrote no books and were extremely cautious about reading them. As
with the Gospel, according to which Jesus wrote nothing, the monks
were part of an oral culture; they held all they needed in their memories. In fact, no one really learns to be a monk only by reading about
it: it is a living tradition personally transmitted, flexible, and vibrant,
though linked always to Christian sources and reflection on how
people actually lived out these principles in their own times. When
in any age monks want to strengthen their proposals for change, they
can distort the past to fit their purpose by turning to books to show
that their predecessors did what they wanted to do. There can be a
lack of perspective about monastic life and writings when traditions
are explored by a kind of monastic archaeology, seeking facts and
practices rather than ideals. It is as well to know about the past, and
for a literate society reading is an invaluable way to have access to it,
but that reading has to be incorporated into life in the present.

Moreover, medieval reading was oral and corporate, not silent
and individual. Tradition was by word of mouth and by example
(*verbum et exemplum docere*). This tradition, this way of handing on
by words and by actions, was established very early in Christian
monastic circles and was best reflected in the many versions of the
apophthegmata patrem, where others recorded what they saw and
heard from the monks.

The desert tradition circulated by word of mouth, with some
written texts by well-known authors. But written texts were rare
at any point, and by the twelfth century, only two could be affirmed:
Cassian's *Conferences* and Athanasius's *Life of Saint Antony*. These
are the books in which William says he had read about the Desert
Fathers. Manuscripts of the *apophthegmata* themselves were very
rare indeed, and it seems they were unknown to William.

William himself was part of the oral tradition of learning by
seeing and hearing, and he referred to "the Egyptian monks of long
ago"[16] when he wanted a parallel for the experience of actually

---

[16] William, Vita Bern 1.34 (CCCM 89B:60; PL 185:247C; Webb and Walker, *St.
Bernard*, 58).

living near his ideal of monastic life, Bernard. Bernard himself rarely referred to the early monastic tradition. Once, in his *Apologia* to Peter of Cluny, he cited the desert as a rebuke about lack of asceticism in the present: "Did Macarius live like this? Did Basil teach this? Did Antony teach this way? Was this the way of life of the fathers in Egypt?"[17] This grouping of Macarius, Basil, and Antony seems to have become a *topos* of the times. But when Bernard expressed nostalgia for the simpler days of the early church, he meant Athanasius and Augustine, not Antony and Arsenius.

It is necessary to look elsewhere for someone who had actually read the *apophthegmata*. It is an ironic fact that the one who knew them well was Peter Abelard, to whom William referred with contempt in his *Golden Letter*.[18] In the letters between Abelard and Heloise it is possible to find someone who really had read the *libris et documentis* of the desert itself and gained from them the same love of silence and individual solitude as was held by the first Christian monks. It may seem that to present Abelard as the true heir to the tradition of the Desert Fathers rather than William or Bernard is to incur the condemnation of Bernard himself (as one would always be reluctant to do), who when writing about Abelard described him as "a most doubtful character, having nothing of the monk about him except the name and the habit."[19] But it is a fact that while William of Saint-Thierry saw both Clairvaux and Mont-Dieu through rosy spectacles, these had gained no tinge of their color from the simple records of *Sayings* from the desert. It seems that Abelard, on the other hand, knew and appreciated the desert hermits well. William knew of Antony, Macarius, and Paul, but Abelard quoted from many other Desert Fathers not found in the standard sources.

After he became a monk, *malgré lui*, Abelard took to it with relentless energy. As a monk of Saint Denis and later at Saint Gildas

---

[17] Bernard, *Apologia* 23 (SBOp 3:100; CF 1:58–59).

[18] William, Ep frat Praef. 10 (CCCM 88:226; CF 12:6).

[19] Bernard, Ep 193 to Cardinal Ivo (SBOp 8:45; *The Letters of St. Bernard of Clairvaux*, trans. Bruno Scott James [London: Burns and Oates, 1953], #241, p. 321).

he had monastic libraries before him and applied his whole mind to reading and thinking about the tradition in which he now found himself; as someone who seems to have been chronically unable to live for long in community, no doubt he found the hermit material especially congenial. Moreover, he wanted Heloise, an even more reluctant nun, also to immerse herself in the monastic and eremitic tradition. It is therefore in Letters Seven and Eight, which he wrote to her on the tradition of monastic life, that one can see what texts Abelard, contemporary and enemy of William, knew from this earliest tradition of Christian monasticism, how well he knew them, and what parts he quoted for Heloise's benefit.[20]

Heloise's reaction to this material needs longer treatment than is possible here, but a summary of the desert themes in their correspondence is relevant. Letters Seven and Eight can be seen as two parts of Abelard's answer to Letter Six, from Heloise, written when she was living with her nuns at the Paraclete in the 1130s. In his letter Abelard says that he is writing in response to her request for information about the origin of the monastic tradition as well as for her entirely practical plea for help in arranging the daily life of the nuns at the Paraclete. She says, reluctantly enough, that she will replace her emotional demands for his attention with this more objective request: "teach us how the order of nuns began and what authority there is for our profession. . . . Prescribe some Rule for us and write it down, a Rule which shall be suitable for women."[21]

Behind this plain and indeed explicit demand was Heloise's determination to attract Abelard's attention and involve Abelard in her life at the Paraclete in some way. Abelard was aware of this desire, and in reply he also had a more personal theme in mind: he was writing, he said, "so that you may more warmly embrace the

---

[20] Abelard, *Epistolae*, PL 178:113–380, here 225–326; Abelard's seventh letter has been edited by T. P. McLaughlin, "Abelard's Rule for Religious Women," *Mediaeval Studies* 18 (1956): 241–92. For abbreviated English translations of these letters, see *Letters of Abelard and Heloise*, rev. ed., trans. Betty Radice, Introduction and notes by Michael Clanchy (New York: Penguin, 2004) (hereafter Radice, *Letters*).

[21] Heloise, Ep 6 (Radice, *Letters*, 94).

calling of your profession through better understanding of its excellence."[22] These two letters, which contain Abelard's long account
of monasticism, were written with a definite intention of propa-
ganda, and this theme affected his selection when he quoted from
the Desert Fathers.

Abelard began the letters with a general description of an ideal-
ized past, quoting Jerome (a special favorite of both himself and
Heloise) from his letter to Heliodorus. With hindsight, it is possible
to see that Abelard was setting up a tradition reaching from the
Old Testament prophets through the disciples in Acts to the Desert
Fathers, thereby appealing to Heloise's biblical scholarship: "after
them Paul, Antony, Macarius and all those who have been preem-
inent among us, fled from the tumult of their times and the world
full of temptations, and carried the bed of their contemplation to
the peace of the wilderness, so that they could devote themselves
to God more sincerely."[23] How did Abelard know about them? Like
William, through Jerome, Cassian, and Athanasius, but also, I suggest, by reading the *apophthegmata patrum* in Latin. He says that he
will instruct Heloise by using written documents: "I . . . propose
to instruct your way of life through the *many documents* of the holy
Fathers and the best customs of monasteries."[24]

Later Abelard quotes a saying from the *apophthegmata* that de-
plores the fact that monastic life in Egypt was written rather than
lived, but he uses it for his own purposes, quoting the saying to
show that information about the traditions of Egypt had in fact
been set down and still existed in writing: "that elder in the Lives
of the Fathers . . . says: 'The prophets wrote books: and your forebears came after and did much work on them. Then their successors
committed them to memory. But now comes the present generation,
which has copied them on paper and parchment and put them back
to stand idle on the shelves.'"[25]

---

[22] Abelard, Ep 7 (Radice, *Letters*, 129).
[23] Abelard, Ep 8 (Radice, *Letters*, 137).
[24] Abelard, Ep 8 (Radice, *Letters*, 131) (emphasis mine).
[25] Abelard, Ep 8 (Radice, *Letters*, 202).

The inference is that these documents still existed and were available to him, since, after referring to the "*many documents* of the holy Fathers," he says, "I have abundant riches in the *records* of the Fathers."[26] In the first case the word is *documentis*, which can only mean written documents.

What were these documents like? Manuscripts of the Latin version of the *vitae patrum* were circulating in Paris in the early twelfth century, combined with other early monastic texts. I have recently compared Abelard's quotations from the Desert Fathers with three such manuscripts in Oxford's Bodleian Library.[27] All of Abelard's desert quotations are there, and they are mainly taken from the section of the Latin translation of the *Sayings* by Pelagius and John; moreover, the manuscripts are so similar as to be representative of a genre. I suggest that a manuscript like these was known to Abelard either at Saint Denis or possibly at Saint Gildas. He could also have known the sayings orally, since he says so himself, but he may well have quoted it from memory rather than copying from the written text.

It seems to me that, like William's references to the Desert Fathers, Abelard's, while more deeply based on the *Sayings* than William's, are entirely typical of the use made of the Desert Fathers in the twelfth century. The "new monks" and those who wrote about them had in mind what they wanted to do, and then they used the texts to back it up. In his references to the desert, William was not exploring the Egyptian monasticism of the fourth century but praising the new orders of monks in the twelfth. Abelard, in his use of the desert material, said equally little about the tradition of early Christian monasticism itself but a great deal about the monastic ideals and practices he recommended for his own time.

It is perhaps a warning to be careful about the use of desert traditions, since they are based on writings that were copied by later monks. After all, the Greek, Syriac, and Latin texts of the desert

---

[26] Abelard, Ep 8 (Radice, *Letters*, 131) (emphasis mine).

[27] Oxford, Bodleian Library, MS. Hatton 84, fols. 27ʳ–112ʳ; Oxford, Bodleian Library, MS. Douce 351, fols. 6ʳ–153ʳ; and Oxford, Bodleian Library, MS. Bodleian 386, fols. 58ʳ–162ʳ.

that now exist were made well after the fourth century. They may not have been made or used with quite the pure desire for objectivity that we think we ourselves have. William of Saint-Thierry and Abelard were not copying the details of early monastic life in any specific way; they were, rather, people who knew about and responded to the air of Egypt and saw the East shedding a light that illuminated not only the East and Egypt of long ago but also the West in its present and future ways. Ultimately the connection between Egypt, Mont-Dieu, Clairvaux, and the Paraclete is beyond all their external similarities: "We are stimulated and drawn on by his love or the love of his love to speak and to think of him."[28]

---

[28] William, Ep frat 299 (CCCM 88:298; CF 12:105).

7

BERNARD MADE A COVENANT WITH HIS EYES
THE SAINT AND HIS BIOGRAPHER,
WILLIAM OF SAINT-THIERRY

James France

How agreeable the affection arising in me for that person, how great the desire to share his lodging in that poverty and simplicity! Had a wish been offered me that day, nothing would I have so wished as to remain there with him and be his servant forever.[1]

These are the words of William of Saint-Thierry in describing the impact of Saint Bernard's personality on him at their first meeting, which took place some time between 1118 and 1120. On entering the modest hut in which Bernard lived he was filled with "as much reverence as if I were stepping up to the altar of God."[2]

William's adulation of Bernard, coupled with William's own modesty and sense of unworthiness, has resulted in his being considerably less well known than his mentor, to whom much of William's work was until relatively recently attributed. Bernard's

---

[1] William, Vita Bern 1.33 (CCCM 89B:58–59; PL 185:246D; William of Saint-Thierry, *Bernard of Clairvaux: Early Biographies, Vol. I by William of St. Thierry*, trans. Martinus Cawley [Lafayette, OR: Abbey of Our Lady of Guadalupe, 1990], 44 [hereafter Cawley, *Bernard*]).

[2] William, Vita Bern 1.33 (CCCM 89:58; PL 185:246D; Cawley, *Bernard*, 44).

charisma inevitably overshadowed William's more withdrawn and retiring nature. Although William describes his relationship with Bernard as that of a pupil to a teacher, the flow of knowledge and ideas was by no means only in one direction. William undoubtedly had an influence on Bernard. He was, for example, responsible for Bernard's involvement in two important areas: the defense of the ideals of the revitalized monasticism as expressed in the *Apologia*, written at the request of William and addressed to him, and the later attack on Peter Abelard leading to Abelard's condemnation at the synod of Sens. William's true worth has been established by modern scholars, notably E. Rozanne Elder, according to whom "William is recognized as a spiritual master of the first rank, in some ways the equal—in some the superior—of Saint Bernard."[3] This assessment is corroborated by other scholars: according to Adriaan Bredero, William's "writings have had a major influence on medieval mystical theology,"[4] and Louis J. Lekai says that he "must be recognized as an outstanding monastic theologian of the twelfth century."[5] And yet William is perhaps still best known as Bernard's biographer.

It is in this capacity that William is depicted in the only two known medieval portraits of him. In the first he is presented in the lower half of the initial *B(ernardus)* (fig. 1), the opening word of book 1 of the *Vita prima*, which he wrote between 1145 and his death in 1148, five years before Bernard's. It is in a manuscript from the Austrian abbey of Zwettl dated ca. 1189—one of the earliest representations of Bernard. A youthful Bernard is depicted in an authoritative frontal position, holding his crozier with one hand and his left hand raised in blessing. William is shown sitting at a desk holding a pen and knife in what is a traditional author portrait.

---

[3] E. Rozanne Elder, Introduction to *The Mirror of Faith* by William of Saint-Thierry, trans. Thomas X. Davis, CF 15 (Kalamazoo, MI: Cistercian Publications, 1979), xi–xxxi, here xi.

[4] Adriaan H. Bredero, *Bernard of Clairvaux: Between Cult and History* (Grand Rapids, MI: William B. Eerdmans, 1996), 118.

[5] Louis J. Lekai, *The Cistercians: Ideals and Realities* (Kent, OH: Kent State University Press, 1977), 231.

Fig. 1. Bernard and William in *Vita prima* dated ca. 1189 (Zisterzienserstift Zwettl, Cod. 144, fol. 26r)

The other image is in a late thirteenth-century composite manuscript that belonged to the Cistercian nuns of Lövenbrueck. Here the small image of William in a black cowl with his hood over his head kneels before the much larger figure of Bernard in a grey cowl, holding a crozier in his left hand and a book in his right (fig. 2).

The two men are depicted within the opening initial S(CRIPTVRUS *Vitam serui tui . . .*) ("It is my aim to write the life of your servant to the honor of your name"). William's identity is indicated by the text in red above, which announces the "beginning of the Prologue of the Life of Saint Bernard [*Incipit prologus*] abbot of Clairvaux, by William, abbot of Saint-Thierry." Although William is referred to as the abbot of Saint-Thierry and is depicted in the black Benedictine habit, by the time he wrote book 1 of the *Vita prima* he was a simple Cistercian monk at Signy following his resignation of the abbacy in 1135. The difference in status is suggested in both images: in the one by the more authoritative frontal position of Bernard, in the other by the distinct difference in

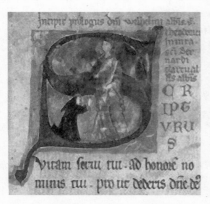

Fig. 2. Bernard and William in *Vita prima* from the nuns' abbey of Lövenbrueck (Berlin, Staatsbibliothek-Preussischer Kulturbesitz MS. Lat. fol. 754, fol. 1r)

scale between the large Bernard and much smaller William, and in both by Bernard's being above William.

The writing of Bernard's *Life* was initiated by Bernard's secretary and travel companion, Geoffrey of Auxerre, who gathered the early biographical material, the so-called *Fragmenta Gaufridi,* which he handed to William. More important as a source, however, was the material William gathered from "certain brothers" during his visits to Clairvaux, a debt he acknowledged in the preface: "They it is who have been reporting to me materials obtained by diligent investigation and inquiry, reporting other episodes too that they were present for and saw and heard for themselves."[6] Most important, however, was the material William obtained firsthand as a consequence of the friendship that developed between him and Bernard.

The wish William had expressed at his first meeting with Bernard—that of remaining with Bernard—was to be partially fulfilled. Some years after his initial visit to Clairvaux, Bernard heard that William was sick and sent his brother Gerard to fetch him. Bernard and William were together for a long period during which they were both ill. This time together would have given them the opportunity of sharing their thoughts and experiences.

The tradition of hagiological illustration in the form of pictures featuring episodes and legendary anecdotes from the lives of saints goes back a long way. The earliest known narrative cycle featuring Saint Bernard is the altarpiece in the church of the Templars in Palma, Majorca, dated ca. 1290, but the most comprehensive is the much later stained glass from the former cloisters of the Cistercian monks of Altenberg in the Rhineland and the Cistercian nuns of Saint Apern in Cologne, both cycles made in Cologne in the first third of the sixteenth century.[7]

---

[6] William, Vita Bern 1.Pref. (CCCM 89B:31; PL 185:225C–226A; Cawley, *Bernard*, 2).

[7] All of these images are reproduced on the CD appended to James France, *Medieval Images of Saint Bernard of Clairvaux,* CS 210 (Kalamazoo, MI: Cistercian Publications, 2005), the Altenberg glass as GL1–GL57, and the Saint Apern glass as GL58–GL67.

The Altenberg glass originally consisted of approximately seventy panels with scenes from the life of Bernard. Following the secularization of the abbeys in 1803, the Altenberg cloister glass panels were sold, and again in 1824, after which they were dispersed. Fifty-eight depicting Bernard are known to have survived, including fourteen that were destroyed in the Second World War, while the remaining forty-four are now in six different locations. The largest number—eighteen—are now in Saint Mary's Church in Shrewsbury, England, having been purchased in 1845 by the vicar. The smaller cycle from Saint Apern is known to have consisted of fifty-four panels, of which eleven still exist, seven of them in Cologne cathedral. A number of these were almost identical to those from Altenberg, replicating the same incidents from the saint's life, while others depicted the same episodes in a totally different way. The source for the narrative depictions was mainly the *Vita prima*—more than half the panels are from book 1, by William.

Among the early stories are three of Bernard's chastity's being tested by the devil, who, in the words of William, "strewed his path with the snares of temptation, at every possible juncture lying in wait for his heel."[8] All three episodes are represented in the Altenberg cycle. The first recounts how Bernard once looked curiously at a woman, but, realizing what he was doing, he blushed, ashamed of himself, and leapt into a pool of freezing water. He remained there until he had cooled down from the heat of carnal longing. At the end of the story William quotes Bernard in the words of Job, who is said to have developed a great love of chastity: "I had made a covenant with my eyes not to linger on any virgin" (Job 31:1).[9] The event was depicted in Altenberg glass that was destroyed during the Second World War. It is only known from a black-and-white photograph. William's suggestion that the adolescent Bernard had an eye for women is curious, for it is in total contrast to the later well-known stories in his *Life* of his almost total inattention

---

[8] William, Vita Bern 1.6 (CCCM 89B:37; PL 185:230C; Cawley, *Bernard*, 11).
[9] William, Vita Bern 1.6 (CCCM 89B:37; PL 185:230B; Cawley, *Bernard*, 11). Biblical translation taken from the *New Jerusalem Bible*.

to his surroundings. William recounts that Bernard never noticed the vaulting of the ceiling in the novices' room where he spent a whole year and that he thought that there was only one window in the sanctuary of the church, whereas there were really three.[10] William's point in presenting these contrasting images was to highlight the transformation from the carefree life of early manhood to Bernard's extraordinary ability to concentrate on his devotions to the exclusion of all that went on around him.

In the first chastity story, Bernard took the initiative. In the two other episodes, he was exposed to temptation as a result of the admiration and attentions of women on account of his great good looks and his charm. Two remarkably detailed accounts of Bernard's physical appearance by his closest friends have survived. If they are to be believed—and there is no reason to doubt their veracity—the attraction was quite natural. According to William, "his physique was elegant, he was good-looking, his manners delightful."[11] Bernard's other biographer, Geoffrey of Auxerre, provides a more detailed description: "His inner beauty was so great that it revealed itself clearly in his outward appearance. He had an air of inner purity full of grace. His body was very thin, and he seemed gaunt with a complexion so pale that there was hardly any color on his cheeks."[12]

The *Exordium Magnum* has another reference to Bernard's appearance. Commenting on the difference between Bernard's horse and that of Henry of Lausanne, Bernard remarked that the two men should not be judged by the necks of their horses but by their own. Conrad of Eberbach writes, "Saying this, he threw back his hood and bared his head to his shoulders, displaying his long and slender neck. This was thin and emaciated, but by heaven's grace

---

[10] William, Vita Bern 1.20 (CCCM 89B:48; PL 185:238D; Cawley, *Bernard*, 28).

[11] William, Vita Bern 1.6 (CCCM 89B:37; PL 185:230B; Cawley, *Bernard*, 28).

[12] Geoffrey of Auxerre, Vita Bern 3.1.1 (*St. Bernard of Clairvaux: The Story of His Life as Recorded in the* Vita Prima Bernardi *by Certain of His Contemporaries, William of St. Thierry, Arnold of Bonnevaux, Geoffrey and Philip of Clairvaux, and Odo of Deuil,* trans. Geoffrey Webb and Adrian Walker [London: A. R. Mowbray, 1960], 20; CCCM 89B:133; PL 185:303C).

it was as white and beautiful as that of a swan."[13] That two of the three chastity stories refer to the effect Bernard's good looks had on women comes as no surprise, but William included them in his *Life* in order to satisfy one of Bernard's main claims to sanctity, his ability to remain chaste in the face of overwhelming temptation.

In the second chastity story a naked girl, incited by the devil (*instinctu daemonis*),[14] climbed into Bernard's bed. When Bernard turned his back on her and went back to sleep she began stroking and stimulating him (*palpans et stimulans*).[15] When Bernard still made no move, the girl blushed with shame, got up, and fled away. Figure 3 first shows her in the bed in which Bernard had yielded

Fig. 3. The second chastity story from Altenberg, now in the Schnütgen Museum, Cologne

[13] Conrad of Eberbach, *Exordium Magnum cisterciense sive Narratio de initio Cisterciensis Ordinis* 2.17, ed. Bruno Griesser, SSOC 2:110–11 (Rome: Editiones Cistercienses, 1961); *The Great Beginning of Cîteaux: A Narrative of the Beginning of the Cistercian Order*, trans. Benedicta Ward and Paul Savage, ed. E. Rozanne Elder, CF 72 (Collegeville, MN: Cistercian Publications, 2012), 151.

[14] William, Vita Bern 1.7 (CCCM 89B:37; PL 185:230D; Cawley, *Bernard*, 12).

[15] William, Vita Bern 1.7 (CCM 89B:38; PL 185:230D; Cawley, *Bernard*, 12).

her the space, turned round, and gone to sleep; it then shows her on the right, leaving the room.

The third story refers to an occasion when Bernard and some companions lodged with a certain matron. William describes Bernard as handsome in looks (*decorum aspectu*) and says that the woman "was caught in the trap of her own eyes and was inflamed with lust towards him."[16] She made three attempts to invade his bed, but Bernard managed to thwart her by each time shouting "Robbers! Robbers!" (*Latrones! Latrones!*),[17] so alerting his companions, who instigated a search and thus frightened her away. The following day, Bernard told his companions that there had indeed been a robber, "for our hostess was out to deprive me of what is most precious to me in this life, my incomparable treasure, my chastity."[18] In figure 4, in the left-hand panel Bernard, wearing a white cap, sits with his two companions at table laden with food and drink. He is watched by the landlady on the far left. The scene on the right shows Bernard in bed with the woman approaching. The scroll reads "Latrones, latrones."

Fig. 4. The third chastity story from Altenberg, now in the Ludwig Collection, Schnuetgen Museum, Cologne

[16] William, Vita Bern 1.7 (CCCM 89B:38; PL 185:231A; Cawley, *Bernard*, 12).
[17] William, Vita Bern 1.7 (CCCM 89B:38; PL 185:231A; Cawley, *Bernard*, 12).
[18] William, Vita Bern 1.7 (CCCM 89B:38; PL 185:231B; Cawley, *Bernard*, 13).

Like the previous panel, this one is divided by a column into two sections in which the story unfurls in two consecutive episodes, a medieval device commonly used to illustrate the lives of saints. The unfolding in time is handled by a sequence in which the chief character, here Bernard, reappears in a succession of scenes. Two lines of text at the foot of the panel describe the scene in abbreviated form: "The young Bernard was a guest with his companions of a certain married lady who was inflamed with desire for him. She approached him three times during the night, and with a loud voice he cried: 'Thieves! Thieves!'"

Little is known about an almost identical panel now in the east window of the small village church of Saint Leonard in Marston Bigot, Somerset. The seating here is reversed with Bernard on the far left and the landlady on the right, and in the right-hand scene the landlady is shown on her way out. The scroll is the same as that in figure 4 (fig. 5).

Fig. 5. The third chastity story from St. Apern, Cologne, now in Saint Leonard's Church, Marston Bigot, Somerset, England

Although the exact provenance of the fifth image is not known, it was almost certainly purchased by the Earl of Cork, whose family had built the church in 1789 next to the ancestral home, Marston House, and it was installed when the church was remodeled in the nineteenth century—one of the many late-medieval German windows that found their way to England following the secularization of monasteries in 1803. It clearly represents the same scene as the fourth, and as there would not have been two identical scenes at Altenberg, it almost certainly belongs to the Saint Apern cycle, a judgment reinforced by the fact that several of the incidents shown in the Altenberg cycle are replicated at Saint Apern.

The treatment of the three chastity stories by the Cologne artists closely follows William of Saint-Thierry's *Vita prima*. The importance attached to the theme in Cistercian monasteries is evidenced by their inclusion in the hymn *Bernardus inclitis*, assigned to Compline on his feast—with almost every line a cameo containing a complete story. The three stories are referred to in the following order: the third story first, then the first, and finally the second:

> When a woman knocked on his bedroom
> He cried out "Thieves!"
> They searched the home with lanterns.
> He threw himself into freezing water.
> He despised lewd songs
> And relinquished displays of splendor.
> He turned away from the woman in the bed.

Most of the panels have an abbreviated version of the whole story at the foot of each panel covering the full width. But there are a few exceptions, such as at Marston, where the text is contained within a rectangular area with a number of lines and placed elsewhere on the panel. The text on the panel, seen in figure 6, reads: "When once the saint discovered a girl, who had got naked into his bed at the instigation of the devil, he yielded to her the part of the bed which he had occupied, and, resting on the other side, went to sleep. Finally she dug her nails into him and drew blood. He still made no move, and she blushed with shame, arose, and fled away."

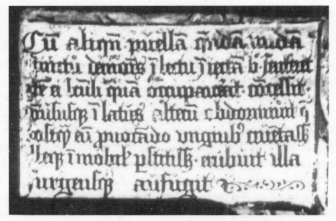

Fig. 6. Text of second chastity story from Saint Apern, now in
St. Leonard's Church, Marston Bigot, Somerset, England

Strangely, this picture does not refer to the scene depicted within
the panel, but it is clearly recognizable as the second of the three
stories. It is evidence that there must also previously have been a
panel featuring this story at Saint Apern, as at Altenberg. While
the writer of the Marston text has not repeated the *palpans et stimulans* of the *Vita prima*, he has added the *lacerans et cruentans* that
is found in some *Vita prima* manuscripts but not in others and that
is notably also absent in the Migne edition.[19]

Interestingly, the text at Altenberg is almost identical to the Marston text: "When once a naked girl had got into the bed while he
was asleep, the young saint moved to the other side. She then
clawed him with her nails in order to stir him, but he remained
immobile." It is slightly shorter than the Marston text, and there is
no mention that the girl acted at the instigation of the devil. It thus
deviates from the original *Vita prima* account but includes the detail
of drawing blood. This seemingly trivial divergence is nevertheless

---

[19] William, Vita Bern 1.7 (CCCM 89B:38; PL 185:230D; Cawley, *Bernard*, 12).
I have checked the late twelfth-century manuscript of the *Vita prima* at Mount
Saint Bernard Abbey, England, which, like Migne, does not include the *lacerans
et cruentans* found in the new critical edition in CCCM 89B.

significant in that it establishes a link between the two similar treatments of the same episode in the two cycles.

The covenant that Bernard made with his eyes and that his biographer explored in the three chastity stories may be just another example of hagiological narrative following the traditional rules of the genre. They may be clichés, examples of cultic images reflecting the duality in the presentation of Bernard's *Life*. Michael Casey has said that "the 'temptations' of Bernard are more literary than historical, and perhaps reveal more about the writers than they do about Bernard himself."[20] Ability to withstand the temptations of the flesh was one of the favorite hagiological themes, a *sine qua non* in satisfying the demands of the genre, that of Bernard's ability to remain chaste in the face of overwhelming temptation. William's purpose in writing Bernard's *Life*, like that of those who continued the work after his death, was to further Bernard's canonization and at the same time show him to be a model to be emulated by future generations of monks. In his Prologue, William described his aim with regard to Bernard as to limit himself "to some external testimonies of his life,"[21] that is, to express his sainthood through his outward deeds. While never deviating from his aim, William nevertheless managed to portray Bernard as thoroughly human.

During the long time he had spent with him, William would have gotten to know the saint well enough to have become aware of his failings. He was, however, sufficiently secure, indeed unswerving, in his faith in Bernard's sainthood that he felt able to reveal some of the ways in which Bernard was less than perfect.[22] Indeed, because of not being afraid to recount stories critical of

---

[20] Michael Casey, *Athirst for God: Spiritual Desire in Bernard of Clairvaux's Sermons on the Song of Songs*, CS 77 (Kalamazoo, MI: Cistercian Publications, 1987), 8–9.

[21] William, Vita Bern 1.Pref (CCCM 89B:32; PL 185:226B; Cawley, *Bernard*, 3).

[22] For a detailed textual analysis of this hypothesis, see E. Rozanne Elder, "Making Virtues of Vexing Habits," in *Studiosorum Speculum: Studies in Honor of Louis J. Lekai, O. Cist*, ed. Francis Swietek and John R. Sommerfeldt, CS 141 (Kalamazoo, MI: Cistercian Publications, 1993), 75–94.

Bernard, he in fact accents Bernard's sainthood rather than diminishing it. He tells of the occasion when Bernard's abbot, Stephen Harding, reprimanded Bernard for failing to recite the psalms he had promised to say for his mother, and he criticizes Bernard for the excessive mortification that undermined his health, both episodes depicted in both cycles. William also draws attention to Bernard's stubbornness in five times refusing bishoprics that he was offered, saying that "no one was able to get him to do anything contrary to his will."[23]

William says that during their close proximity at Clairvaux, Bernard shared with him his emotional experiences and that each day he would write down what he could remember. Considering the amount of time they must have spent together, Bernard may well also have found time to recount episodes from his youth. Accounts of the three occasions in which Bernard is said to have been exposed to temptation may be characterized as hagiological clichés. Nevertheless, it is equally possible, in the same way that William portrayed some of the flawed human side of Bernard's character, that he based the substance of the three chastity stories on Bernard's own account. The third story in particular, as depicted in the glass from both Altenberg and Saint Apern, has a ring of authenticity about it that would support this hypothesis. Whether or not that is true, however, William presents these three stories—as he does narratives throughout the *Vita Prima*—in such a way as to convey his admiration for Bernard while pointing to Bernard's life as truly a saintly one.

---

[23] William, Vita Bern 1.69 (CCCM 89B:82; PL 185:265B; Cawley, *Bernard*, 86).

8

MEDIATING A PRESENCE
RHETORICAL AND NARRATIVE STRATEGIES IN THE VITA PRIMA BERNARDI

Marjory Lange

M any medieval *vitae* survive; it was a popular genre.[1] Read in monasteries for edification, read outside for instruction and entertainment, the saint's life was an established literary form. Some surviving *vitae* are pedantic and dull, using the genre's conventions as an uninspiring model for stereotypical reports. Others, however, are outstanding not only for their content but also for the level of the author's artistic achievement. One such is William of Saint-Thierry's account of the life of Bernard of Clairvaux, the first book of the *Vita prima Sancti Bernardi*.[2] William was a skilled writer, and his subject was certainly famous. Bernard's reputation and William's relationship with him have kept the *Vita prima* central in Bernard scholarship. It is the first life, written by a colleague; those facts create assumptions of authority. Those facts also create stresses

[1] Many thanks to the Mount Angel Abbey Library and its staff, where I have found meditative work space, wonderful resources, and extremely helpful souls.

[2] William of Saint-Thierry, *Vita prima Sancti Bernardi*, ed. Paul Verdeyen, CCCM 89B (Turnhout: Brepols, 2011). English translations are mine, with some assistance from William of Saint-Thierry, *Bernard of Clairvaux: Early Biographies, Vol. I by William of St. Thierry*, trans. Martinus Cawley (Lafayette, OR: Abbey of Our Lady of Guadalupe, 1990) (hereafter Cawley, *Bernard*).

on its interpretation. Historians have asked repeatedly how objective a friend can be, what sort of truth does William present, and even what *is* William doing? Rarely has the *Vita prima* been read from a literary perspective, to examine William's choices in organization, presentation, and rhetoric to see how they might transform or clarify the historical issues.

The *Vita prima* has been the subject of more controversy than most medieval Cistercian *vitae*. It remains vulnerable to an unusually wide range of readings for several reasons. Conventions of the *vita* genre have become so unfamiliar and strange that its features and function appear foreign. Even Dom Jean Leclercq, a fine reader of William's work, can write that

> as William was always an author and a thinker of some originality, he tried to cover up the fact that he was adopting the conventional model. Yet, if we compare his work to earlier or contemporary *Lives*, and even with the other books of this *First Life*, we can recognize many a traditional theme in what he says about the way Bernard prayed, became absorbed in meditation, refrained from eating and sleeping, or [what he says] about his brothers' opposition to his healing activities.[3]

Certainly William employs *vita* conventions, but his choices in no way cover up his use of his model; to the contrary, he openly exploits the cardinal facets of the genre, making them work for him. William's originality is showcased by the conventions' presence.

A second challenge to interpretation is the role played by William's personal feeling for Bernard. Friendship clearly influenced William's artistic choices; a friend praises—and criticizes—differently than an outsider. The literary merit of the *Vita prima* has been obscured by these types of legitimate concern that have hidden its quality as a piece of excellently crafted persuasive writing.

This essay explores how William's artistic choices shape the way he chose to represent the life of his fellow abbot and friend within the thematic rubrics of the *vita* genre. It has three sections: (1) dis-

---

[3] Jean Leclercq, *A Second Look at Bernard of Clairvaux*, trans. Marie-Bernard Said, CS 105 (Kalamazoo, MI: Cistercian Publications, 1990), 5.

cussion of the genre of hagiographical *vitae* ("sacred biography")[4] and generic implications for current debates over the nature of the *Vita prima*, (2) consideration of William's rhetorical strategies in the manipulation of the storyline and his placement of *aliquando* episodes, the ones that have no clear chronological location, and (3) an examination of William's use of himself within the text. When William's work is placed within its context and its strategies are recognized for the roles they play, the *Vita prima* emerges as a carefully crafted, highly successful life that transcends its model as well as the modern controversies surrounding it.

The Genre of Hagiographical *Vitae* and the Debate Surrounding the *Vita prima*

The Vita *Genre*

During the twentieth century, scholars vigorously debated William's purposes in composing his book of the *Vita prima*. For centuries it had simply been accepted as the primary source for firsthand, contemporary information about Bernard's life, but during the later twentieth century its generic nature came into question: Is it biography or hagiography? That question itself is modern: until the seventeenth century the word *life* designated histories of individuals and context served to distinguish whether a work was sacred or secular. Subsequently, the term *biography* became customary for describing works that set out the factual events of a person's life.

Hagiography entered mainstream English even later. Beginning in the sixteenth century, the Latin word (*hagiographa*) named the section of Hebrew Scriptures now called *Writings* (*Ketuvim*): the Law, the Prophets, and Hagiographa. In its English form, the earliest references in the *Oxford English Dictionary* are to nineteenth-century quotations about the writing of saints' lives. Robert

---

[4] Thomas J. Heffernan, *Sacred Biography: Saints and Their Biographers in the Middle Ages* (New York: Oxford University Press, 1988), is the most comprehensive resource for this genre. His term, "sacred biography," neatly avoids the chasm gaping between *hagiography* and *biography*, but it has not quelled the debate.

Southey's 1821 reference to miracle stories as tales that are "common in Romish hagiography" is characteristic.[5] This negative connotation associated (in Protestant and many academic circles) with hagiography has beleaguered the entire discussion of the purpose of the *Vita prima*. If considered a biography, is it factual enough to be reliable by modern historiographical standards? And if hagiography, does the archaic *vita* genre have anything to say about Bernard that would be relevant now?

Two examples of modern generic expectations can draw attention to often-unconscious difficulties in appreciating conventions of the hagiographic agenda. Today's literature students, for instance, struggle to understand why, in *Pride and Prejudice*, Lydia Bennett's living with Wickham a week before they married troubled her family and society. Social conventions have changed greatly since the early nineteenth century. Literary conventions change as well, so that elements of hagiography, like miracle episodes, can seem artificial and unbelievable. In a different interpretive framework, assumptions regarding the arrest of a serial killer have evolved to the point of convention. When a suspect is identified, authorities confidently expect to find a record from childhood of maternal neglect, bedwetting, torturing small animals, etc. These signs substantiate and support the arrest because they have been associated over time with many other serial killers.

Just as modern psychological profilers anticipate conventional traits in a serial killer, a medieval audience would expect any sacred *vita* to provide a birth narrative at least verging on the miraculous, evidence of unusual youthful studiousness if not actual piety, successful resistance against temptations (especially, but not limited to, sexual ones), and examples of natural laws being suspended in the subject's presence. Each feature demonstrates that God's grace operated with unusual strength in the protosaint. Sanctification, after all, was never merely a human designation but rather the

---

[5] Robert Southey, "Art. IX. The Works of the Reverend William Huntington, S.S., Minister of the Gospel, at Providence Chapel, Gray's Inn Lane, Completed to the Close of the Year 1806," *The Quarterly Review* 24, no. 48 (1821): 462–510, here 476.

human acknowledgment of a divine nomination. These elements were not obstacles but a solid basis for audience satisfaction with the *vita*.

Ironically, characteristics of the *vita* that defined its appeal to its original audience can cause the most difficulty now. Robert T. Meyer, the translator of Bernard's *Vita sancti Malachiae*, describes these conventions:

> The purpose of the *vita* was to edify. A prologue prefixed to the composition generally tells us that the author had been asked to give an account of some pious person who had died in the state of sanctity. He often protests his inability to write a good account: his Latin is too poor, he is unskilled in literary composition. But he will write under obedience and to praise God's wonderful grace working in a human being. When a miracle is performed we are reminded that it was God's own working through the agent of a person who was very close and dear to him. . . . Herein a hagiographical document differs from the modern biography, which gives us factual information of a person's birth, life and death.[6]

From this list it is clear how the primary focus of a *vita* (God's grace displayed in a human life) and the medium (an unworthy, but humbly obedient writer) separate hagiography from modern biography.

Thomas Heffernan, writing about the artistic choices involved in writing sacred biography, suggests that the equilibrium between the human and the God-graced elements in a *vita* is crucial: "The sacred biographer sought to maintain a difficult balance between the narrative depiction of a not-quite demigod (if the expression is permitted) and a moral everyman. If this characterization . . . is weighted too far toward the supernatural, we lose the man, while if the exemplary is underemphasized, we end up without our saint."[7] Although not writing specifically about Bernard, Heffernan

---

[6] Robert T. Meyer, "Introduction," in *The Life and Death of Saint Malachy the Irishman*, by Bernard of Clairvaux, trans. Robert T. Meyer, CF 10 (Kalamazoo, MI: Cistercian Publications, 1978), 1–7, here 6.

[7] Heffernan, *Sacred Biography*, 30.

underscores the challenges of maintaining accuracy and credibility, which are multiplied when the subject of a *vita* is as multifaceted and complex as William found his to be.

From a different perspective, and with a twinkle in his eye, Fr. Chrysogonus Waddell proposes a clearer picture of what hagiography sets out to accomplish. A hagiographer created a model for others to follow. This task required discernment to choose qualities and events worthy of emulation: "The chief difference between our twelfth-century hagiographer and our modern biographer is that, whereas we insist on the truth, nothing but the truth, and the whole truth—warts and all—the medieval biographer was more selective, and more liable to conform to models supplied from the past. He was, so to speak, painting an icon rather than taking a photograph."[8] *Icon* is particularly useful, since iconography is a highly stylized art form, where the conventions actually carry the meaning. Seeing hagiography as verbal icon provides an excellent metaphor for reading the genre.

Genre and the Vita prima

The *fons et origo* for the generic debate as it relates specifically to the *Vita prima* appears in the explanatory *subscriptio* to book 1, written shortly after William's death by Abbot Burchard of Balerne. William, he explains, had gathered and organized Bernard's life to the conflict between Peter Leonis (Anacletus II) and Pope Innocent II (ca. 1130). He continues: "This faithful man had as his particular motive for writing the friendship and familiarity in which he had been joined to the Man of God for a long time. . . . William evidently also had a more powerful general motive: usefulness to the whole Church of God; lest if this vessel full of desirable treasure were concealed the treasure itself should be hidden also."[9] Burchard explicitly recognizes that both William's personal friendship for Bernard and his awareness of Bernard's power as a community

---

[8] Chrysogonus Waddell, "The Exegetical Challenge of Early Cistercian Hagiography," CSQ 21, no. 3 (1986): 195–212, here 201.

[9] Vita Bern, *Subscriptio* (CCCM 89B:84; PL 185:266CD; Cawley, *Bernard*, 89).

model operated in his decision to write the *vita*. He concludes by saying that the reader will discover a portrait of Bernard as a matured man, painted as well as the painter was capable of doing before he predeceased his subject and left his work unfinished.[10]

The opening salvo in the twentieth-century controversy over the genre of the *Vita prima* comes from Adriaan Bredero, who has written extensively urging that William's use of the *vita* genre is explicitly for "saint making" and insists that "the problem is that in evaluating this treatise, until recently no attention was given to the fact that it had originally been written to promote Bernard's canonization, that is—literally—to write him heavenward."[11] He further proposes that the election of the Cistercian Eugenius III in 1145 created a climate favorable for a *vita* of Bernard: "A request for Bernard's canonization, provided it was supported by a *vita*, would have more chance of being approved during this pontificate than when Eugenius would have been succeeded by a non-Cistercian."[12] The limit Bredero places on William's work is excessive: he sees only overt political writing.

Leclercq, with his interest in psychoanalytical criticism, responds to Bredero's assessment but approaches the issue from a different perspective. He asserts that "from among the facts he knew, William made a selection. . . . He does not say a word about the

[10] Vita Bern, *Subscriptio* (CCCM 89B:85; PL 185:266CD; Cawley, *Bernard*, 90).

[11] Adriaan H. Bredero, *Bernard of Clairvaux: Between Cult and History* (Grand Rapids, MI: William B. Eerdmans, 1996), 7. This quotation is from the most recent of Bredero's books, but he has developed the argument since his 1960 dissertation, published as *Études sur la "Vita Prima" de Saint Bernard* (Rome: Editiones Cistercienses, 1960).

[12] Bredero, *Bernard of Clairvaux*, 34–35. Leclercq acknowledges the *Vita prima Bernardi* as an example of the "intentional legend-making, which was, very early on, practiced in cistercian [sic] circles" (Leclercq, *Second Look*, 6). Written before 1148, William's work predates Innocent III's bull of January 12, 1199, which mandated that names proposed for canonization be accompanied by a *vita*. This bull completed the shift from popular recognition of a saint endorsed by the local bishop to papal authorization of sainthood. See André Vauchez, *Sainthood in the Later Middle Ages*, trans. Jean Birrell (Cambridge, UK: Cambridge University Press, 1997), esp. 22–32.

Apologia which he urged Bernard to write, nor does he mention the keen controversy to which it was linked." Simultaneously, "on matters on which he decided to speak [William] goes about what has been called 'conscious legend-making.'"[13] Following Burchard, Leclercq sees in the *Vita prima* a personal interaction between author and subject but observes William's strong tendency to "stress the ambiguity in Bernard and the problematic sides" of his personality.[14] Because he is interested in reconciling "the requirements and limitations of both history and psychology," in discovering the "'historical' Bernard," Leclercq examines William as much as he does Bernard.[15] He appreciates the rhetorically conscious nature of the *Vita prima*, in which William's choices and interpretations emphasize simultaneously the holiness and the humanity of his subject:

> Was [William] not trying to suggest at once his own mystery and Bernard's and to set his own before the reader using Bernard's merely as a pretext? On this level objective historicity no longer counts. When he presents Bernard "doubting his own zeal"[16] was he not giving an illustration of his own knowledge of man? . . . putting theory into images? Could Book One of the *First Life* be, so to speak, the cartoon of his own anthropology? . . . In some way it is an exercise in applied anthropology, and the actual events were, for William, of only secondary importance.[17]

It is useful to juxtapose Waddell's "icon" and Leclercq's "cartoon," with its emphasis on "caricature" (the French *la bande dessinée* does not carry the artistic sense of "model" or "design" available within

---

[13] Leclercq, *Second Look*, 5.

[14] Leclercq, *Second Look*, 7.

[15] Leclercq, *Second Look*, 18–19.

[16] Vita Bern 29 (CCCM 89B:55; PL 185:243D; Cawley, *Bernard*, 16).

[17] Leclercq, *Second Look*, 19–20; "Le livre I de la *Première Vie* est-il autre chose que, pour ainsi dire, *la bande dessinée* de son anthropologie?" (*Nouveau visage de Bernard de Clairvaux: Approches psycho-historiques "Essais"* [Paris: Les Éditions du Cerf, 1976], 32).

the English *cartoon*); both point to artistic manipulation of information or a specific purpose. Each conceives of that purpose differently. Waddell's hagiographer paints a portrait of his subject. Leclercq would agree that William is painting a portrait; however, he would say it is his own portrait, not Bernard's, that William uses Bernard as the pretext for studying his own psychology.

At the same time, Leclercq's recognition of William's deep personal involvement with his subject's life can recontextualize Bredero's accusations of political craftsmanship, even though Leclercq minimizes the factual importance of the events recorded. Where Burchard discovers a portrait intended to enlighten a community, Leclercq envisions an author's exploring what it means to be "man." Like Bredero, Leclercq diminishes the historical value of particular events in the portrait of Bernard's life: for both Bredero and Leclercq, William is not, ultimately, writing *about* Bernard at all, except incidentally.

E. Rozanne Elder's important contribution to the discussion stems from her recognition of how far reader perspective colors the text, so that an *"amica Guillelmi"* (herself) will see notably different features of the portrait than do members of her audience who are friends of Bernard. Certainly, the *Vita prima* can portray a young Bernard who is not entirely engaging:

> If we read the *Vita Prima* determined not to be distracted by the miasma of holiness which William has cast about his subject, and if we lay aside any prejudice in favor of Saint Bernard—the handsome, aristocratic, keen-witted, eloquent, well-mannered young man who could have succeeded at any career—and put ourselves instead in the place of, say, *amici Abaelardi*, we discover a Bernard who is—among other things—stubborn, anorexic, and improvident; a young man who lacked practical and pastoral skills, suffered mood swings, sulked or was reduced to tears when frustrated; someone whose behavior irritated and embarrassed his own family.[18]

[18] E. Rozanne Elder, "Making Virtues of Vexing Habits," in *Studiosorum Speculum: Studies in Honor of Louis J. Lekai, O. Cist*, ed. Francis Swietek and John R.

Elder's reading creates a different balance between the author's personal voice and the sense of overt eulogizing, urging readers to look beyond any "saint-making" to what William actually says about his subject as a multifaceted human being. Her argument occupies a mediating position between Leclercq's version of William's self-interested portrayal and Bredero's Cistercian-Order-centered appraisal.

This triangle of interpretive stances shapes the generic debate as it applies to the nature of the *Vita prima*. Bredero presents hagiography as a politicized enterprise of promotion. For Leclercq, William's own history and psychological preoccupations color the result in ways that may do injustice to Bernard as the subject of the *Vita*. Elder sees a William who is not blinded by the reputation of his subject and tries to produce an admiring but balanced portrait. Ultimately, each of these readings relies on different nuances for understanding the genre of hagiographical writing, of what it is to write sacred biography. Each also depends on a distinct understanding of William's rhetorical and structural devices.

Any question of what the *Vita prima* is or accomplishes ultimately begins with the text itself. From its opening, William asserts that the *Vita prima* is a work in progress, to be completed after Bernard's death. He establishes his purpose as unambiguously as is possible for any writer. First, he observes the *vita* conventions in acknowledging his unworthiness for the task, as he carefully explains in his Prologue:

> For ages I have wanted to do what bit of service one in my position might, but until now fear has held me back, or else shame. At one moment, I felt the topic to be above me, reserved for craftsmen more worthy than I; at another, I thought to outlive him: after his death, I could deliberate better, could do a more competent job. At that point the man would not be embarrassed by praises of him and would be safe from human confusion, and from contradicting tongues.[19]

Sommerfeldt, CS 141 (Kalamazoo, MI: Cistercian Publications, 1993), 75–94, here 76.

[19] Vita Bern, Prologue (CCCM 89B:31; PL 185:225AB; Cawley, *Bernard*, 1).

William's avowed unworthiness mingles with the constraints imposed by friendship. It would be easier to write about a Bernard who is not present, not vulnerable to anything his chronicler could say about him.

William continues by explaining his aim in writing:

> What I am undertaking is by no means the Man of God's entire life but only a part, only a few experiences of the Christ who lives and speaks in him—that is to say, certain deeds of his outer interaction with people, deeds seen by those to whom it has been granted. And, to some extent, we have seen and have heard, and our hands have touched, as well. . . . I have not planned to tell the story of the invisible life of Christ living and speaking in him, but just some outward experiences of his life, which show the purity of his inward holiness and invisible consciousness shining through the works of the exterior man. These deeds of his are common knowledge, available to any to write down as best they may.[20]

William does not expound Bernard's thoughts, prayers, sermons, or exhortations; he does not discuss his subject's ideas. In fact, it would be hard to know what Bernard thought from reading the *Vita prima*. Instead, William provides what an observer could see and what someone who spoke with Bernard's associates could hear. It is his organization and presentation of these events that interpret Bernard's life in terms of "a few experiences of the Christ who lives and speaks in him."

A more unusual feature in the *Vita prima* is the author's friendship with his subject, which makes William both more and less appropriate as Bernard's biographer. The relationship between author and generic model is crucial. A good author always adapts the genre to his subject, not the other way around, and an author who is contemporary with his subject can see him more clearly in his context than any later writer can. A friend, however, both knows and may excuse more than a detached interpreter. The temptation to mitigate or justify unpleasant features of the friend's character

---

[20] Vita Bern, Prologue (CCCM 89B:32; PL 185:226B–227A; Cawley, *Bernard*, 3).

must be great. It is impossible to know what William chose to omit because of his affection for Bernard; what he does include presents both sunshine and a good deal of the shadow in his subject's character.

William's Rhetorical Strategies

Three characteristic narrative strategies highlight William's individual talent for manipulating generic material in remarkable ways. He connects stories of Bernard's sexual temptations, prefacing them with the death of his mother, Aleth, and both entering and exiting the series by means of references to the serpent—a tactical use of contrast. Using *aliquando* ("at some time or other") as a strategy, he places various stories about the miracles Bernard performed where they can achieve the greatest dramatic effects. By these means, William takes typical, even stereotypical, episodes and infuses them with an artistic vitality that brings Bernard's individuality to life within the hagiographic genre. Finally, William creatively includes himself in the *vita* at key moments. This strategy allows him to mediate Bernard directly for his readers.

Temptations: Serpent-Surrounded Sex Stories

Although tales of holy men who overcome sexual seduction are standard tropes in *vitae*, William does much more than simply demonstrate the strength of Bernard's sanctity through his continence. He constellates four vivid stories into one tight section in which the youthful Bernard innovatively overcomes sexual temptation, and he frames the section with two powerful contrasting elements—the death of Aleth, Bernard's mother, at the outset, and Bernard's recognition that he needs to escape the world's opportunities at the conclusion of the section.[21] References to the tempting serpent pull the two details together even more tightly.[22] Although

---

[21] Vita Bern 5–8 (CCCM 89B:36–38; PL 185:228D–231C; Cawley, *Bernard*, 9–13).

[22] Vita Bern 6, 8. At the outset, "the envious twisting serpent" [*inuidens coluber tortuosus*] (CCCM 89B:37; PL 185:230C; Cawley, *Bernard*, 11), and at the

these stories clearly belong to the young Bernard, they have no specific temporal anchor. Instead, they are revelations of Bernard's growing sanctity, portrayed by means of sexual encounters. Generically, they add evidence to the explanation of Bernard's arrival in the monastery. Symbolically, sexual temptations stand in for all the lures of the world, those things Bernard's rank, appearance, and gifts entitled him to expect. Being elegant of body, extremely distinguished in appearance, polished in manner, intelligent, charismatic, and eloquent, this young man had before him all the world's opportunities.[23]

The narration of Aleth's faithful death foreshadows several dominant themes that William subsequently develops. Before her death, Aleth had become a monastic as far as possible for an obedient wife. She wore cheap clothing, ate sparingly, and spent as much time as she could in prayer, fasting, vigils, almsgiving, and other works of mercy. In writing Aleth's death, William uses various euphemisms: *migrauit* ("moved," as in "changed residence"), *obdormiuit* ("fell asleep"), and finally, *emisit spiritum* ("sent forth her spirit"). This diction represents her death as part of her son's ongoing journey, ignoring human grief. His mother made his first home on earth; then she precedes him to the heavenly one. William first defines her life as Bernard's principal model, then presents Bernard's life as a model for others.

Placing Bernard's sexual history immediately after Aleth's death is critical because William moves directly thereafter to Bernard's introduction to Cîteaux and the life of love under the yoke of Christ (*sub iugo Christi*). The association offers a parallel with Isaac, whose marriage to Rebecca—specifically taking her into Sarah's tent—comforted him for the death of his mother (Gen 24:67). Bernard's escape (*fugam*) into Cîteaux, away from the world's temptations, echoes Isaac's story: in both, a new, compelling love brings comfort for the loss of the first, most influential one. Aleth's death is itself exemplary. Surrounded by clerics, Aleth joins them in chanting

---

end, "it is unsafe to dwell with a snake" (*non esse tutum diu cohabitare serpenti*) (CCCM 89B:38; PL 185:231B; Cawley, *Bernard*, 13).

[23] Vita Bern 6 (CCCM 89B:37; PL 185:230B; Cawley, *Bernard*, 11).

psalms until her last breath; as her final gesture she crosses herself at the petition in the Litany: "Set her free through your Passion and cross, O Lord."[24] Her death occurs as Bernard has become a young man; William indicates that, in effect, her work was then done, having brought her children to the threshold of their adult paths. By moving directly from her death to Bernard's awakened and ultimately subjugated sexuality and thence to the monastery, William juxtaposes positive and negative models of the feminine and of love that transcends gender.

Four stories of Bernard's sexual temptation epitomize what the young man faced in growing up. With his mother gone, Bernard confronts the world and its temptations without human assistance. William describes Bernard's elegant and handsome appearance and polished manners, emphasizing the intellectual gifts and eloquence that promised a bright worldly future. William suggests that Bernard would have enjoyed a prosperous success in any career he chose and that many careers were open to him. His comrades were apparently as prosperous and leisured as he, but different in their essential values. They wanted him to adopt their ways, and William admits that, if their lifestyle had grown sweeter to Bernard, his most prized gift, chastity, would have become bitter to him. But, continues William, "mainly the envying, coiling serpent [*coluber tortuosus*] spread alluring traps for him and at various places ever lay in wait for his heel."[25] By prefacing the account of four sensual temptations with the enticing possibilities of career and advancement available to Bernard, William signifies many varieties of temptation facing the young man. Sexual temptation, however, embodies all other lures the world offers; it functions as an efficient literary device because the stories are compactly related and incomparably personal, and they quickly illustrate the many-faceted development of Bernard's self-discipline.

---

[24] Vita Bern 5 (CCCM 89B:36; PL 185:229D–230A; Cawley, *Bernard*, 10).

[25] Vita Bern 6: *Cui praecipue inuidens coluber tortuosus spargebat laqueos tentationum, ac uariis occursibus calcaneo eius insidiabatur* (CCCM 89B:37; PL 185:230B; Cawley, *Bernard*, 11).

William recreates the four episodes in a tantalizing progression. In the first, Bernard responds to seduction by talking until he can flee; in the second, he actively freezes his reaction to temptation. By the third, however, he needs to do nothing. The culminating story shows him actively averting a looming danger with a humorous outburst. William's strategy shows that rather than becoming more sensitive to the attractions of women and sexuality, Bernard grows increasingly detached, more adept at deflecting dangerous situations. In terms of their use within William's agenda, several things about this group are worth noting. He uses literary compression to create a tight, tense presentation of a young man's sexual history. The details present a dramatic narrative crescendo. References to the serpent, whose coils wait to trap all people struggling for virtue, enclose the four vignettes, reminding readers of the ultimate source for temptation. By extension, Bernard's sexual temptations become tropes for all the temptations likely to beset every person.

The first episode links directly to the serpent named immediately before; the first word, "whence" (*Vnde*), can only refer to the serpent. Bernard's participation in the attempted seduction is shaped as a strategy to heighten the suspense in this initial temptation story: "Whence [from the serpent] when on one occasion a certain woman, offering the enticements of desire and sin with her beauty, riches, elegance and other things of this sort, assailed him in a rather private room in the house, that she might lure him into sin, he, caressing her with gentle words until he could slip from her hands and embraces, fled and escaped, and in the middle of fire he was not burnt."[26] The language in this short narrative is sensuous and challenging. Describing Bernard as playing along with the seduction by "caressing" the woman with gentle words (*lenibus*

---

[26] Vita Bern 6: *Vnde cum aliquando matrona quaedam pulchritudine diuitiis cultu et aliis huiusmodi irritamenta praeferens concupiscentiae et peccati, in secretiori domus cubiculo eum aggressa, pertraheret ad peccatum, ille lenibus eam uerbis demulcens, donec e manibus eius et amplexibus elaberetur, fugit et euasit, et in medio ignis non est aestuatus* (CCCM 89B:37). This vignette is not in the Patrologia Latina or Cawley's translation.

eam uerbis demulcens) until he can escape heightens the tension and suspends the outcome. The narrative is lean and taut; in a single sentence, the main verbs—she would lure (*pertraheret*), he fled (*fugit*) and escaped (*euasit*)—divide the action clearly and keep the energy fluid. William's presentation illustrates an inexperienced man coping with a difficult situation.

The second event connects with the first by means of the heat and cold but not in terms of time; it merely happens "on another occasion." It is unique among the four stories, because Bernard does something he perceives as sinful:

> On another occasion [*aliquando*] he held his eyes fixed on someone for a while with a prying gaze before suddenly returning to himself; blushing at himself, he, the avenger, flamed out fiercely against himself. Nearby was a pool of freezing water: into it he leapt, neck-deep, and stayed in until he was nearly bloodless. Through the power of cooperating grace he fully cooled down from the heat of that carnal longing. Thus did he clothe himself in the same passion for chastity as surrounded the one who said, "I made a covenant with my eyes that I would not even think upon a virgin" [Job 31:1].[27]

Unlike the first occasion, where Bernard shows unpracticed imagination and a willingness to trick his temptress, here he applies a brutally effective remedy to his own desires.

William demonstrates the long-term effectiveness of this cure in the next story (which happens "at just about the same time" [*circa idem tempus*]), where Bernard remains completely unmoved in spite of intense provocation. By juxtaposing the two events, William illustrates just how quickly Bernard learns self-control. The reintroduction of demonic influence, absent since the serpent in the prefatory section, reinforces the suspicion that these episodes are more threatening than any natural situations an attractive young man might experience:

---

[27] Vita Bern 6 (CCCM 89B:37; PL 185:230C; Cawley, *Bernard*, 11).

At just about the same time, at the inspiration of a demon, a naked girl was introduced into the bed in which Bernard was sleeping. Noticing her there, he yielded to her the part of the bed she had invaded; in all peace and calm he just rolled on to his other side [*se convertit*] and slept. The wretched girl lay there a while, waiting and expectant, and then she began stroking and arousing, at last even scratching him with her nails and drawing blood. Finally, seeing that he continued unmoved in spite of her enormous effrontery, she blushed. Drenched in great horror and admiration, she abandoned him, and rising, she fled.[28]

William's strategies here are complex. Bernard is not responsible for the girl's presence; she is put into his bed. His only action during the story is to turn away. Using *se convertit* carries all the connotations of *conversion* without interrupting the flow of the action. The girl's escalating attempts at seduction, from caresses to assault, underline the potency of Bernard's immobility.

If the third story illustrates Bernard's powers of detachment, William presents the fourth in a manner that indicates how incorruptible Bernard has become. So far from being tempted by or even concerned about the woman's attempts, he can make a meaningful joke out of it:

Similarly it happened [*Contigit item*] that Bernard and some companions once lodged with a certain matron. This woman, noticing his appearance, was caught in the trap of her own eyes and flamed with lust towards the good-looking youth. She treated him as the honored one among her guests and prepared a bed for him. Then, during the night, she arose and shamelessly approached him. Bernard, sensing this and not short on ideas, began to shout, "Robbers, Robbers!" At the cry, the woman runs off, the household all get up, the lantern is

---

[28] Vita Bern 7 (CCCM 89B:37–38; PL 185:230D; Cawley, *Bernard*, 12). The description of the girl's scratching Bernard is missing from the PL and from Cawley (*Misera uero illa aliquamdiu iacuit sustinens et exspectans, deinde palpans et stimulans,* demum etiam unguibus eum lacerans et cruentans; *emphasis mine*).

lit, the robber is sought for but hardly [*minime*] discovered. They each return to their beds. Silence falls, it is as dark as before; the others repose, but that wretched woman did not rest.

She gets up and again makes for Bernard's bed. Once more he calls out, "Robbers, Robbers!" Again the robber is sought and again escapes detection; again she lies hidden, nor did he who alone knew the truth make it public. With a third attempt thus repulsed, the wicked woman ceased, scarcely defeated in the end even by anxiety or despair.

The following day, while journeying, his companions, complaining, asked Bernard who the robbers were he had dreamed up so often in the night. His answer was: "Truly there was a robber present. Our hostess strove to seize from me what is most precious to me in this life, that incomparable, irreparable treasure, my chastity!" [*Veraciter, inquit, aderat latro, et quod mihi pretiosius est in hac uita, castitatem uidelicet, hospita nitebatur auferre, incomparabilem irreparabilemque thesaurum.*]

Meanwhile, he was thinking and weighing the popular saying that it is unsafe to live with a snake [*non esse tutum diu cohabitare serpenti*]. And so he began to contemplate flight.[29]

This longest of the four episodes concludes William's presentation of the temptations Bernard endured. He links it to the third only with the word *similarly* (*item*). He alternates past and present tenses, increasing the tension and making the narrative appear more immediate. Following stories of three successful evasions of sexual disaster, readers would not expect Bernard to fail now; accordingly, William's tension-building techniques become more anecdotal and rely on a less formal rhetoric. Bernard's creative solution to the repeated assaults illustrates how little they affect him. Equally, his talking about the night's events with his companions demonstrates that their values no longer tempt him either; he is no longer one of them. Bernard can now contemplate a new life because he is free of the former one. As a closing gesture, William gives Bernard himself the summary statement: being present to

[29] Vita Bern 7–8 (CCCM 89B:37–38; PL 185:230D–231B; Cawley, *Bernard*, 12–13).

sexual temptations and allures of the world is like living with a snake. This neutralizes the issue of temptation once and for all.

Inserting Wonder—*aliquando* Moments

The four temptation narratives provide in one complete and polished section the varieties of rhetorical and organizational decisions William practices to negotiate the distance between stating the simple facts of Bernard's life and depicting his burgeoning holiness. Throughout his book of the *Vita prima*, William carefully manipulates two sorts of narrative—stories bound in place by chronology and those outside a chronological frame—*aliquando* ("sometime-or-other") narratives. These *aliquando* narratives occur where they are most useful or where they link with other events most effectively. For example, the second of the sexual temptation stories is an *aliquando* narrative; it clearly fits into the group as a whole, but the text offers no evidence that it had to occur in the order presented. By placing it immediately after the first story, William exploits its potential for contrast and overall development.

In the second half of the *vita*, William gathers a number of stories without chronological mooring. He could easily have reorganized them or replaced any story with a later one that seemed more appropriate. This group of tales is the strongest reminder that the *Vita prima* remained unfinished at William's death. Even as it stands, however, it provides evidence that William structured the section thoughtfully and effectively selected tales to showcase salient aspects of Bernard's character and holiness.

William begins the section by summarizing significant features of Bernard's life: his efforts to restore monasticism to its old fervor, the consequences of his illness (separating him from his community while bringing him into more contact with people outside it), and his maturity displayed in preaching, prophecy, and achievement. William emphasizes that each of Bernard's deeds (miraculous or not) manifested the Holy Spirit in a useful action.[30] Such utility is

---

[30] Vita Bern 42 (CCCM 89B:65–66; PL 185:252A; Cawley, *Bernard*, 56). William has used the word *miracle* sparingly until this point, only two or three times. From here on, however, the word occurs frequently, even where it seems unusual.

a key concept throughout the *Vita prima*; every episode William recounts adds depth and detail to his image of a Bernard whose every act combined holiness with usefulness.

As is the case with many miracles reported of Cistercians, Bernard's are more down to earth than those associated with other groups of saints: as William presents them, many depend on clairvoyance (or clairaudience), a solid awareness of human nature, and a preternatural sense of good timing, or luck. Here, for the first time since the Prologue, William mentions his reliance on informants, men close to Bernard at Clairvaux as well as people associated with his activities beyond the monastery. These two groups act as a virtual invisible narrator for much of the *Vita*.[31] They provide authority for the stories and also substantiate William's own authority when he speaks without naming his sources.

William anchors some of these miraculous stories in Bernard's real-time chronology—deaths, for example. Others have no necessary factual anchor, and William controls their positioning to give them a clear rhetorical trajectory. Bernard's healing of a crippled child's hand serves as a good case in point. William locates the incident between two situations where Bernard's actions have caused concern among his brethren. The story itself is typical of healing stories in *vitae*: "One time [*aliquando*] as Bernard returned from the meadows he met up with a woman who was carrying her little son in her arms . . . because from his mother's womb he had a withered hand and distorted arm. Moved by the mother's tears and prayers, Bernard . . . engaged in prayer, continually signing [the cross] over the boy and his arm and hand."[32] When, on Bernard's orders, the woman called her son, he could embrace her with both hands and was completely healed from that moment. Healing stories are the core of *vitae*. No kind of tale speaks of grace more unequivocally than one in which the subject heals a sufferer.

This characteristic miracle, however, is as valuable because of its position in the narrative as for its content. Immediately before the healing, William describes how Bernard guided his avaricious

---

[31] Vita Bern 42 (CCCM 89B:66; PL 185:252A; Cawley, *Bernard*, 56).

[32] Vita Bern 44 (CCCM 89B:67; PL 185:253A; Cawley, *Bernard*, 58).

neighbor, Josbert, through a final conversion to a good death by insisting that Josbert return revenues taken from the church and confess, in order to die well.[33] Immediately after the healing, William introduces the story of Bernard's performing a similar service for his gyrovague Uncle Gaudry, an early supporter. Gaudry's illness also occurred *aliquando*, but by placing it at this point in his narrative, William underscores the nature of Gaudry's earlier defection, showing him to have been one of those "zealous in reproaching" the relatively young Bernard for making a public spectacle of himself. When Gaudry actually died is not relevant to Bernard's story, but the narration of his death is pertinent to the *vita* here.

William presents these two deaths as being at least as miraculous in the context as Bernard's restoring a withered hand to life, and all three episodes are linked by his family's worry on account of "his youthful age and his still new *conversatio*."[34] Putting the unexpected healing of the anonymous child between the stories of Josbert and Gaudry creates space for them and illustrates Bernard's spontaneous compassion. William has less concern for historical chronology than for creating a balanced display of Bernard's graced actions.

Not all the tales William includes are miraculous; some instead draw attention to Bernard's humanity. One example of this lesser sort of wonder occurs during Bernard's meeting with the infant Walter of Montmirail at his parents' house. While Bernard visits with the parents, this baby in his mother's lap keeps reaching out for his moving hand: "To the wonderment of all, Bernard made his hand available for the baby to seize as he had wanted. With remarkable reverence, the infant put one of his own hands under Bernard's and used the other to maintain his grip, while he drew the hand to his mouth and kissed it. Nor was it just the once that he did this, but as often as he was allowed to hold Bernard's hand."[35]

Only someone divorced from the realities of childrearing could call this a miracle—and William does not—but anyone can, I think,

---

[33] Vita Bern 43 (CCCM 89B:66; PL 185:252BD; Cawley, *Bernard*, 57–58).

[34] Vita Bern 45: *iuuenili eius aetati et nouae adhuc conuersationi, spirituali sollicitudine metuebant* (CCCM 89B:67; PL 185:253B; Cawley, *Bernard*, 58).

[35] Vita Bern 56 (CCCM 89B:73; PL 185:257CD; Cawley, *Bernard*, 68–69).

recognize it as wonderful (as anything to do with babies can be): putting moving or shining things in their mouths is what babies naturally *do*. The story is consummately useful, because through it William can illustrate a child's recognizing and reacting to the unusual grace emanating from Bernard; it also demonstrates Bernard's innate gentleness with the baby.

Many examples of both miraculous and wonderful stories appear in the latter sections of William's book. Although their details are varied and the narrative style is alternately energetic and contemplative, they all share this common motive: William uses them to delineate the human and saintly man whose actions are infused with grace in ways no doctrinal discussion or scriptural parallel could do with such color and creativity.

William in the Frame: First Recorded Meeting

Besides his varied use of stories, the most distinctive strategy William employs is his use of himself in the body of the narrative. At almost the geographical center of his book, William enters the story for the first time since the Prologue. Although this episode has often been treated as if it recounted the first meeting of these two figures, neither the text nor the circumstances make that reading mandatory. It occurs during the period when, because of illness, Bernard has been relieved of all responsibility and is convalescing in isolation from his community. It seems unlikely that a stranger would have been permitted to penetrate his sanctum, while an established friend might. Whether the first encounter or not, this meeting marks an epiphanic moment in William's life, and he uses it as a powerful persuasive strategy.

By placing the narrative of his entry at the center of Bernard's *vita*, William calls attention to himself and to his interpretation of the events of Bernard's life in a way that rarely occurs in *vitae* of the period. His language of amazement extends to describing the place, his own attitude, and the paradoxes he observes. "I began," he writes,

> to haunt [*frequentare*] Clairvaux and Bernard himself. Once when paying him such a visit, accompanied by another abbot,

I found him in a shack such as is built for lepers at a public crossroads. I found him, just as had been the order of the bishop and the abbots, furloughed [*feriatum*] from all concern for the house, from internal affairs as well as external. He was at leisure [*uacantem*] for God and for himself and seemed to be exulting in the delights of Paradise.

When I stepped into that royal bedchamber and took stock of both the house and the inhabitant, God is my witness that the building itself stirred in me as much reverence as if I were stepping up to the altar of God. I was so moved by the sweetness surrounding that man, and so great was my desire to share his lodging in that poverty and simplicity that, had a choice been offered me that day, I would have wished for nothing so much as to remain there with him and serve him always.[36]

This was a momentous—pivotal—meeting for William, who here reveals his discovery of a love that will endure until his own death. He becomes a character as well as the author. The contrasts in the first paragraph, like the opposition of a leper's shack to a palace, or the difference between Bernard's paradisal quiet and his unbounded energy in other episodes, underscore the extraordinary nature of the moment for its participating narrator.

William offers his vivid reactions in the next paragraph. Placing such an emotional moment here, at the narrative heart of the *vita*, shifts the interpretive focus for just a moment away from the ailing Bernard to what the awestruck William sees; William becomes his own witness, his own informant. As he moves into the later sections of the *vita*, his account of Bernard's remarkable actions and miraculous deeds is supported by the extraordinary experience he shares here.

At this moment in the *vita*, with this revelation, William allows readers to view the scene through his eyes instead of only hearing the voice of an invisible, detached narrator. William enters from the wings, where he has been anonymously narrating, captures center stage, holds it long enough to position himself as authoritative observer, and then withdraws. This brief appearance

---

[36] Vita Bern 33 (CCCM 89B:58–59; PL 185:246CD; Cawley, *Bernard*, 44).

provides him the opportunity to castigate Bernard's caregivers, praise Bernard's patience and humility, and establish both the neutrality of an observer and the concern of an intimately involved witness. He declares his outrage at Bernard's treatment, his awe at Bernard's patience, and, perhaps, his exasperation for the way in which the great man has been pushed aside.

William's Second Entrance

The second time William places himself in the narrative occurs much later, but it is written in a way that echoes the earlier encounter. This description of Bernard and William's shared convalescence at Clairvaux demonstrates both Bernard's power to heal and William's identification with his friend. Although many of the *vita*'s original audience could probably have anchored the event in time, William's narration of this *aliquando* episode floats without a solid chronological anchor. By removing any calendar context, William achieves a narrative numinosity: it seems as though it could have come at any time and resonates with its timelessness.

William explains that he had been long ill when Bernard sent for him to be brought to Clairvaux, "vowing that, once there, I would either be cured or would die. To me the opportunity seemed a Godsend."[37] As Bernard is also ill,[38] William enjoys the unprecedented pleasure of an opportunity for serious conversation with his mentor:

> How can I name the good this illness brought me: the respite [*feriae*], the leisure [*uacantem*]? . . . All during my own infirmity, he expounded the Canticle of Canticles. . . . Each day I wrote down whatever God enabled me to recall of what I had heard, lest it slip away. He expounded it for me with

[37] Vita Bern 59: . . . *spondens me ibi cito aut curandum aut moriturum. Ego uero quasi diuinitus accepta uel oblata facultate* (CCCM 89B:74; PL 185:259A; Cawley, *Bernard*, 72).

[38] Vita Bern 59: *Nam et cooperabatur necessitati meae toto illo tempore infirmitatis meae apud eum infirmitas eius, qua et ipse tunc temporis detinebatur* (CCCM 89B:74; PL 185:259B; Cawley, *Bernard*, 72–73).

goodwill and warmth, sharing his intellectual convictions and the feelings he had experienced, making every effort to teach my inexperienced self the realities that can be learned only through experience. Although I could not fully understand what he presented to me, he made me better understand the gaps in my previous understanding of them. But that is enough to say about this topic.[39]

The repetition in this passage of the words *feria* and *uacatio* first used in his narration of Bernard's illness underlines William's desire to model his own sickness on Bernard's as precisely as possible. For each, recuperation at Clairvaux is shown to be a time for study and peace, a time to enjoy the delights of paradise. William continues to parallel his and Bernard's illnesses when he reports the miracle of his own healing. William had wanted to return to monastic dietetic austerities sooner than Bernard thought he should: "I wanted to abstain [from meat], but he would not allow it. . . . He would advise and I would not agree; he would plead and I would not listen; he would command and I would not obey. That is how things stood, that Saturday evening, as we parted on our separate ways. . . . And then, my illness, oh, with what a raving rage it rebounded!"[40]

Only then does William accept Bernard's authority and eat the prescribed meat—and is cured. William clearly believes the coincidence of his obedience with his return to health to be a miraculous manipulation of natural phenomena, grounded in the extraordinary grace granted to Bernard. His account is replete with relish and a self-abasing pride in Bernard's achievement. The passage is shaped to parallel Bernard's own behavior in illness: placed under obedience to a caregiver who treated him abominably, Bernard complied. Placed under his most beloved friend's direction, William rebels. Only violent recurrence of his illness makes him yield. William's disobedience highlights his subject's obedience.

[39] Vita Bern 59: *quod mihi boni contulit infirmitas illa, feriae illae, uacatio illa!* . . . (CCCM 89B:75; PL 185:259BC; Cawley, *Bernard*, 73).

[40] Vita Bern 60 (CCCM 89B:75; PL 185:260B; Cawley, *Bernard*, 73).

In both of his entrances into the narrative, William becomes his own rhetorical device, first as reliable eyes and second as an example of Bernard's power, both as healer and as teacher. William uses himself to display Bernard more fully than description alone could do by contrasting their actions.

Conclusion

William's book of the *Vita prima* is supremely well crafted, and, wherever it is placed in the realm of modern scholarship, it has its own valuable personality. At the very least, it is a memoir recording the personality of a friend; as such, it is a document only William could have written. He absorbed the conventions of generic hagiography and made them his own. In the process, by introducing himself so vulnerably into his text, he mediated Bernard with his own person.

Because William was a conscientiously good writer, he approaches his task with at least as much care for literary values as for hagiographic ones. The literary aspects of the *Vita prima*, however, show that the hagiographical/biographical model has become for William an armature for his portrait, not something either ignored or stumbled over, but also not something controlling the writer. At some moments, his friendship with his subject trips him up; in others, his desire to offer an unvarnished portrait pushes him toward the opposite extreme. Only a dear friend, for example, could take the facts of Bernard's digestive difficulties during office and turn them into an instance of self-denial:

> For with that persistent eruption from his ruined stomach, with the undigested raw matter coming up through his mouth, he soon became quite bothersome to others, especially in choir at the psalmody, but he did not at that time quit the gatherings of the brethren; instead he arranged to have a container dug into the ground alongside his place in choir, and for some time he managed in this way to deal with the exigencies of the situation.[41]

[41] Vita Bern 39 (CCCM 89B:63; PL 185:250B; Cawley, *Bernard*, 52).

An objective observer would simply report the spectacle, while a single-minded hagiographer would ignore the situation altogether since it does nothing to express the holiness of the sufferer. William takes the more difficult middle road. He discusses the community's discomfort and the effect of illness on Bernard's own spirituality without eliminating one nauseating detail.

In the final analysis, I would stand in accord with Fr. Chrysogonus Waddell's wise comment: "Our appreciation of this [hagiographic] literature depends much on the frame of mind in which we approach it. In the intention of the authors, these lives of holy men and women served less to provide a life-story than to mediate a presence. . . . It is through these lives, which mirror the saints, and which give spice and flavor to our own existence—*speculum et . . . condimentum*—that the saints live on in our midst, even after their deaths."[42]

William negotiates the fine line between praising Bernard beyond what was due to a man and minimizing the manifestation of a holy figure. Because he knew Bernard personally, he had all the resources of personal observation and experience to draw on. Because he was an excellent writer, he used his materials in multifaceted ways. Because Bernard's journey was not finished when William laid down his pen, he could not propose a final summation of the life: every conclusion in his book of the *Vita prima* is provisional. He wrote of what Bernard had done but could not evaluate how those actions would make a saint. He went, however, beyond Waddell's vision to include the life story as the means of reconciling the fallible man and the emergent saint. As Elder has demonstrated, William created a biography that showed Bernard at his best but included his shortcomings, too.[43] Such tensions make the text incandescent.

In the *Vita prima Sancti Bernardi*, William made Bernard live, as man and as saint, through the strategies he selected and molded so masterfully. Doing that, he mediated our genres of biography and hagiography as no one else in the period succeeded in doing.

---

[42] Waddell, "Exegetical Challenge," 199–200.
[43] Elder, "Making Virtues," 86.

9

Unitas Spiritus and the Originality of William of Saint-Thierry[1]

F. Tyler Sergent

The phrase *unitas spiritus*, "unity of spirit," appears numerous times in Christian works from the fourth through the twelfth centuries. Although it originates historically in the Latin version of the New Testament (Eph 4:3), it also appears in patristic and medieval authors outside of biblical quotations and the biblical context. In William of Saint-Thierry's writings and thought, *unitas spiritus* describes the highest attainable state of spiritual progress in this life, and therefore it conveys a principal concept for understanding William's ideas on spiritual life and its fulfillment. Does William draw this language and concept from an inherited literary tradition, or do these come from his own creativity? To answer this question—one that relates directly to William's sources and influences—I here trace the literary transmission of *unitas spiritus*, investigate its meaning and context in each occurrence, and then compare these instances with William's own writings in which he

---

[1] This article is based on the chapter "*Unitas Spiritus*—Union with God" in my dissertation, "*Signs of Spiritual and Divine Realities*: The Sources and Originality of William of St. Thierry's Ascetic Language," PhD dissertation, Roskilde Universitet, Denmark, 2009, 135–72. A version was also presented at the 2010 Cistercian Studies Conference of the forty-fifth International Congress on Medieval Studies, Western Michigan University, Kalamazoo, Michigan, May 14, 2010. Most important, I include this article to honor my teacher, colleague, and friend, Dr. E. Rozanne Elder.

uses *unitas spiritus*, develops its meaning and context, and applies it to spiritual life.

Both the Old Latin and the Vulgate translations of the Greek New Testament use this phrase in Ephesians 4:3.[2] The Greek version,[3] with introductory verses for context, reads:

[4:1] Παρακαλῶ οὖν ὑμᾶς ἐγώ ὁ δέσμιος ἐν κυρίῳ ἀξίως περιπατῆσαι τῆς κλήσεως ἧς ἐκλήθητε [4:2] μετὰ πάσης ταπεινοφροσύνης καὶ πραΰτητος μετὰ μακροθυμίας ἀνεχόμενοι ἀλλήλων ἐν ἀλάπῃ [4:3] Σπουδάζοντες τηρεῖν τὴν ἑνότητα τοῦ πνεύματος ἐν τῷ συνδέσμῳ τῆς εἰρήνης.

In Latin, it reads:

[4:1] Obsecro itaque vos ego vinctus in Domino ut digne ambuletis vocatione qua vocati estis, [4:2] cum omni humilitate et mansuetudine, cum patientia subportantes invicem in caritate, [4:3] *solliciti servare unitatem spiritus in vinculo pacis.*

Each version translates the same into English:

[4:1] I, therefore, the prisoner in the Lord, beg you to lead a life worthy of the calling to which you have been called, [4:2] with all humility and gentleness, with patience, bearing with one another in love, [4:3] *careful to preserve the unity of spirit in the bond of peace.*

Ostensibly written by the Apostle Paul, this passage concerns unity within the church at Ephesus.[4] The text exhorts the people toward

[2] *Vetus Latina: Die Reste der altalateinischen Bibel,* ed. H. J. Frede (Freiburg: Herder, 1962–1964); *Biblia Sacra: Iuxta Vulgatum versionem* (Stuttgart: Deutsche Bibelgesellschaft, 1983). Neither edition reports any variants for verse 3.

[3] *Novum Testamentum Graece,* 27th ed., ed. Eberhard Nestle, Erwin Nestle, Kurt Aland, et al. (Stuttgart: Deutsche Bibelgesellschaft, 1996). This critical edition reports no variants for verse 3.

[4] Consensus among New Testament scholars, however, rejects Pauline authorship for the epistle to the Ephesians. See Bruce M. Metzger, *The New Testament: Its Background, Growth, and Content,* 3rd ed. (Nashville, TN: Abingdon Press, 2003), 270.

unity, a "unity of spirit," and continues in vv. 4-5: "There is one body and one spirit, just as you have been called in one hope of your calling: one Lord, one faith, one baptism."[5] The point of the text is the unity of believers in community and God's calling to be part of that community through a unity of faith and rite of baptism.

This biblical verse is quoted hundreds of times in extant Christian texts throughout the patristic and medieval eras. William himself, however, never quotes it directly. It appears one time in his *Ænigma fidei*,[6] but only in a verbatim quotation from Augustine's *De Trinitate*,[7] where Augustine himself quotes the biblical verse. Because William does not himself use *unitas spiritus* within a scriptural quotation, it is not necessary to investigate other patristic and me-

---

[5] Eph 4:4-5: *unum corpus et unus spiritus sicut vocati estis in una spe vocationis vestrae unus Dominus una fides unum baptisma* (Vlg).

[6] William, Ænig 98 (CCCM 89A:190; CF 9:115). John D. Anderson, the English translator, indicates the reference to Augustine and describes William's quotation as a "paraphrase," but as n. 7 below shows, the quotation is more identical than paraphrased (CF 9:115n330).

[7] Augustine, Trin 6.7 (CCSL 50:235; PL 42:928). In the two quotations below, boldface indicates the parts of the Augustinian passage that William quotes verbatim.

Augustine writes:

> Sive enim sit **unitas amborum** sive sanctitas sive **caritas** sive ideo unitas quia caritas et ideo caritas quia sanctitas **manifestum est quod non aliquis duorum** est **quo uterque coniungitur quo genitus a gignente diligatur** generatoremque **suum diligat** sint**que non participatione sed essentia** sua neque **dono** superioris alicuius **sed suo proprio "servantes unitatem spiritus in vinculo pacis."**

William writes:

> Cum ergo sit Spiritus sanctus spiritus Patris et Filii, et ab utroque procedat sitque **caritas** et **unitas amborum, manifestum est, quod non** sit **aliquis duorum, quo uterque coniungitur quo genitus a gignente diligitur**, genitoremque **suum diligit**, ut sint non participatione aliena sed propria **essentia**, nec alterius **dono sed suo proprio "servantes unitatem spiritus in uinculo pacis"** (Ænig 98 [CCCM 89A:190; CF 9:115 (§88)]).

dieval quotations of this verse. Yet in order to find possible antecedents for William's use of the phrase *unitas spiritus*, it is necessary
to investigate all nonbiblical occurrences that could have been
available to William.

Apart from the biblical verse and William's own uses of *unitas
spiritus*, this phrase appears only twenty-two times from the mid-
fourth through the mid-twelfth centuries (it does not occur in the
tenth century). All of these occurrences fall into one of three categories: (1) the intra-trinitarian unity among Father, Son, and Spirit, (2)
the unity among believers in the universal church or local community, and (3) spiritual union between the individual soul and God.

The first two authors to use the phrase provide examples of the
first two different meanings. Chronologically, the first appearance
is in *De Trinitate* by Hilary of Poitiers (ca. 315–ca. 367).[8] Written
between 356 and 360,[9] this work on the Trinity provides an often
scathing rebuke to Arians and other non-Nicene trinitarians while
defending the Nicene position regarding Christ as the consubstantial Son of God the Father; thus Hilary uses the language of *unitas
spiritus* for trinitarian purposes:

> Extend now your quivering and hissing tongues, serpents of
> heresy, whether of Sabellius or Photinus, you who now preach
> that the only-begotten God is a creature. Whoever denies the
> Son will be told "one God the Father," because a father may
> not be a father unless through a son; through this a son is
> signified in a father. Certainly one who takes away from the
> Son the unity of an undifferentiated nature recognizes "one
> Lord Jesus Christ." For unless there is one Lord through the
> unity of the Spirit [*per unitatem Spiritus*], it will not be left for
> God the Father to be Lord.[10]

[8] Hilary of Poitiers, *De Trinitate*, ed. Pierre Smulders, CCSL 62 (Turnhout:
Brepols, 1979) (hereafter De Trin) and CCSL 62A (Turnhout: Brepols, 1980); for
a complete English translation, see *St. Hilary of Poitiers, Select Works*, ed. Philip
Schaff and Henry Wace, NPNF series 2, vol. 9 (New York: Scribner, 1899), 40–233.
[9] Smulders, Introduction to Hilary of Poitiers, De Trin, CCSL 62:1.
[10] Hilary, De Trin 8.40 (CCSL 62A:40). For an alternative translation, see NPNF
2.9, 149.

Hilary thus argues against those denying the unity of nature between God the Father and Jesus Christ the Son, and he uses the phrase *unitas spiritus* to describe the means by which there is one Lord, "through the unity of the Spirit."[11] His context is trinitarian theology, and his meaning for the phrase describes the Holy Spirit as the means by which the Father and Son exist in unity.

The second author to use the phrase is the unknown "Ambrosiaster," so called from a traditional false attribution of these writings to Ambrose of Milan. The phrase *unitas spiritus* appears in a *Commentary on the Epistles of Paul* dated ca. 366–378.[12] Commenting on Ephesians 2:17-18, this author writes of the community of believers:

> Yet [Christ] has died for all, as much for the Jews as for the Gentiles. Indeed, the death for all provides the benefit of salvation. And so, rising from the dead, having condemned death, which encompasses everyone, [Christ] shows the hope that those believing in him have. Henceforth he commissioned preaching, through which all have been called to God the Father in the unity of the Spirit [*in unitate spiritus*] with discord torn away, so that whether Jews—who are called from nearby because the promise was made by their very own Patriarchs— or Gentiles—who are called from far off because they did not receive the law of God given through Moses—with the ritual of the past lifted away, they accept faith in Christ, through whom they are made one.[13]

In these comments on Ephesians 2, the author does not define *unitas spiritus* but uses it simply in the same context and with the same apparent meaning as in Ephesians 4:3, referring to the unity

---

[11] Hilary, De Trin 8.40, line 7 (CCSL 62A:40). As a minor variant, some manuscripts read *spiritus unitatem* rather than *unitatem spiritus*.

[12] Ambrosiaster, *Commentary on the Epistles of Paul* (hereafter Comm Ep Paul) (CSEL 81.3); for the dates, see *Vetus Latina*, 136–40, cited in Ambrosiaster, Comm Ep Paul (*summa notarum* in the Library of Latin Texts—Series A, www.brepolis.net [Turnhout: Brepols, 2012]).

[13] Ambrosiaster, Comm Ep Paul 2.17–18 (CSEL 81.3, 85).

of believers who share in the faith and are united by the Holy Spirit. This unity supersedes even the diversity between Jews, who are described as "nearby" to God because of the ancient, pre-Christian covenant and Mosaic Law, and Gentiles, who are "far off" from God because they had not, until the work of Christ, been granted knowledge of God. Unlike Hilary, this author uses the phrase *unitas spiritus* not to describe God or the trinitarian unity but rather the community of believers who are unified first by the work of Christ and then by the unity of the Holy Spirit.

The next author to use *unitas spiritus* is Augustine of Hippo (354–430), who uses the phrase no fewer than fifty-five times, yet only twice apart from quoting Ephesians 4:3. In one of these passages, Augustine addresses trinitarian unity, in the other the community of believers. The first appears in his incomplete second effort at writing a literal interpretation of the creation narrative in Genesis, *De Genesi ad litteram.*[14] In his opening paragraph, explaining that he is seeking in his commentary not to go beyond established boundaries of the catholic faith (*catholicae fidei*), he discusses the Trinity as part of that faith:

> Moreover, this is [that faith]: that God the Father almighty made the universe and constituted the creation through his only-begotten Son, and he is God's wisdom and virtue, consubstantial and eternal to Godself, and in the unity of the Holy Spirit [*in unitate spiritus sancti*], consubstantial and coeternal himself. Therefore the Catholic discipline bids that it be believed that

---

[14] Augustine, *De Genesi ad litteram imperfectus liber* [De Gen litt imp], Liber 1 (CSEL 28.1, 457–503; PL 34:219–46). Roland J. Teske provides a chronology to Augustine's Genesis commentaries, the writing of which spanned nearly forty years from 388 to 427. The first was *De Genesi contra Manichaeos*, 388 or 389; then the work cited here, *De Genesi ad litteram imperfectus liber*, begun ca. 393, with the last two paragraphs added in 427; the last section of *Confessions*, 397–401; the lengthy *De Genesi ad litteram*, 404–20, and finally book 11 of *De civitate Dei*, 418 (*Saint Augustine on Genesis: Two Books on Genesis against the Manichees and On the Literal Interpretation of Genesis: An Unfinished Book*, trans. Roland J. Teske [Washington, DC: The Catholic University of American Press, 1991], 3, 6).

this Trinity be declared one God and that God has made and created all the things that exist, inasmuch as they exist.[15]

Here Augustine addresses the relationship between the nature of the Trinity and the nature of the creation, asserting that although made by the Trinity, creation does not share the nature of the Trinity *per se* and is neither coeternal nor consubstantial. The persons of the Trinity, however, are indeed coeternal and consubstantial "in the unity of the Holy Spirit." For Augustine, here this phrase expresses the intra-trinitarian unity between Father and Son by the Holy Spirit.

Augustine also uses the phrase *unitas spiritus* in his *Tractate* 6 on the epistles of John, dated perhaps 407–408. Considering the community of believers, he writes:

> If he loves a brother, the Spirit of God remains in him. Let him see that the eyes of God approve his own heart. Let him see that if the love of peace and unity is in him, the love of the church is diffused through the whole earth. It does not put him out[16] to love a brother who previously put himself out [on the other's behalf]. For we do not see many of our brothers, and yet in the unity of the spirit [*in unitate spiritus*] we unite closely to them. Is that any wonder, just because they are not with us? We are in one body; we have one head in heaven.[17]

Here Augustine uses *unitas spiritus* to describe the unity of believers in the Christian community, a meaning and context that fit the biblical meaning and context of the phrase in Ephesians 4:3. Therefore, in these two texts Augustine uses *unitas spiritus* in two different ways, once to describe trinitarian unity and once to relate it to Christian unity in the church.

---

[15] Augustine, De Gen litt imp 1.1 (CSEL 28.1, 457; PL 34:219).

[16] Literally, "bend him to the floor" (*adtendat eum solum*).

[17] Augustine, *In Iohannis epistulam ad Parthos tractatus* [In ep Ioann] 6 (PL 35:2025). For date of composition, see Peter Brown, *Augustine of Hippo: A Biography*, 2nd ed. (Berkeley, CA: University of California Press, 2000), Chronological Table C, 180, and Chronological Table D, 280.

Caesarius of Arles (d. 542) uses the phrase one time in his *Exposition on the Apocalypse* in fourteen homilies.[18] Commenting on Revelation 17:6, he too writes of the community of believers: "'And I saw a woman drunk by the blood of the saints and by the blood of the martyrs of Jesus.' Indeed there is one body, which is turned into the church from within and also from without, that is, Christians formed within the church, and heretics and pagans outside the church. Although the body appears separated by location, nevertheless, in the persecution of the church, the body builds unity of spirit [*unitatem spiritus*]."[19] Caesarius's concern here is the ways in which the church community, the "body" (*corpus*), is formed and unified. There is one body, and it is defined both by those within the church and, by negation, by those outside the church. Even in the midst of persecution—as in the context of Revelation 17:6—the community builds "unity of spirit" (*unitatem spiritus*) within the church. And so for Caesarius, *unitas spiritus* refers to the unity of believers within the church, following the biblical meaning in Ephesians 4:3 (though without reference to this verse) applied to the context of Revelation 17:6.

The next occurrence of the phrase is in the lengthy commentary on the Apocalypse in five books by Primasius of Hadrumetum (d. ca. 560). As Primasius writes on Revelation 6:14, he too speaks of the community of believers:

> "And heaven went away as a book unraveled." Heaven, that is the church, rightly went away as a book unraveled and not wrapped up. Indeed, whatever will have been wrapped up is

[18] Caesarius of Arles, *Expositio in Apocalypsim* [hereafter Exp Apoc], in *S. Caesarii Opera Omnia*, ed. Germain Morin, vol. 2 (Bruges: Desclée, Brouwer, et Cie, 1942), 210–77; PL 35:2417–22. Migne erroneously—but without certainty— attributes this work to Augustine. Morin demonstrates that this commentary is authentically by Caesarius by appealing to what he labels as the only authentic manuscript of the work, which dates to the late eighth century, and attributes it to Caesarius. He points out as well that the manuscript tradition attributes the work to various authors.

[19] Caesarius, Exp Apoc, Hom 14 (Morin, *S. Caesarii Opera*, 2:256–57; PL 35:2442).

not at all able to be recognized from anywhere, for what is
unraveled is proclaimed [to be] revealed directly. Thus when
these have been manifested, the living will retreat separately
from persecution so that they do not seem hidden from strangers, so greatly . . . known to themselves through the unity of
the spirit [*per unitatem spiritus*], they take precautions toward
those unknown and strangers and hide themselves through
the discretion of the spirit, lest recognized they be betrayed.[20]

Primasius thus interprets the apocalyptic text in relation to the universal church community under persecution, as described in the
book of Revelation, and explains how Christians still remain known
to one another as members of the faith community, although they
are hidden and not revealed to those outside the community of
believers. For Primasius, the "unity of the Spirit" is the means by
which the community members are known to one another within
the church community. Therefore Primasius uses *unitas spiritus* to
describe the unity of the Christian community on the whole.

In the last decade of the sixth century, Pope Gregory the Great
(d. 604) uses *unitas spiritus* in his Letter 41, dated June 1, 595, addressed both to Anastasius, bishop of Antioch, and to Eulogius,
bishop of Alexandria. After quoting Ephesians 4:3, in the next paragraph Gregory urges church unity: "Let us therefore, with a united
mind, attack the evil of pride in humanity so that it may itself first
be freed from its enemy, that is, its error. Our almighty redeemer
will provide strength for our charity and justice, and he will provide
for us the unity of his own Spirit [*unitatem spiritus sui ipse*], though
we are placed far from each other."[21]

---

[20] Primasius, *Commentariorum super Apocalypsim* 2.6 (PL 68:839–40). For the
second half of the paragraph, I translate the singular nouns and verbs as plural for a more natural English style: *per unitatem spiritus cognita, incognitos et
alienigenas praecavet, se que per discretionis spiritum, ne intellecta prodatur, occultat*
(PL 68:840A).

[21] Gregory, Ep 41 (*Registrum epistularum*, ed. Dag Norberg, CCSL 140A [Turn-
hout: Brepols, 1982], 323); for a complete English translation, see *The Letters of
Gregory the Great*, 3 vols., trans. John R. C. Martyn (Toronto: Pontifical Institute
of Mediaeval Studies, 2004), 2:361.

In this letter, Gregory addresses the issue and fact that the patriarch of Constantinople, John, has claimed the title of "universal" bishop (*se universalem appellare*) among the patriarchates.[22] He considers John's use of the title to result from the "evil of pride" (*malum superbiae*) that causes disunity among the patriarchs and diminishes the honor of them all. Gregory, therefore, asks the patriarchs of Alexandria and Antioch to refrain from calling anyone among them universal and points out that the Council of Chalcedon (451) granted the title to the bishop of Rome alone.

Here Gregory argues that Christ will provide strength for love and justice against human vice and error and, more important, that Christ also provides the "unity of his own Spirit" for them, even though they are distanced from one another. In fact, Gregory adds, this unity extends beyond the bishops alone to include the whole church, which can withstand such internal and external obstacles to unity. Gregory, therefore, uses this phrase this single time in order to describe the unity of believers within the church, of both the bishops of the patriarchal cities and the members of the church at large.

About a century after Gregory, Bede (d. 735) provides the next two occurrences of the phrase *unitas spiritus*. Both appear in biblical commentaries, the first one in his commentary on the Song of Songs. Bede writes of the unity of the church:

> Luke teaches, saying, "Indeed, all the churches, edified and walking in the fear of the Lord, had peace through the whole of Judea and Galilee and Samaria, and they were replenished in the consolation of the Holy Spirit. . . ." Whence [the church] is openly accessible because from then on it is called the Universal [*catholica*] Church, which, through every part of the world, is edified in one peace and one fear of the Lord and is replenished by one consolation of the one and the same

---

[22] Anastasius had been removed from his episcopal see by the emperor in 570 and reinstated only two years before Gregory wrote this letter in 593. Eulogius had been patriarch since 580 and had received other letters from Gregory (*Letters of Gregory*, 2:359nn116, 117).

> Holy Spirit, by which unity even the Dove itself is rightly
> called the Spirit [*a qua unitate spiritus ipsa etiam Columba recte
> vocatur*].[23]

Although *unitas spiritus* appears in this text—and thus I include
this quotation—it appears more likely, as my translation shows,
that these two words, *unitate* and *spiritus*, are simply proximate
words in the sentence rather than a phrase; here *spiritus* is in the
nominative case rather than the genitive. It is possible—though
awkward—to translate the last sentence differently by taking *spiritus* as the genitive case: "by which unity of spirit even the Dove
itself is rightly called." Either way, Bede refers to the unity of the
church, in peace, in the fear of the Lord, in the consolation of the
Holy Spirit. Yet I would argue for my original translation on the
basis of the context of the passage, of his previous explanation of
the dove (*columba*) as the Holy Spirit, and of the syntax, which
suggests that Bede does not intend to link the two words.

Bede's next use of the phrase comes in yet another commentary,
his *Explanatio Apocalypsis*, compiled between 703 and 709.[24] This
occurrence, however, does not add anything original to the literary
transmission of the phrase *unitas spiritus* because it is merely a
near-verbatim duplication of the earlier *Expositio in Apocalypsim* by
Caesarius of Arles.[25] The fact that Bede quotes Caesarius here, how-

---

[23] Bede, *In Cantica canticorum* 4.6 (*Opera* 2:2B; CCSL 119B:309).

[24] Bede, *Expositio Apocalypseos*, ed. Roger Gryson, 3.30 (CCSL 121A:467). For
the dating, see "Beda Venerabilis, Explanatio Apocalypsis," *summa notarum*,
in the Library of Latin Texts—Series A, www.brepolis.net (Turnhout: Brepols,
2012), www.brepolis.net, acc. October 19, 2012.

[25] For comparison, boldface indicates parts of the passage that Bede quotes
verbatim.

Caesarius, *Expositio in Apocalypsim*, Homily 14 (PL 35:2441):

> **Habentem capita septem, et cornua decem** [Rev 17:3]: **id est, haben-
> tem mundi reges et regn**um, cum quibus diabolis visus est in
> caelo. . . . **Quid sit denique intra hanc pulchritudinem**, sic **exponit,
> dicens**: et **habens poculum aureum in manu sua, plenum abomina-
> tionum** et inmunditiarum fornicationis eius [Rev 17:4]. **Aurum in-**

ever, may be a new discovery, because no one in the scholarly literature on Bede, Caesarius, or medieval commentaries on Revelation—including the editor of the critical edition of Bede—has made note of it.[26] The only notable difference between the texts is that the two authors do not use the same Latin version of the book of Revelation; Bede uses the Vulgate and Caesarius, presumably, an older Latin version.[27] For the present study, however, this

---

munditiarum hypocrisis est; quia foris quidem parent hominibus quasi iusti, intus autem pleni sunt omni inmunditia. . . . Nam quis talem titulum aperte inponat? Mysterium enim dixit esse, quod interpretatus est dicens: **et vidi mulierem ebriam sanguine sanctorum et sanguine martyrum Iesu** [Rev 17:6]. **Unum est** enim **corpus,** quod **adver**satur ecclesiae **intus ac foris,** id est, in ecclesia ficti christiani, et extra ecclesiam heretici vel pagani. **Quod licet** corpus **videatur loco separatum, in** persecutione **tamen** ecclesiae **unitate spiritus operatur.**

Bede, *Expositio Apocalypseos* 3.30 (CCSL 121A:467):

Habentem capita septem et cornua decem [Rev 17:3], **id est habentem reges mundi et regna,** quorum et domino gloriam in monte monstravit. . . . **Quid sit denique intra hanc pulchritudinem exponit dicens: habens poculum aureum in manu sua plenum abominationum** [Rev 17:4]. **Aurum** plenum **inmunditiarum hypocrisis est, quia foris quidem parent hominibus quasi iusti, intus autem pleni sunt omni** spurcitia; . . . **et vidi mulierem ebriam de sanguine sanctorum et de sanguine martyrum Iesu** [Rev 17:6]. **Unum est corpus adversum intus ac foris, quod licet videatur loco separatum, in** commune **tamen unitate spiritus operatur.** . . .

[26] T. W. Mackay says that Bede relied on Gregory, Augustine, and Jerome in his commentary, as well as using the *Vetus Latina* Bible or a "hybrid" of the Vulgate, but he does not name Caesarius or mention that Bede borrowed from him (T. W. Mackay, "Augustine and Gregory the Great in Bede's Commentary on the Apocalypse," in *Northumbria's Golden Age*, ed. Jane Hawkes and Susan Mills [Stroud (UK): Sutton, 1999], 396–405). Roger Gryson, the editor of the CCSL critical edition, notes in his introduction that Bede quotes verbatim from Primasius's commentary (see 151–52 above) in a later section when he comments on Rev 22:20—as is true—but, again, Gryson has no note about Caesarius's commentary (CCSL 121A:160n38).

[27] This difference is shown in their respective quotations of Rev 17:3. Bede's Vulgate reads *et abstulit me in desertum in spiritu*. Caesarius's Latin version reads

occurrence provides one more possible antecedent for William, since it comes from one additional author possibly available to him.

In the century following Bede, Agobard of Lyons (769–840), who became archbishop in 816, provides the next literary reference for *unitas spiritus*. Agobard grew up to enjoy the educational and literary fruits of the Carolingian Renaissance under Charlemagne, probably in a monastery at Narbonne.[28] He himself then played a role in rebuilding Lyons at the end of the eighth century while also combating the trinitarian doctrine of Adoptionism.[29] As archbishop of Lyons, he carried on the work of the first generation of intellectuals who gave birth to the Carolingian Renaissance (e.g., Boniface, Alcuin, and Benedict of Aniane), even supervising the abbatial election at Aniane after Benedict's death.[30] In the last decade of his life, Agobard became abbot of Saint Medard monastery before being exiled to Italy (834–838).[31]

Agobard's only use of *unitas spiritus*[32] appears in the lengthy *Sermo exhortatorius ad plebem de fidei veritate et totius boni institutione*,

---

et tulit in heremo in spiritu. The Vulgate has no textual variants for this verse that match Caesarius's version.

[28] Allen Cabaniss, *Agobard of Lyons: Churchman and Critic* (Syracuse, NY: Syracuse University Press, 1953), 4.

[29] Cabaniss, *Agobard of Lyons*, 9, 5.

[30] Cabaniss, *Agobard of Lyons*, xi.

[31] Cabaniss, *Agobard of Lyons*, xii.

[32] The two terms *unitas* and *spiritus* do appear together in another of Agobard of Lyon's works, *De modo regiminis ecclesiastici ad clericos et monachos Lugdunenses* 7 (CCCM 52:330), written sometime between 816 and 839 as a pastoral encyclical. Although focused on the unity of the church, Agobard's use of these two terms does not actually form the phrase *unitas spiritus*: *Etenim in uno Spiritu omnes nos in unum corpus baptizati sumus sive Iudei sive gentiles sive servi sive liberi et omnes in uno Spiritu potati sumus quia videlicet hanc unitatem Spiritus Christi facit*. In this case, *Spiritus* is nominative and, together with the genitive possessive *Christi*, functions as the subject of the final verb *facit*. Thus the passage translates: "'For we all have been baptized in one Spirit into one body, whether Jews or Gentiles, whether slaves or free, and we have all drunk in one Spirit' [1 Cor 12:12], wherefore the spirit of Christ undoubtedly creates this unity." There is no consensus among scholars for the date of this work. Adrien Bressolles gives sometime after 816 (*Doctrine et action politique d'Agobard: I. Saint*

written perhaps ca. 829–830.[33] Quoting and commenting on Colossians and Galatians, Agobard argues for Christian unity when he writes,

> Moreover, the mediation of our Lord Jesus Christ, mediator between God and humankind, joined to the Father all the elect of creation, so that in this ineffable unity of Spirit there may be no diversity of race, condition, or gender [*ita ut in ista ineffabili unitate Spiritus nulla sit diversitas generis*], but indeed there may be one house of angels and human beings and one city of God, and even in their great and wonderful unity there may be one head, Christ.

Agobard, whose interest throughout this text is to advocate for church unity, thus uses *unitas spiritus* to describe the Christian unity, based on baptism into Christ, that supersedes the individuality of church members.[34] For Agobard, the phrase *unitas spiritus* refers to the unity that is shared by Christian believers in Christ and the Holy Spirit.

The next author to use *unitas spiritus* does not come until the eleventh century. Peter Damian (ca. 1007–1072) uses it seven times in three sermons and three letters. Spanning the latter half of his life, these texts all date between 1041 and 1067. One example from each genre will suffice.[35] The earliest occurrence appears in Sermon

---

Agobard, Evêque de Lyon (760–840) [Paris: J. Vrin, 1949], 124n1). Cabaniss suggests ca. 826 (*Agobard of Lyons*, 103); more recently, Egen Boshof indicates that it was written during Agobard's exile, 834–39 (*Erzbischof Agobard von Lyon. Leben und Werk* [Cologne: Böhlau, 1969], 261, 301–5).

[33] Agobard of Lyons, *De fidei veritate et totius boni institutione* 10 (CCCM 52:251–79). A certain date, however, is indeterminable according to L. Van Acker (Introduction to CCCM 52:XLIV) and Cabaniss, who also notes that the manuscript title is simply *Agobardi sermo* (*Agobard of Lyons*, 105).

[34] Agobard, *De fidei veritate* 10 (CCCM 52:261).

[35] Other occurrences include Ss 38.8 and 41 and Epp 40.42 and 153.62. For the sermons, see Peter Damian, *Sanctus Petrus Damianus sermones*, ed. Ioannis [Giovanni] Lucchesi, CCCM 57 (Turnhout: Brepols, 1983); for letters, see *Die Briefe des Petrus Damiani*, ed. Kurt Reindel, 4 vols. (Munich: MGH, 1983–1993; www.brepolis.net), 4:1–4.

14, *In festivitate Sancti Marci Evangelistae, sermo primus*, dated 1041/1042, referring to the unity of all the faithful:

> But this has been made for teaching the magisterium, so that the Holy Spirit in the beginning of its very own Gospel, whose very author it was, may show itself to be one and the same as had been spoken by the mouth of all the prophets, so that what has been said by one particularly was revealed by all collectively. Therefore whatever Malachy said, so also Isaiah said, and at one time the words were revealed by all through the unity of the Spirit [*per unitatem spiritus*].[36]

Here Peter Damian uses *unitas spiritus* in a way that appears different from previous authors. Yet he argues that the message that came from the prophets of ancient Israel and also from the Christian Gospel is unified because the same Holy Spirit was the author of that message, through the prophets and through the evangelists. Therefore he seems to use *unitas spiritus* to describe the unity of believers in the community, not only the Christian community but also the community of the faithful both before and after Christ. The general meaning here is unity within the community, and the specific meaning goes beyond most other occurrences of *unitas spiritus* by including those before the advent of Christ (but see Ambrosiaster above). Even so, this idea is shared—perhaps even assumed—by other Christian writers (e.g., Agobard, above) who also appeal to the message of the prophets to elucidate the message of the gospels, and vice versa. So Peter Damian does not provide a new concept but rather states the traditional concept in a different way.

The first of Peter Damian's letters to use *unitas spiritus*, Letter 39, dated ca. 1051, does so twice.[37] He addressed the letter to canons at the cathedral of Fano, Italy, in the light of schisms that were arising among them. Peter writes of the desirability of Christian

---

[36] Peter Damian, S 14.3 (CCCM 57:62–73).

[37] For the dating, see Giovanni Miccoli, *Chiesa Gregoriana. Ricerche sulla riforma del secolo XI* (Florence: La Nuova Italia, 1966), 98n1.

unity: "If one is surrounded by the enemy and leaves the tightly drawn battle line, one exposes oneself to the enemy and becomes a target for the enemy's errors. Certainly the churches of Christ, as prophetic utterances attest, are strongholds of God that undoubtedly the assault of the enemy will not invade so long as the soldiers of Christ, armed with weapons of virtue, rally together in love and unity of spirit [*in unitate spiritus*]."[38]

A few paragraphs later, Peter writes again of the unity of the community:

> Wherefore, my loved ones, if you would stand before the people of God as possessing the words of life, a people for whom you were appointed to give good example and among whom you should shine as lights in this world—if you should wish, I repeat—to gather a harvest of souls among them and call back the errant to the right path of religious practice, you should first straighten what is awry in your own lives, if that be necessary, and, gathering in the school of Christ, you should remain together in a common life and in the unity of spirit harmoniously [*unitate spiritus concorditer*]. Let there be no division of houses among you, no divisions of mind, no diversity of inherited property.[39]

Although he does not refer specifically to Ephesians 4:3, Peter Damian's meaning for *unitas spiritus* in both places here fits the biblical meaning when he refers to the unity of the brothers in the community. Overall, Peter Damian uses *unitas spiritus* to refer generally to Christian unity—as in the biblical passage—and specifically to religious communities.

The next occurrence of the phrase brings the discussion to William's own day and is by his older contemporary and one-time correspondent Rupert of Deutz (ca. 1070–1129/30), who uses the

---

[38] Peter Damian, Ep 39.8 (*Die Briefe*, 4.1, 378); for an English translation of the complete corpus, see Peter Damian, *The Letters of Peter Damian*, trans. Owen J. Blum and Irven M. Resnick, 7 vols. (Washington, DC: The Catholic University of America Press, 1989–2005).

[39] Peter Damian, Ep 39.13 (*Die Briefe*, 4.1, 382).

phrase *unitas spiritus* twice in his *Commentary on the Gospel of St. John*, written ca. 1115.[40] Commenting on John 4:24, Rupert describes the unity of the church community as *unitas spiritus*, a unity from which one may be cut off, as is the schismatic, by not confessing the truth about Christ in the Spirit. In this case, for Rupert, *unitas spiritus* simply refers to the unity of believers in the (orthodox, catholic) church.[41]

The next occurrence appears when Rupert comments on John 6:54 (in the Vulgate, 6:53 in English versions), writing, "[Jesus] did not say *you* but *of you*; you have similar murmurers and life of the quarrelsome among you, but my one people, who are united to me in the unity of the Spirit [*unitate spiritus*], my one church, for which they eat my flesh and drink my blood, have eternal life."[42] As in his earlier use of *unitas spiritus*, Rupert uses the phrase here to describe the unity of the church in the context of Jesus' command to eat his flesh and drink his blood for eternal life. For Rupert, the words of Jesus also relate to the unity of the believers through the Holy Spirit and through the Eucharist.

Three other twelfth-century contemporaries of William use the phrase, but only one or two times each outside of biblical quotations. After Rupert, Bernard of Clairvaux (1090–1153) uses *unitas spiritus* a total of fifteen times, yet all but one of these occurrences are in a direct quotation of Ephesians 4:3.[43] The one exception appears in his *Sermon on the Annunciation of the Lord:*

[40] Rupert of Deutz, *Commentaria in Evangelium Sancti Iohannis*, ed. Rhabanus Haacke, CCCM 9 (Turnhout: Brepols, 1969) (*Comm in Evang Ioh*); for the date of composition, see Haacke's Introduction, viii.

[41] Rupert, *Comm in Evang Ioh* 4 (CCCM 9:210).

[42] Rupert, *Comm in Evang Ioh* 6 (CCCM 9:361).

[43] In *The Mystical Theology of Saint Bernard*, trans. A. H. C. Downes, CS 120 (Kalamazoo, MI: Cistercian Publications, 1990; originally published in 1940), Étienne Gilson—rather misleadingly—titles a chapter "Unitas Spiritus," explaining (1) Bernard's mysticism as spiritual union between the soul and God (126–27), (2) this spiritual union as the *unus spiritus* from the phrase *tam suaviter quam secure ligatus, adhaerens Deo, unus spiritus est cum eo* (127), which he indicates comes from 1 Cor 6:17, *Qui autem adhaeret Domino, unus spiritus est* (239n177), and (3) "pure love" as the basis for this spiritual union (142–45). It

Certainly "mercy and truth have met each other." And certainly this [is so] in order that you may turn aside from evil. Already you may certainly do good for yourself with the timbrel, and the gradual in choir is itself a mortification of your flesh, and fruit of penance and also works of righteousness, and let them be done in unity and harmony—because the unity of spirit is the bond of perfection [*unitas spiritus, vinculum est perfectionis*]—you will turn aside neither to the right nor to the left.[44]

Although Bernard's use of *unitas spiritus* is not a direct quotation from Ephesians in this text, the language is almost identical to the biblical verse, even adding the term *vinculum*, making this passage a clear allusion to the biblical verse.

The next twelfth-century author to use the phrase is Peter the Venerable (1092/94–1156), abbot of Cluny and ardent correspondent of Bernard of Clairvaux. Peter uses the phrase only once, in his Letter 35, writing of monastic unity: "And because I did not have a clear path, through the grace of God, with jealousy melting away, God gave effectiveness to my sermons, and God, who made the hearts of our brothers one, each and the other, has thus united us in the unity of the Spirit [*unitate spiritus*] to God, so that the congregation might be able to believe as by faith and love, thus not two but one."[45] Peter reflects the tradition already seen above as he uses the phrase to describe the unity of the brothers in the monastery. This unity results from God's work in human hearts, a work that leads to the singularity of community in spite of the plurality of members.

The final twelfth-century author to use the phrase is contemporary to William and a fellow Cistercian, Guerric of Igny (1080–1157). In his *Sermo in Adventu*, Guerric writes,

---

appears that "Unitas Spiritus" is simply Gilson's own shorthand for the concept expressed by the *unus spiritus* phrase (127), but, again, *unitas spiritus* does not appear in Bernard's own writings in the form Gilson implies (Gilson, *Mystical Theology*, 119–52). Gilson devotes Appendix 5 to a discussion of William's "mystical theology" (198–214).

[44] Bernard of Clairvaux, *Sermones in adnuntiatione dominica* 1.5 (SBOp 5:16).

[45] Peter the Venerable, *The Letters of Peter the Venerable*, ed. Giles Constable, 2 vols. (Cambridge, MA: Harvard University Press, 1967), 1:114.

> Concerning the final [coming of the Lord] . . . the Apostle
> writes: "But we all, beholding the glory of the Lord, are trans-
> formed into the same image from glory into glory as by the
> Spirit of the Lord." Utterly wonderful and lovable it is when
> God, the Love of the lover, is grasped even in the senses, when
> the Bridegroom embraces the Bride in the unity of the Spirit
> [*in unitate spiritus*] and she is transformed into the same image,
> in which as in a mirror she sees the glory of the Lord.[46]

Guerric uses *unitas spiritus* here in a context and with a meaning
wholly different from those of previous authors. For him, the
phrase describes the union between the bride and bridegroom,
which can be understood as that between the soul and Christ.

Guerric's use, however, echoes William's, as Guerric seems to
understand the unity of spirit to be between the soul and Christ—
echoes because this sermon was not published until perhaps 1145–
1148,[47] at least twenty years after William had written his first work,
De contemplando Deo, in 1121–1124, describing *unitas spiritus*. Guerric's use was thus at best contemporary with and possibly subsequent to William's last work to articulate this idea, *Epistola Aurea*,
in 1147. Even if this sermon was composed (or even preached)
earlier, its publication date indicates that William could have received it only after his own writing career was nearing its end. If
there is a direct connection, the influence is from William to
Guerric.

These twelve authors up to the mid-twelfth century collectively
use the phrase *unitas spiritus* only twenty-two times (apart from
biblical quotations of Eph 4:3). Only two authors, Hilary of Poitiers
and Augustine of Hippo, write of trinitarian unity, all others except
Guerric of Igny write of unity of believers, and Guerric alone (not

---

[46] Guerric of Igny, "Sermo in Adventu" 2.4, in *Sermons*, ed. John Morson and
Hilary Costello, 2 vols., SChr 166 (Paris: Les Éditions du Cerf, 1970), 1:114–71
(CF 8:12).

[47] John Morson and Hilary Costello, Introduction, *Liturgical Sermons by Guerric of Igny*, vol. 1, trans. the monks of Mount Saint Bernard Abbey, CF 8 (Kalamazoo, MI: Cistercian Publications, 1970), xxii–xxiii.

yet counting William) writes of spiritual union between the soul and Christ.

By comparison, William of Saint-Thierry uses the phrase *unitas spiritus* nine times in four different works, from his first work, *De contemplando Deo* (ca. 1121–1124), to his final work, *Vita prima Bernardi* (1147).[48] The first occurrence, *De contemplando Deo* 7, shows William explaining just what the union of the soul with God is and calling it *unitas spiritus*:

> O the happy and most fortunate soul that merits so to be acted on by God, so that through the unity of the Spirit [*per unitatem Spiritus*] it loves in God not just some property of God's, but God's very self, and even loves itself only in God. Like God, [the soul] loves and approves in itself what God must approve and love, that is to say, Godself. Or, to put it another way, it loves and approves in itself that which must be loved both by God the Creator and by God's creature. In a word, neither the name of love nor the love itself belongs by right to anyone, nor is owed to any, save to you alone. O you who are true Love, love-worthy Lord, this also is the will of your son in us, this is his prayer for us to you his father: "I will that, as you and I are one, so may they themselves be one in us." This is the final goal, this is the consummation, this is perfection, this is peace, this is the "joy of the Lord," this is joy in the Holy Spirit, this is the "silence in heaven."[49]

Here William describes what he calls the "final goal" (*finis*) of spiritual life, its culmination a complete union with God through love and in the Holy Spirit. He connects this goal once again with the fulfillment of Jesus' prayer for Christian unity (John 17:21), which

---

[48] Jacques Delesalle explores the concept of the soul's union with God in *De natura et dignitate amoris*, noting the absence of the phrase *unus spiritus* from that work while focusing for his discussion of the concept on William's use of 1 Cor 6:17 (*Qui autem adhaeret Domino unus Spiritus est*) ("L' 'in-hésion' à Dieu. Un langage de l'union à Dieu dans le traité *De Natura et dignitate amoris* de Guillaume de Saint-Thierry." Coll 71, no. 4 [2009]: 300–314).

[49] William, Contem 10 (CCCM 88:159–60; CF 3:48 [§7]).

William without exception interprets to mean the union of the individual soul with God. Even at this early stage of William's literary career, he shows an enthusiastic and profound concept of spiritual union. He seems unable to find enough predicates to describe this indescribable experience: the final goal, consummation, perfection, peace, joy, silence in heaven.

Not until 1139, in his *Expositio super Cantica Canticorum*, does William return to *unitas spiritus*, although he mentions it only one time in this work. Commenting on Song 1:16, "The beams of our houses are cedars," he writes,

> In the houses of virtues, the beams of incorruptible cedar are faith and the hope of eternity; beneath the roof of God's protection, they are raised toward heaven by the strength of a right intention. The rafters of cypresses by their beautiful workmanship and strong fragrance signify the interior adornment of carefulness to preserve the unity of spirit [*unitatem spiritus*]. This unity, in the charity of God, is the mutual charity of the children of the Bridegroom for one another, in that they love one another and uphold one another, just as the wooden rafters in the ceiling are embraced by other timbers to achieve the interior adornment and likewise the interior defenses—so that nothing may enter surreptitiously or thrust itself in to disturb the dwellers in the house, since one single charity disposes them for mutual giving and receiving.[50]

Within the grand allegory of the Song of Songs—as William understands it—lies the story of spiritual union between the Bride and the Bridegroom, that is, the soul and Christ. Although William's overall commentary focuses on this interpretation of the biblical text, in the section quoted above he adjusts his interpretation to include the community of believers ("the children of the Bridegroom," who dwell in the "houses of virtues") and their unity, to which he refers here as "unity of Spirit," rather than applying the phrase to the individual soul and Christ. This use of *unitas spiritus* fits squarely within the literary tradition and other uses of the phrase.

[50] William, Cant 101 (CCCM 87:75; CF 6:83–84 [§105]).

William uses the phrase *unitas spiritus* frequently in his *Epistola Aurea*, written 1144–1145, where he also lays out more systematically what he means by *unity of spirit*. William explains that the human will "is a natural appetite of the soul" (*naturalis . . . animi appetitus est*) and can thus be directed toward various objects, to God and spiritual life or to the body and corporeal things.[51] When one's will is directed properly, he says, one can make profound progress in spiritual life, progress that can lead to spiritual union:

> When the will mounts on high, like fire going up to its place, that is to say, when it unites with truth and tends toward higher things, it is love [*amor*]. When it is fed with the milk of grace in order to make progress, it is love [*dilectio*]; when it lays hold of its object and keeps it in its grasp and has enjoyment of it, it is love [*caritas*], it is unity of spirit [*unitas spiritus est*], it is God, for God is love [*caritas*]. But in these things, when one has completed them, then one merely begins, because nothing of these things in this life comprises the fullness of perfection.[52]

In this brief paragraph, William summarizes his idea of spiritual life and the progression from will to *amor* to *dilectio* to *caritas* to *unitas spiritus*—spiritual union with God. This is the fullest experience of spiritual life one can have *in hac vita*. It is not complete, as it will be in the next life, but it is still a powerful and profound union between the human soul and the divine reality—in truth (*veritas*), in love (*caritas*), in enjoyment (*fruitio*).

In the next chapter of the *Epistola Aurea*, William again explains the connection and progression between will, love, and union. In the context of the human will (*voluntas*) and capacity to desire (*velle*), when one desires God "to the point of despising the self and everything that either exists or can exist,"[53] the human will expands itself to become more than will: love (*amor*), love (*dilectio*), love (*caritas*),

---

[51] William, Ep frat 234 (CCCM 88:276; CF 12:87).
[52] William, Ep frat 235 (CCCM 88:276; CF 12:88).
[53] William, Ep frat 256 (CCCM 88:280; CF 12:94).

and unity of spirit (*unitas spiritus*).[54] He then defines each of these types of love and explains their place in the progression of the human will and soul toward God, resulting in spiritual union with God:

> For God ought to be loved in this way. For a great will toward God is love [*amor*]; love [*dilectio*] is a clinging to or joining together [with God]; love [*caritas*] is the fruition [of God]. Indeed, unity of spirit with God [*Vnitas uero spiritus cum Deo*], for the person having a heart raised up, is the perfection of the will progressing to God, when it at last not only desires what God desires and is not just so great an *affectus* but is a perfected *affectus*, so that it is unable to desire except what God desires.[55]

William continues to say that to desire what God desires is to be like God[56] and that likeness to God is humanity's ultimate goal: "For because of this end alone were we created and do we live: in order that we may be like God, for we were created in the image of God."[57] Every human being has a certain likeness (*similitudo*) to God that comes through nature, through creation itself, regardless of will or desire or effort.[58] But there is also a more important likeness that can be gained by desire and the will, one that "consists in the virtues and inspires the soul, as it were, to imitate the greatness of the Highest Good."[59]

William describes *unitas spiritus* as the consummation, the culmination of spiritual progress in this life:

> In addition to this there is yet another likeness, of which something has already been said. It is so close in its resemblance that it is styled not merely a likeness but a unity of spirit [*unitas spiritus*]. It makes a person one with God, one spirit, not only

---

[54] William, Ep frat 256: *ut iam voluntas plus quam voluntas sit, ut amor sit, ut dilectio sit, ut sit caritas, sit unitas spiritus* (CCCM 88:280; CF 12:94).

[55] William, Ep frat 257 (CCCM 88:281; CF 12:94).

[56] William, Ep frat 258 (CCCM 88:281; CF 12:94).

[57] William, Ep frat 259 (CCCM 88:281; CF 12:95).

[58] William, Ep frat 260 (CCCM 88:281–82; CF 12:95).

[59] William, Ep frat 261 (CCCM 88:282; CF 12:95).

with the unity that comes of desiring the same thing but, with a greater fullness of virtue, as has been said, the inability to desire anything else.

This is called unity of spirit [*haec unitas spiritus*] not only because the Holy Spirit brings it about or inclines a person's spirit to it, but because it is the Holy Spirit itself, the God who is love [*caritas*], who is the love [*caritas*] of the Father and the Son, their unity, sweetness, goodness, kiss, embrace, and whatever else they can have in common in that supreme unity of truth and truth of unity. This becomes for the human person toward God in his or her own way what the Holy Spirit is for the Son to the Father, or the Father to the Son in consubstantial unity, when the blessed conscience finds itself in a certain way in the middle of the embrace and the kiss of the Father and Son, when in an ineffable and imponderable way the person of God merits to become not God but, nevertheless, what God is. The person becomes by grace what God is by nature.[60]

Throughout these paragraphs the phrase *unitas spiritus* expresses the very purpose of human existence: deification. And it also expresses the very purpose of the incarnation of Christ—as described by the Christian theological tradition since the fourth century—through which humanity becomes by grace what God is by nature. In William's thought, *unitas spiritus* is deification.

William's last two uses of *unitas spiritus* appear in his final work, *Vita prima Bernardi*, the *ante mortem* hagiography of his friend and fellow Cistercian, Bernard of Clairvaux, written in 1147. This work is a carefully constructed theological and spiritual text in which William portrays Bernard as a person who perfectly fits William's own concept of spiritual life and progress. A close reading of the text, compared with William's other writings, shows how Bernard moves through the stages of spiritual life—animal, rational, spiritual—and how both his interior and his exterior life provide an image of spiritual perfection.[61] As E. Rozanne Elder explains in detail, however,

---

[60] William, Ep frat 262–63 (CCCM 88:282; CF 12:95–96).
[61] See Tyler Sergent, "*Vita prima Bernardi:* Portrait of a Spiritual Journey?" paper presented at the 1998 Cistercian Studies Conference of the thirty-third

William's *Vita prima* does not entirely gloss over the "vexing habits" of Bernard's life inside and outside the monastery.[62]

In *Vita prima* 4, William describes Bernard's efforts at manual labor after joining the community at Cîteaux. Bernard did manual labor (e.g., digging or chopping wood) in spite of his physical frailty, and he found himself able to meditate and contemplate while doing the physical work. William says that Bernard not only tolerated the labor but, in his humility, also found it good. In this way Bernard was different from others, William explains, for even spiritually perfected people can be distracted by the physical senses and mentally distracted by manual labor:

> Hence they necessarily suffer some undoing of their inner unity of spirit [*interiore unitate spiritus*]—not perhaps as regards their basic orientation but certainly in terms of mindfulness and thought. Bernard, on the contrary and as has already been mentioned, mortified those senses. Thus being privileged in the grace and the power of the Spirit, he could somehow be outwardly totally at work and inwardly totally at leisure for God. He could cater at one and the same time to his conscience and to his devotion. During work time, therefore, he was inwardly praying or meditating without interrupting the outward labor and was likewise outwardly laboring without sacrificing his inward sweetness.[63]

William uses *unitas spiritus* here to refer to the individual spiritual state "of the perfect" (*perfectorum*), those who have achieved the

---

International Congress on Medieval Studies, at Western Michigan University, Kalamazoo, Michigan, May 8, 1998.

[62] E. Rozanne Elder, "Making Virtues of Vexing Habits," in *Studiosorum Speculum: Studies in Honor of Louis J. Lekai, O. Cist*, ed. Francis Swietek and John R. Sommerfeldt, CS 141 (Kalamazoo, MI: Cistercian Publications, 1993), 75–94.

[63] William, Vita Bern 1.23 (CCCM 89B:50; PL 185:240C; *Bernard of Clairvaux: Early Biographies, vol. 1 by William of St. Thierry*, trans. Martinus Cawley [Lafayette, OR: Abbey of Our Lady of Guadalupe, 1990], 31 [hereafter Cawley, *Bernard*]). This passage is Cawley's translation except for the last phrase, *iactura interioris suauitatis*, which Cawley translates as "upsetting his inner relish."

spiritual reality and union William describes so vividly in *De contemplando Deo* and *Epistola Aurea*. Just as that state reflects the unity between the human will and the divine will, so too it shows the spiritual focus of the soul that cannot be distracted by the physical senses even when doing manual labor.

In *Vita prima*, William describes the community at Clairvaux under Bernard's abbacy and spiritual direction:

> Indeed, all of them were solitaries, even within the multitude. For their charity was well ordered, a charity that, thanks to well-ordered observance, turned that valley so full of people into a solitary place for each one of them. Just as one disorderly person, even when alone, is a crowd unto himself or herself, so too that multitude of people had been made orderly thanks to its unity of spirit [*unitate spiritus*] and thanks to the law of regular silence. Indeed the orderly observance of silence was the bulwark of each one's solitude of heart.[64]

This final occurrence of *unitas spiritus* in William's writings describes not the individual soul in union with God but the communal harmony and unity among Bernard's monks at Clairvaux Abbey.

All occurrences of *unitas spiritus* from the fourth century to the first half of the twelfth century, taken in the aggregate, convey only three different meanings and contexts: trinitarian unity, unity of Christian believers, and union of the soul with God. Two authors— Hilary of Poitiers and Augustine of Hippo—use the phrase to describe trinitarian unity. Twelve authors (all but Guerric of Igny) use the phrase to describe Christian unity, either within the church at large or in a local community or monastery—as does William on three occasions (once quoting Augustine). Only Guerric and William use *unitas spiritus* to describe spiritual union between the human soul and God. William does so six times between 1121–1124 and 1147, and Guerric does so one time between 1145 and 1148. In

---

[64] William, Vita Bern 1.35 (CCCM 89B:60–61; PL 185:248B; Cawley, *Bernard*, 48). Loosely following Cawley's translation, which renders *unitate spiritus* as "oneness of spirit" rather than "unity of spirit."

this case, chronology strongly suggests that Guerric borrows this meaning of the phrase for *unitas spiritus* from William.

One of William's key phrases and most important concepts, *unitas spiritus* has a long literary tradition beginning in the fourth century and transmitted through all but one century to his own twelfth century. The phrase has a biblical origin, and that origin provides the most common meaning and context in the literary tradition: unity of Christian believers. Yet William does not draw on the biblical text himself, never quoting Ephesians 4:3 directly in any of his extant writings; nor does he merely recite the received tradition. He does not borrow from or rely directly on any of these antecedents or contemporary authors for his use of *unitas spiritus*. Instead, he takes the biblical language and context, along with the transmitted context, and changes them to suit his own purposes for describing spiritual life and progression. With his *unitas spiritus* defining not only spiritual union with God but ultimately deification, William makes an original and significant contribution to the Christian spiritual tradition.

Afterword

CÎTEAUX AT KALAMAZOO
ROZANNE ELDER AND THE EARLY DAYS OF THE INSTITUTE OF CISTERCIAN STUDIES AND OF CISTERCIAN PUBLICATIONS

John R. Sommerfeldt

As I remember, the year was 1969 when I received a letter from a hitherto unknown correspondent named M. Basil Pennington. I do not know how Basil knew of me—perhaps through Jean Leclercq, with whom I had been exchanging communiqués. At any rate, Basil invited me to come from Kalamazoo to St. Joseph's Abbey in Spencer, Massachusetts, and speak of my work on Cistercians. I was not the only one so invited, but I remember the name of only one other: Bernie McGinn.

Basil told us of his plans to translate the Cistercian Fathers into English in response to the call of Vatican II to return to the sources of the Order's spirituality. Deeply impressed by Basil's project and equally impressed by the response of the Cistercian scholars in attendance, I invited everyone to come to Western Michigan University the next—sixth—Conference on Medieval Studies, as the meeting was then known. I promised to sponsor a Cistercian conference within the Medieval Institute's conference.

My invitation was accepted, and 1971 saw the descent of the Cistercians on Kalamazoo. Basil chaired one of the Cistercian sessions, I the other. Delivering papers were Louis Lekai and Bede Lackner, both distinguished Cistercian historians from Our Lady of Dallas Abbey. Roger De Ganck left his hermitage/trailer at Red-woods to speak to us. Bernie McGinn and Elizabeth Kennan also delivered papers. The response of the Cistercians who came was astonishment at the number of scholars who flocked to hear about Bernard and William, about Aelred and Alan of Lille.

Cistercian scholarship found a place within what is now called the International Congress on Medieval Studies, and the number of papers and attendees has grown greatly since. By 1976, five years after the first of the Cistercian conferences, there were six sessions of Cistercian papers. Among those on the program were Edward McCorkell, Keith Egan, Chrysogonus Waddell, William Paulsell, Lawrence Braceland, David Bell, and Meredith Lillich.

By this time Basil had experienced firsthand that editing, pub-lishing, and distributing Cistercian translations and studies was more than a one-monk job. He approached me with what I thought was a great idea. Basil and I agreed to set up an institute of Cister-cian Studies at Western Michigan University, which would house Cistercian Publications and a Cistercian library and would arrange the annual Cistercian conference.

The Abbey of Gethsemani donated its precious Obrecht Collec-tion of manuscripts and incunabula to the library as a permanent loan. Several Cistercian houses served as hosts to meetings of Cis-tercian scholars, enabling those layfolk and clerics alike to experi-ence the life of the Order they had studied.

Who, then, was to do the real work of editing the books submit-ted to Cistercian Publications? I had a candidate but did not reveal her name until the Cistercian-Western Michigan link had been firmly established. My very first—and the most brilliant—of my graduate students had received her MA in Medieval Studies in 1969. It will not surprise you to learn that her splendid thesis was on William of Saint-Thierry. Rozanne Elder had then done two stints as an instructor in history at Western Michigan University. It was during her first stint, as I remember, that we were assigned to share an office. The very first day of the semester I gently re-minded her that we were now colleagues and therefore she need not address me as "Dr. Sommerfeldt." Her reply was: "Yes, Dr. Sommerfeldt."

The second semester Rozanne taught for us we no longer shared an office. I was curious to learn why. It seems that she had a choking aversion to the three-cent cigars I then smoked. Rozanne then left WMU for two years of course work at the University of Toronto, where in 1972 she received a doctorate in Medieval Studies with a brilliant dissertation—also, it will not surprise you, on William of Saint-Thierry. The title was "The Image of Invisible God: The Evolving Christology of William of Saint Thierry," a work cited by William scholars ever since. In the meantime, Rozanne had gone from assistant director to associate director of the Medieval Institute.

Rozanne was, of course, my choice for the post of editor of Cistercian Publications, and Basil readily agreed. In the years between 1972 and 1978, Rozanne and I shared duties, she as editor of Cistercian Publications and director of the Institute of Cistercian Studies, and I as director of the Medieval Institute and executive director of ICS.

Cistercian Publications continued year after year to dangle on the thinnest of threads. Rozanne subsisted on the salary of an adjunct and, later, affiliate faculty member. For years Karen McDougall and her secretarial office were not supported by the university. Bookkeeping and other financial functions were provided by my wife Pat, who, though unpaid, took several courses learning to balance the books or, at least, to explain the ever-recurring CP deficit.

The highlight of the CP year was the annual meeting of the board of directors. This took place on the Wednesday before the Congress and was characterized by much handwringing at the persistently inadequate financing of our operation. But after the handwringing and soul searching were finished, we partied. As soon as Rozanne appeared with the last of the participants and with the vestments, the abbots, abbesses, nuns, monks, and layfolk on the board would concelebrate Mass at Pat's dining room table. I still have a clear image of Jean Leclercq, wearing a stole and stirring not one whit while my daughters Ann and Elizabeth sat cross-legged on the floor next to his chair and singing with the accompaniment of the guitars. I never could figure out how Michael's rowing the boat ashore could be interpreted as a hymn, but Jean did not seem to mind.

Then the mountains of hors d'oeuvres would be distributed by our sons Jim and John, and libations would be poured. The banter between Chrysogonus Waddell and Louis Lekai was invariably hilarious, Louis attempting to imitate Armand de Rancé with a pseudo-French accent that was almost completely disguised by his very thick Hungarian.

One year Pat served boeuf bourguignon. Louis took exception to her preparation. "The beef cubes are too small" was only one of his complaints. Pat said nothing. But when Louis turned to me to criticize my choice of wine, Pat could restrain herself no longer. She suggested that the next year he do the cooking. Sure enough, the next year Louis showed up at our house. He was greeted at the door by a present from Rozanne: a tall chef's hat. There was also a gift from my daughters: a white apron with a black scapular.

My children came to know many Cistercians and their eccentricities both at the annual board meeting and through frequent visits by our monastic sisters and brothers. When Elizabeth was in fifth grade, her teacher regaled the class with a description of the strictest order in the church. "They eat little and don't talk at all," he said. At this Elizabeth began to wave her hand frantically. When recognized she said: "I know lots of Cistercians, and they all chatter like magpies and drink like fish."

Through all this time, and more so when I left Kalamazoo in 1978, Rozanne Elder was the very model of great industry combined with intelligence and insight. She took over the task of organizing the Cistercian Conference in 1978 and has proved herself a gracious and elegant hostess. All the while she continued to provide us with translations of the Cistercian Fathers and Mothers and splendid studies on them and all matters Cistercian.

Another service she has given us is less known. The tenure of deans at WMU seems shorter than the longevity of Italian governments. This means that Rozanne has continued to fight with new administrators for the very existence of the Institute of Cistercian (now: and Monastic) Studies and thus of our enterprise. That she has succeeded is tribute to her perseverance, to her wisdom, and to her talent. We are truly grateful to a scholar who deserves all honor and the highest praise.

Curriculum Vitae
of E. Rozanne Elder

Professional Experience

Director, Center for Cistercian and Monastic Studies, Western Michigan University (WMU)	2010–2015
Professor of History, WMU	1999–2015
Director, Institute of Cistercian Studies, WMU	1973–2009
Editorial Director, Cistercian Publications	1973–2008
Associate Professor of History, WMU	1993–1999
Affiliate Professor of History, WMU	1991–1993
Affiliate Associate Professor of History, WMU	1989–1991
Adjunct Assistant Professor of History, WMU	1973–1989
Member, Board of Editors, Cistercian Publications	1972–2008
Member, Board of Editors, The Medieval Institute, WMU	1969–1977
Associate Director, The Medieval Institute, WMU	1973–1976
Assistant Director, The Medieval Institute, WMU	1970–1973
Instructor in History, WMU	1965–1966, 1968–1972
Instructor in German and Religious Knowledge, St. Mildred's College, Toronto	1966–1968

Academic Training and Honors

PhD	University of Toronto, 1972 (Medieval Studies)
MA	Western Michigan University, 1964 (Medieval Studies)
Fellow	Fulbright Grant. Albert-Ludwigs-Universität, Freiburg-im-Breisgau, West Germany, 1962–1963
AB	Western Michigan University, 1962 *magna cum laude*
Stipendiatin	Deutsche Sommerschule am Pazifik, Portland State University, 1960

PhD Dissertation

"The Image of Invisible God: The Evolving Christology of William of Saint Thierry." The University of Toronto, 1972.

Publications

"The Eye of Reason—The Eye of Love: 'Divine Learning and Affective Prayer' in the Thought of William of Saint Thierry." In *Prayer and Thought in Monastic Tradition: Essays in Honour of Benedicta Ward SLG*, edited by Santha Bhattacharji, Rowan Williams, and Dominc Mattos. London: Bloomsbury T & T Clark, 2014. 229–42.

"Early Cistercian Writers." In *The Cambridge Companion to the Cistercian Order*, edited by Mette Birkedal Bruun. Cambridge, UK: Cambridge University Press, 2013. 199–217.

"Formation for Life, Not Education for Knowledge." In *Religious Education in Pre-Modern Europe*, edited by Ilinca Tanaseanu-Döbler and Marvin Döbler. Numen Book Series 140. Leiden: Brill, 2012. 183–211.

"Bernard and William of Saint Thierry." In *The Brill Companion to Bernard of Clairvaux*, edited by Brian Patrick McGuire. Leiden: Brill, 2011. 108–32.

"Mary in the Common Latin Tradition: Agreement, Disagreements and Divergence." In *Studying Mary. The Virgin Mary in Anglican and Roman Catholic Theology and Devotion: The ARCIC Working Papers*, edited by Adalbert Denaux and Nicholas Sagovsky. London and New York: T & T Clark, 2007. 73–109.

"Communities of Reform in the Province of Rheims: The Benedictine 'Chapter General' of 1131." In *The Making of Christian Communities in Late Antiquity and the Middle Ages*, edited by Mark F. Williams. London: Anthem Press, 2005. 182–88.

"Shadows on the Marian Wall: The Cistercians and the Development of Marian Doctrine." In *Truth as Gift: Studies in Medieval Cistercian History in Honor of John R. Sommerfeldt*, edited by Marsha L. Dutton, Daniel M. La Corte, and Paul Lockey. CS 204. Kalamazoo, MI: Cistercian Publications, 2004. 537–74.

Introduction. *Mary Most Holy: Meditation with the Early Cistercians*. CF 65. Kalamazoo, MI: Cistercian Publications, 2003. ix–xxxi.

"*Macula nigra et virgo immaculata*: Bernard's Tests for True Doctrine." CSQ 38, no. 4 (2003): 425–38.

"Authoritative Standards. The Historical Documents in the Book of Common Prayer." *The Anglican* 32, no. 1 (2003): 11–16.

"Trappisten." In *Theologische Realenzyklopädie*. Berlin-New York: Verlag Walter de Gruyter, 2002.

"Guillaume de Saint-Thierry et le 'Chapitre général' bénédictin de 1131." In *Signy l'abbaye et Guillaume de Saint-Thierry. Actes du Colloque international d'Études cisterciennes 9, 10, 11 septembre 1998, Les Vieilles Forges (Ardennes)*, edited by Nicole Boucher. Signy l'abbaye: Association des amis de l'abbaye de Signy, 2000. 487–504.

"Christologie de Guillaume de Saint-Thierry et vie spirituelle." In *Signy l'abbaye et Guillaume de Saint-Thierry. Actes du Colloque international d'Études cisterciennes 9, 10, 11 septembre 1998, Les Vieilles Forges (Ardennes)*, edited by Nicole Boucher. Signy l'abbaye: Association des amis de l'abbaye de Signy, 2000. 575–87.

"Bernard of Clairvaux." In *The International Encyclopedia of the Church*, I. Grand Rapids, MI: Eerdmans, 1998.

"*Conversatio*. Cistercian Monastic Life in Berryville, Virginia." *Cîteaux* 46, no. 3–4 (1995): 359–60.

"Cistercian Order," "Trappistine Sisters," and "Trappists." In *The Harper-Collins Encyclopedia of Catholicism*. San Francisco: Harper San Francisco, 1995.

"Making Virtues of Vexing Habits." In Studiosorum Speculum: *Studies in Honor of Louis J. Lekai, O.Cist*, edited by Francis R. Swietek and John R. Sommerfeldt. CF 141. Kalamazoo, MI: Cistercian Publications, 1993. 75–94.

"The Christology of William of Saint-Thierry." *Recherches de théologie ancienne et médiévale* 58 (1991): 79–112.

"Séminaire tenu à l'abbaye de Gethsemani sur les documents cisterciens primitifs, 19–26 janvier 1983." *Collectanea Cisterciensia* 45, no. 3 (1983): 221–30.

"A Seminar on Early Cistercian Documents." CSQ 18, no. 3 (1983): 250–59.

"Bernard of Clairvaux." In *Dictionary of the Middle Ages*. New York: Scribner, 1983.

"William of St. Thierry." In *The Westminster Dictionary of Christian Spirituality*. London-Philadelphia: Westminster Press, 1983.

"Monastic Scholasticism." *Publishers Weekly* 4 (March 1983): 44–45.

Introduction to William of St. Thierry, *The Mirror of Faith*, translated by Thomas X. Davis. CF 15. Kalamazoo, MI: Cistercian Publications, 1979. xi–xxi.

"William of Saint Thierry's Reading of Abelard's Christology." In *Cistercian Ideals and Reality*, edited by John R. Sommerfeldt. CS 60. Kalamazoo, MI: Cistercian Publications, 1978. 106–24.

"William of Saint-Thierry: Rational and Affective Spirituality." In *The Spirituality of Western Christendom*, edited by E. Rozanne Elder. CS 30. Kalamazoo, MI: Cistercian Publications, 1976. 85–105, 197–200.

"William of Saint Thierry and the Greek Fathers: Evidence from Christology." In *One Yet Two: Monastic Tradition, East and West—Orthodox-Cistercian Symposium*, edited by M. Basil Pennington. CS 29. Kalamazoo, MI: Cistercian Publications, 1976. 254–66.

"William of St. Thierry: The Monastic Vocation as an Imitation of Christ." *Cîteaux* 26 (1975): 9–30.

"The Way of Ascent: The Meaning of Love in the Thought of William of Saint-Thierry." In *Studies in Medieval Culture* 1, edited by John R. Sommerfeldt. Kalamazoo, MI: Medieval Institute Publications, 1964. 39–47.

Books Edited

Mary Most Holy. Meditating with the Early Cistercians. CF 65. Kalamazoo, MI: Cistercian Publications, 2003.

Praise No Less Than Charity: Studies in Honor of M. Chrysogonus Waddell. CS 193. Kalamazoo, MI: Cistercian Publications, 2002.

The New Monastery. Texts and Studies on the Early Cistercians. CF 60. Kalamazoo, MI: Cistercian Publications, 1998.

Common Witness to the Gospel: Documents on Anglican-Roman Catholic Relations 1983–1995. Washington, DC: United States Catholic Conference Publishing Services, 1997 (with Jeffrey Gros and Ellen Wondra).

Receiving the Vision: The Anglican-Roman Catholic Reality Today: A Study by the Third Standing Committee of the Episcopal Diocesan Ecumenical Officers (with David Bird, R. William Franklin, Joan McGuire, Dennis Mikulanis, and Emmanuel Sullivan). Collegeville, MN: Liturgical Press, 1995.

The Contemplative Path: Reflections on Recovering a Lost Tradition. CS 147. Kalamazoo, MI: Cistercian Publications, 1995 (with Robert Lehmann).

The Joy of Learning and the Love of God: Studies in Honor of Jean Leclercq. CS 160. Kalamazoo, MI, and Spencer, MA: Cistercian Publications, 1995.

From Cloister to Classroom: Monastic and Scholastic Approaches to Truth; The Spirituality of Western Christendom, III. CS 90. Kalamazoo, MI: Cistercian Publications, 1986.

Guide to Cistercian Scholarship. 2nd ed. Kalamazoo, MI: Cistercian Publications, 1985 (with Benoît Chauvin).

Goad and Nail: Studies in Medieval Cistercian History, X. CS 84. Kalamazoo, MI: Cistercian Publications, 1985.

The Spirituality of Western Christendom, II: The Roots of the Modern Christian Tradition. CS 55. Kalamazoo, MI: Cistercian Publications, 1984 (with Jean Leclercq).

The Way of Love. Photographs by Patrick Hart. Texts selected by E. R. Elder. CF 16. Kalamazoo, MI: Cistercian Publications, 1977.

The Spirituality of Western Christendom. CS 30. Kalamazoo, MI: Cistercian Publications, 1976.

A Guide to Cistercian Scholarship. Kalamazoo, MI: Cistercian Publications, 1974.

Book Reviews

Rievaulx Abbey and Its Social Context 1132–1300: Memory, Locality, and Networks, by Emilia Jamroziak. *Church History: Studies in Christianity and Culture* 77 (2008): 160–61.

The Essential Writings of Christian Mysticism, edited by Bernard McGinn. *Anglican Theological Review* 89, no. 3 (2007): 513–14.

Help My Unbelief, by Fleming Rutledge. *The Anglican* 31 (2002): 30.

Rievaulx Abbey: Community, Architecture, Memory, by Peter Fergusson and Stuart A. Harrison, with Glyn Coppack and Paul Mellon. *Anglican Theological Review* 84, no. 4 (2002): 777–78.

Prayer and Community: The Benedictine Tradition, by Columba Stewart, and *The Way of Simplicity,* by Esther de Waal. *Anglican Theological Review* 82, no. 1 (2000): 203.

The Boundaries of Charity: Cistercian Culture and Ecclesiastical Reform 1098–1180, by Martha G. Newman. *The Journal of Religion* 78, no. 1 (1998): 111–13.

Fasti ecclesiae gallicanae. Répertoire prosopographique des évêques, dignitaires et chanoines de France de 1200 à 1500. Vol. 1, *Diocèse d'Amiens,* by Pierre Desportes and Hélène Millet, et al. *Medieval Prosopography* 19 (1998): 224–25.

Herman of Tournai: *The Restoration of the Monastery of Saint Martin of Tournai,* translated with an introduction and notes by Lynn H. Nelson. *The Medieval Review* (http://quod.lib.umich.edu/t/tmr/), December 3, 1996.

Religion and Devotion in Europe c. 1215–c. 1515, by R. N. Swanson. *The Medieval Review* (http://quod.lib.umich.edu/t/tmr/), December 3, 1996.

Monastic and Religious Orders in Britain 1000–1300, by Janet Burton. *The Journal of Religion* 75, no. 4 (1995): 563–64.

Chronological Data in the Lives of Ida of Nivelle and Beatrice of Nazareth, by Roger de Ganck. CSQ 19 (1984): [638]–[639].

A History of Christian Spirituality: An Analytical Introduction, by Urban T. Holmes, III. *Anglican Theological Review* 64, no. 3 (1982): 133–34.

The Origins of the Christian Mystical Tradition from Plato to Denys, by Andrew Louth. *Anglican Theological Review* 64, no. 2 (1982): 243–45.

Hugo von St. Viktor: Studien zum Geschichtsdenken und zur Geschichtsschreibung des 12. Jahrhunderts, by Joachim Ehlers. *Church History* 44, no. 1 (1975): 105.

Psychological Themes in the Golden Epistle of William of Saint Thierry to the Carthusians. Analecta Cartusiana, by Louis M. Savary, edited by James Hogg. CSQ 9 (1974): 95–96.

The Cistercian Spirit: A Symposium in Memory of Thomas Merton, edited by M. Basil Pennington. *Studies in Religion/Sciences religieuses* 1 (1972): 378–81.

Presentations and Papers

"William of Saint-Thierry with Bernard at Clairvaux: Friendship and Theology." Nonacentenary of the Founding of Clairvaux Symposium, the Cistercian Abbey of Our Lady of New Clairvaux, Vina, CA. June 17, 2015.

"Shifting Theologies in the Late Twelfth Century: Medieval Church and Culture Seminar." Oxford University. November 30, 2010.

"Devoid of this Discipline? William, Bernard, and Dialectics." International Medieval Studies Congress/Cistercian Studies Conference. May 14, 2010.

"Dialectics in the Conflict of Abelard and Bernard." Sixth Annual Conference on New Directions in the Humanities, Faith University, Istanbul, Turkey. July 15–18, 2008.

"Zisterzienser Formungsprozess im zwölften Jahrhundert." Plurality and Representation. Religion in Education. Culture and Society. Joint Conference of the European Association for the Study of Religions and the Deutsche Vereinigung für Religionswissenschaft, Bremen, Germany. September 23, 2007.

"Overview of the Development of Marian Doctrines: Augustinian-Anselmian-Franciscan." Anglican-Roman Catholic International Theological Commission, Paris. August 2000.

"La Christologie de Guillaume de Saint-Thierry." Signy l'abbaye: du terroir ardennais à l'Europe cistercienne, Centre des Congrès du Conseil Gènèral des Ardennes, Lac des Vielles Forges (Ardennes), France. September 9–11, 1998.

"Les abbès reformants de Reims." Signy l'abbaye: du terroir ardennais à l'Europe cistercienne, Centre des Congrès du Conseil Gènèral des Ardennes, Lac des Vielles Forges (Ardennes), France. September 9–11, 1998.

"The Reforming Abbots of the Province of Reims (1131)." The Making of Christian Communities Conference, Calvin College, Grand Rapids, MI. October 22–25, 1998.

"Black Monk-White Monk." International Medieval Congress, The University of Leeds. July 14, 1997.

"An Overview of Anglican-Orthodox Relations." Episcopal-Russian Orthodox Theological Consultation, Moscow. May 26–28, 1997.

"Bernard of Clairvaux and the Twenty-one Abbots of Reims (1131)." International Medieval Studies Congress, Leeds (England). July 10, 1995.

"Making Virtues of Vexing Habits." International Medieval Studies Congress/Cistercian Studies Conference, Kalamazoo. May 1991.

"Cistercian Christology." The Medieval Academy of America, Philadelphia. April 1988.

"Cistercian Asceticism: Animal, Rational, Spiritual." International Medieval Studies Congress/Cistercian Studies Conference. May 1978.

"*Ratio et rationalitas*: The Validity of Reason for William of St. Thierry." Workshop on the Spirituality of Western Christendom, Kalamazoo, MI. August 1975.

"The Cistercian Fathers' Use of the Greek Fathers." A Symposium on Cistercian-Orthodox Spirituality, Mansfield College, Oxford. August 1973.

"William of St. Thierry's Reading of Abelard's Christology." International Medieval Studies Congress/Cistercian Studies Conference. May 1973.

"William of St. Thierry's Concept of Authority." Michigan Academy of Science, Arts, and Letters, History Section. 1966.

Awards and Recognitions

Distinguished Faculty Scholar, Western Michigan University, 2015.

Visiting Academic Fellow at Harris Manchester College, the University of Oxford. 2011–2012.

HLD, *honoris causa*, Nashotah House Theological Seminary. Nashotah, WI. 1995.

The Jerome Award of the Catholic Library Association, to Cistercian Publications. In recognition of its outstanding contribution and commitment to excellence in scholarship which embodies the ideals of the Catholic Library Association. April 21, 1995.

Lectures and Workshops

"Bernard, William, and Abelard"; "The Council of Sens (1141?)"; "The Confrontation between Peter Abelard and the Cistercians." Three lectures, Tautra Mariakloster, Frosta (Norway). February 2011.

"The ARCIC Agreed Statement on Mary," with Dr. Sara Butler. National Workshop on Christian Unity, San Jose, CA. May 8–11, 2006.

"'Lamps Burning in a Dark Place': The Cistercians of the Twelfth Century." Three lectures, Creighton University, Des Moines, IA. October 23, 2004.

"Experiencing Joy: An Introduction to Cistercian Spirituality." Weekend workshop for the Merton Studies Center, Bellarmine College, Louisville, KY, at Gethsemani Abbey, Trappist, KY. November 3–5, 2000.

"The Life and Works of William of St. Thierry." Four-day course at Mount Saint Bernard Abbey, Charnwood Forest, Leicestershire (England). July 1991.

"The Psychology of William of St. Thierry." Two-day workshop for juniors of the Western Region, OCSO, at New Clairvaux Abbey, Vina, CA. February 1991.

"Medieval and Cistercian Bibliography." Two-day workshop for directors of formation, OCSO, at Holy Spirit Abbey, Conyers, GA. January 1991.

"The Theological Anthropology of the Early Cistercians." The Rossiter Lectures, Bexley Hall, Colgate-Rochester Divinity School, Rochester, NY. February 1–2, 1988.

Monastic History. Two-week course presented successively at six West African (Nigerian and Cameroonian) monasteries under the sponsorship of Aide-Inter-Monastère. September–December 1986.

Bernard of Clairvaux's Influence on William of Saint-Thierry. Workshop at New Clairvaux Abbey, Vina, CA. December 1982.

William of Saint-Thierry and Early Cistercian Spirituality. Lecture at Holy Trinity Abbey, Huntsville, UT. September 1981.

The Theology of William of St. Thierry. Workshop led in conjunction with Thomas X. Davis, OCSO, at Santa Rita Abbey, Sonoita, AZ. February 1980.

William of St. Thierry's Place in Early Cistercian Thought. Workshop at New Melleray Abbey, Dubuque, IA. June 1979.

Cistercian Anthropology and William's Theology. Two-week workshop at Redwoods Abbey, Whitethorn, CA. February 1979.

The Theology of William of St. Thierry. One-week workshop at St Mary's Cistercian Priory, New Ringgold, PA. January 1979.

The Spirituality and Theology of William of St. Thierry. One-week workshop at Holy Spirit Abbey, Conyers, GA. October 1978.

The "Stripped" Mentality of Early Cîteaux. Ten-day workshop at Valley of Our Lady Cistercian Monastery, Prairie du Sac, WI. July 1978.

Resource person: International Symposium on Spiritual Fatherhood/ Motherhood and the Monastic Tradition, Abbey of New Clairvaux, CA. June 1978.

La spiritualité de Guillaume de St. Thierry. One-week workshop at Abbaye N.-D. Du Bon Conseil, Levis, Quebec. October 1977.

Guillaume de St. Thierry et l'ascension vers Dieu. Ten-day workshop at Abbaye de l'Assomption de l'Acadie, Rogersville, New Brunswick. November 1976.

"Bernard, William, and Abelard." Lecture at Abbaye N.-D. du Calvaire, Rogersville, New Brunswick. November 1976.

The Spirituality of William of Saint-Thierry: A Cistercian. Workshop, Gethsemani Abbey, Trappist, KY. September 1976.

William of Saint-Thierry and the Early Cistercians. One-week workshop at Mount Saint Mary's Abbey, Wrentham, MA. August 1976.

Reading Early Cistercian Texts. Four-day practicum, Assumption Abbey, Ava, MO. June 1976.

Speaker and panelist: Colloquium on The Love of God and Love of Neighbor in Twelfth-Century Monasticism (with Giles Constable, Caroline Walker Bynum, and Ambrose Wathen), Mount Saviour Monastery, Pine City, NY. March 1976.

The Twelfth-Century World and the Cistercians' Place in It. Ten-day workshop at Abbey of New Clairvaux, Vina, CA, and at Assumption Abbey, Ava, MO. May–June 1975.

The Ascent of God in the Thought of William of Saint-Thierry. Lecture series at Our Lady of the Mississippi Abbey, Dubuque, IA. July 1974.

The Spirituality of William of St. Thierry and The Spirituality of Lancelot Andrewes. St. John's Provincial Seminary, Plymouth, MI. Winter term 1977.

Chair

Annual sessions of International Medieval Studies Congress/Cistercian Studies Conference, 1968–2008.

Editorial Service

Board of Directors, *The Anglican Theological Review*, 1997–2008.

Editorial Advisory Board, Classics of Western Spirituality, Paulist Press, 1977–.

Board of Editors, *Theoforum*, formerly *Eglise et théologie* (Ottawa), 1985–.

Associate Editor, Studies in Medieval Culture, 1972–1976.

Reviewer

National Endowment for the Humanities (various times, most recently 1993).
Mediaeval Studies (Pontifical Institute of Mediaeval Studies), January 2000.
   Theoforum.

Panelist

National Endowment for the Humanities, Translations Division, 1983.

Ecumenical Leadership

Chaplain, Ecumenical Leadership Workshop, The General Theological Seminary, New York. May 27–June 3, 1996.
Anglican-Roman Catholic International Consultation. 1995–2002.
Feature writer: "Called to Be One in Heart and Soul," 1994 Week of Prayer for Christian Unity. Garrison, NY: Greymoor Ecumenical and Religious Institute. 1994–1997.
Anglican-Roman Catholic Bishops' Pilgrimage to Canterbury and Rome (in collaboration with Lorelei Fuchs, SA). November 1994.
Theological Committee: Standing Commission [of the Episcopal Church] on Ecumenical Relations, 1993–1994.
Ecumenical Leadership Workshop II, Mercy Center, Burlingame, CA. February 14–19, 1993.
National Consultation on Ecclesiology, The Bronx, NY. October 17–21, 1993.
Consultation on Ecumenism in the Evangelical Lutheran Church of America, Del Ray Beach, FL. February 28–March 3, 1993.
Ecumenical Committee (Chair and Ecumenical Officer) of the (Episcopal) Diocese of Western Michigan. 1992–.
Steering Committee, Kalamazoo Ecumenical Forum. 1992–1995.
Anglican-Roman Catholic International [Ecumenical] Consultation. 1991–2001.
Fellowship of St Alban and St Sergius/American Branch (Vice-President 1990).
Episcopal-Lutheran Coordinating Committee, Chicago. June 1990.
Michigan Ecumenical Forum, Select Committee 1987, 1995–1997; Secretary, Select Committee. 1988–1989.
Anglican-Orthodox Theological Consultation. 1983–1991.
Standing Commission on Ecumenical Relations (of the Episcopal Church), 1982–1994. Vice President, 1992–1994.

BIBLIOGRAPHY OF THE WORKS OF WILLIAM OF SAINT-THIERRY

**Alphabetical List of Latin Editions
and the Most Recent English Translations**

Ænigma fidei (PL 180:397–440)

Guillelmi a Sancto Theodorico Opera Omnia, V: Opuscula adversus Petrum Abaelardum et de Fide. Edited by Paul Verdeyen. CCCM 89A. Turnhout: Brepols, 2007. 130–91.

Guillaume de Saint-Thierry. *Deux traités sur la foi: Le miroir de la foi, l'enigme de la foi*. Edited and translated by M.-M. Davy. Paris: J. Vrin, 1959. 92–179.

William of Saint Thierry. *The Enigma of Faith*. Translated by John D. Anderson. CF 9. Kalamazoo, MI, and Spencer, MA: Cistercian Publications, 1973.

Brevis commentatio (PL 184:407–36)

Guillelmi a Sancto Theodorico Opera Omnia, II: Brevis Commentatio. Edited by Stanislaus Ceglar and Paul Verdeyen. CCCM 87. Turnhout: Brepols, 1997. 155–96.

De contemplando Deo (PL 184:365–80)

Guillelmi a Sancto Theodorico Opera Omnia, III: De Contemplando Deo. Edited by Paul Verdeyen. CCCM 88. Turnhout: Brepols, 2003. 153–73.

Guillaume de Saint-Thierry. *La contemplation de Dieu, L'Oraison de Dom Guillaume*. Edited and translated by Dom Jacques Hourlier. SCh 61 *bis*. Paris: Les Éditions du Cerf, 1959; rev. ed., 1977; corrected eds., 1999, 2005.

Guillaume de Saint-Thierry. *Deux traités de l'amour de Dieu: De la contemplation de Dieu*. Edited by M.-M. Davy. Paris: J. Vrin, 1953. 31–67.

Prière de Guillaume, Contemplation de Dieu. Edited and translated by Robert Thomas. Pain de Cîteaux 23. Roybon (France): Abbaye de Chambarand, 1965.

William of St. Thierry. *On Contemplating God, Prayer, Meditations.* Translated by Sr. Penelope [Lawson], and introduced by Jacques Hourlier. The Works of William of St Thierry 1. CF 3. Kalamazoo, MI: Cistercian Publications, 1977. 36–64.

De natura corporis et animae (PL 180:695–726)

Guillelmi a Sancto Theodorico Opera Omnia, III: De Natura Corporis et Animae. Edited by Paul Verdeyen. CCCM 88. Turnhout: Brepols, 2003. 101–46.

William of St. Thierry. "The Nature of the Body and Soul." In *Three Treatises on Man: A Cistercian Anthropology,* edited by Bernard McGinn. Translated by Benjamin Clark. CF 24. Kalamazoo, MI: Cistercian Publications, 1977. 101–52.

De natura et dignitate amoris (PL 184:379–408)

Guillelmi a Sancto Theodorico Opera Omnia, III: De Natura et Dignitate Amoris. Edited by Paul Verdeyen. CCCM 88. Turnhout: Brepols, 2003. 175–212.

Guillaume de Saint-Thierry. *Deux traités de l'amour de Dieu: De la nature et de la dignité de l'amour.* Edited by M.-M. Davy. Paris: J. Vrin, 1953. 69–137.

Nature et dignité de l'amour. Edited and translated by Robert Thomas. Pain de Cîteaux 24. Roybon (France): Abbaye de Chambarand, 1965.

William of St. Thierry. *The Nature and Dignity of Love.* Translated by Thomas X. Davis. Introduced by David N. Bell. CF 30. Kalamazoo, MI: Cistercian Publications, 1981.

De sacramento altaris (PL 180:344–66)

Guillelmi a Sancto Theodorico Opera Omnia, III: De sacramento altaris. Edited by Stanislas Ceglar and Paul Verdeyen. CCCM 88. Turnhout: Brepols, 2003. 53–91.

Disputatio adversus Petrum Abaelardum (PL 180:249–82)

Guillelmi a Sancto Theodorico Opera Omnia, V: Opuscula adversus Petrum Abaelardum et de fide. Edited by Paul Verdeyen. CCCM 89A. Turnhout: Brepols, 2007. 17–59.

Epistola ad domnum Rupertum (to Rupert of Deutz) (PL 180:341–46)

Guillelmi a Sancto Theodorico Opera Omnia, III: Epistola Guillelmi ad Rupertum Tuitiensem. Edited by Stanislas Ceglar and Paul Verdeyen. CCCM 88. Turnhout: Brepols, 2003. 47–52.

Epistola ad fratres de Monte Dei (PL 184:307–64)

Guillelmi a Sancto Theodorico Opera Omnia, III: Epistola ad fratres de Monte Dei. Edited by Paul Verdeyen. CCCM 88. Turnhout: Brepols, 2003. 223–89.

Guillaume de Saint-Thierry. *Lettre aux frères du Mont-Dieu (Lettre d'Or)*. Edited and translated by Jean Déchanet. SCh 223. Paris: Les Éditions du Cerf, 1975; rev. and corrected ed., 2004.

Lettre aux frères du Mont-Dieu. Edited and translated by Robert Thomas. Pain de Cîteaux 33–34. Roybon (France): Abbaye de Chambarand, 1968.

William of St. Thierry. *The Golden Epistle: A Letter to the Brethren at Mont Dieu*. Translated by Theodore Berkeley. Introduction by J.-M. Déchanet. The Works of William of St. Thierry 4. CF 12. Kalamazoo, MI: Cistercian Publications, 1980.

Epistola ad Gaufridum Carnotensem episcopum et Bernardum abbatem Claraevallensem (Preface to Adv Abl) (PL 182:531–33)

Guillelmi a Sancto Theodorico Opera Omnia, V: Epistola Willelmi. Edited by Paul Verdeyen. CCCM 89A. Turnhout: Brepols, 2007. 13–15.

Leclercq, Jean, ed. "Les lettres de Guillaume de Saint-Thierry à Saint Bernard." RBen 79 (1969): 375–91, here 377–78.

Epistola de erroribus Guillelmi de Conchis (to Bernard of Clairvaux) (PL 180:333–40)

Guillelmi a Sancto Theodorico Opera Omnia, V: De erroribus Guillelmi de Conchis. Edited by Paul Verdeyen. CCCM 89A. Turnhout: Brepols, 2007. 61–71.

Leclercq, Jean, ed. "Les lettres de Guillaume de Saint-Thierry à Saint Bernard." RBen 79 (1969): 375–91, here 382–91.

Excerpta de Libris Beati Ambrosii super Cantica Canticorum (PL 15:1851–1962)

Guillelmi a Sancto Theodorico Opera Omnia, II: Excerpta de libris beati Ambrosii super Cantica canticorum. Edited by Antony van Burink. CCCM 87. Turnhout: Brepols, 1997. 205–384.

Excerpta ex Libris Beati Gregorii super Cantica Canticorum (PL 180:441–74)

Guillelmi a Sancto Theodorico Opera Omnia, II: Excerpta ex libris beati Gregorii super Cantica canticorum. Edited by Paul Verdeyen. CCCM 87. Turnhout: Brepols, 1997. 344–85.

"Excerpts from the Books of Blessed Gregory on the Song of Songs." Translated by Mark DelCogliano. In Gregory the Great, *On the Song of Songs*. Translated by Mark DelCogliano. CS 244. Collegeville, MN: Cistercian Publications, 2012. 181–240.

Expositio super Cantica Canticorum (PL 180:473–546)

Guillelmi a Sancto Theodorico Opera Omnia, II: Expositio super Cantica Canticorum. Edited by Paul Verdeyen. CCCM 87. Turnhout: Brepols, 1997. 17–133.

Guillaume de Saint-Thierry. *Exposé sur le Cantique des Cantiques.*
Edited by J.-M. Déchanet and translated by M. Dumontier. SCh
82. Paris: Les Éditions du Cerf, 1962; 2nd ed., 1998.

Commentaire sur le Cantique des cantiques. Edited and translated by
Robert Thomas. Pain de Cîteaux 9–12. Roybon (France): Abbaye
de Chambarand, 1961.

William of Saint Thierry. *Exposition on the Song of Songs.* Translated
by Columba Hart. Introduction by J.-M. Déchanet. CF 6. Kalamazoo, MI: Cistercian Publications, 1968.

Expositio super Epistolam ad Romanos (PL 180:547–694)

*Guillelmi a Sancto Theodorico Opera Omnia, I: Expositio super Epistolam
ad Romanos.* Edited by Paul Verdeyen. CCCM 86. Turnhout: Brepols, 1989. 1–196.

Guillaume de Saint-Thierry. *Exposé sur l'Épître aux Romains, 1 (Books
1–3).* Edited by Paul Verdeyen. Translated by Yves-Anselme
Baudelet. SCh 544. Paris: Les Éditions du Cerf, 2011.

Exposé sur l'Épître aux Romains. Edited and translated by Antoine
Bru. Pain de Cîteaux. Paris: OEIL, 1986.

William of St. Thierry. *Exposition on the Epistle to the Romans.* Translated by John Baptist Hasbrouk. Edited and introduced by John
D. Anderson. CF 27. Kalamazoo, MI: Cistercian Publications, 1980.

Meditativae orationes (PL 180:205–48)

*Guillelmi a Sancto Theodorico Opera Omnia, IV: Meditationes Devotissi-
mae.* Edited by Paul Verdeyen. CCCM 89. Turnhout: Brepols, 2005.
1–80.

Guillaume de Saint-Thierry. *Oraisons méditatives.* Edited and translated by Dom Jacques Hourlier. SCh 324. Paris: Les Éditions du
Cerf, 1985.

Oraisons méditées. Edited and translated by Robert Thomas. Pain de
Cîteaux 21–22. Roybon (France): Abbaye de Chambarand, 1964.

William of St. Thierry. *On Contemplating God, Prayer, Meditations.*
Translated by Sr. Penelope [Lawson]. Introduced by Jacques
Hourlier. Kalamazoo, MI: Cistercian Publications, 1977. 87–178.

Oratio domni Willelmi

Guillelmi a Sancto Theodorico Opera Omnia, III: Oratio Domni Willelmi.
Edited by Paul Verdeyen. CCCM 88. Turnhout: Brepols, 2003.
169–71.

Guillaume de Saint-Thierry. *La contemplation de Dieu, l'oraison de Dom
Guillaume.* Edited and translated by Dom Jacques Hourlier. SCh
61 *bis.* Paris: Les Éditions du Cerf, 1959; 2nd ed., 1968; rev. ed.,
1977; corrected eds., 1999, 2005.

Prière de Guillaume, Contemplation de Dieu. Edited and translated by Robert Thomas. Pain de Cîteaux 23. Roybon (France): Abbaye de Chambarand, 1965.

"The Prayer of Dom William: A Study and New Translation." Edited by David N. Bell. In *Unity of Spirit: Studies on William of Saint-Thierry in Honor of E. Rozanne Elder*, edited by F. Tyler Sergent, Aage Rydstrøm-Poulsen, and Marsha L. Dutton. Collegeville, MN: Cistercian Publications, 2015. 21–36.

William of St. Thierry. *On Contemplating God, Prayer, Meditations.* Translated by Sr. Penelope [Lawson]. Introduced by Jacques Hourlier. CF 3. Kalamazoo, MI: Cistercian Publications, 1977. 71–74.

Prologus ad Domnum Bernardum abbatem Claravallis (Prologue to Sac altar) (PL 180:344–45)

   Guillelmi a Sancto Theodorico Opera Omnia, III: Prologus [Ad Domnum Bernardum Abbatem Claravallis]. Edited by Stanislas Ceglar and Paul Verdeyen. CCCM 88. Turnhout: Brepols, 2003. 53.

Responsio abbatum auctore Willelmo abbate Sancti Theodorici (to Cardinal Matthew)

   Guillelmi a Sancto Theodorico Opera Omnia, IV: Responsio Abbatum Auctore Willelmo Abbate Sancti Theodorici. Edited by Paul Verdeyen. CCCM 89. Turnhout: Brepols, 2005. 103–12.

   "Réponse des abbés bénédictins (1131–1132)." In *Documents inédits pour servir à l'histoire ecclésiastique de la Belgique.* Edited by Ursmer Berlière. 2 vols. Maredsous (France): Abbaye de Saint-Benoit, 1894. 1:103–10.

Speculum fidei (PL 180:365–98)

   Guillelmi a Sancto Theodorico Opera Omnia, V: Speculum Fidei. Edited by Paul Verdeyen. CCCM 89A. Turnhout: Brepols, 2007. 81–127.

   Guillaume de Saint-Thierry. *Le miroir de la foi.* Edited and translated by Jean Déchanet. SCh 301. Paris: Les Éditions du Cerf, 1982.

   Guillaume de Saint-Thierry. *Deux traités sur la foi: Le miroir de la foi, l'enigme de la foi.* Edited and translated by M.-M. Davy. Paris: J. Vrin, 1959. 24–91.

   William of Saint Thierry. *The Mirror of Faith.* Translated by Thomas X. Davis. Introduced by E. Rozanne Elder. CF 15. Kalamazoo, MI: Cistercian Publications, 1979.

Vita prima Sancti Bernardi, Liber Primus (PL 185:225–68)

   Guillelmi a Sancto Theodorico Opera Omnia, VI: Vita Prima Sancti Bernardi—Liber primus. Edited by Paul Verdeyen. CCCM 89B. Turnhout: Brepols, 2011. 29–85.

Bernard: Jeunesse et entrée à Cîteaux. Edited by Dominique Guéniot. Langres: Editions Dominique Guéniot, 2012.

Bernard of Clairvaux: Early Biographies, Volume I by William of St. Thierry. Translated by Martinus Cawley. Centennial Edition: 1090–1990. Guadalupe Translations. Lafayette, OR: Abbey of Our Lady of Guadalupe, 1990.

St. Bernard of Clairvaux: The Story of his Life as Recorded in the Vita Prima Bernardi by Certain of His Contemporaries, William of St. Thierry, Arnold of Bonnevaux, Geoffrey and Philip of Clairvaux, and Odo of Deuil. Translated by Geoffrey Webb and Adrian Walker. London: A. R. Mowbray, 1960.

William of Saint-Thierry, Arnold of Bonneval, and Geoffrey of Clairvaux. *The First Life of Saint Bernard of Clairvaux*. Translated by Hilary Costello. CF 76. Collegeville, MN: Cistercian Publications, 2015.

GENERAL BIBLIOGRAPHY

Editions and Translations

Abelard, Peter. "Abelard's Rule for Religious Women." Edited by T. P. McLaughlin. *Mediaeval Studies* 18 (1956): 241–92.

———. *Epistolae.* Edited by J.-P. Migne. PL 178:113–380. Paris, 1855.

———. *Letters of Abelard and Heloise.* Rev. ed. Translated by Betty Radice. Introduction and notes by Michael Clanchy. New York: Penguin, 2004.

Aelred of Rievaulx. *Oratio Pastoralis.* In *For Your Own People: Aelred of Rievaulx's* Pastoral Prayer, edited and introduced by Marsha L. Dutton. Translated by Mark DelCogliano. CF 73. Kalamazoo, MI: Cistercian Publications, 2008.

Agobard of Lyons. *Commentarius in Pauli epistulas. Summa notarum.* Library of Latin Texts—Series A. www.brepolis.net. Turnhout: Brepols, 2012.

———. *Opera Omnia.* Edited by L. Van Acker. CCCM 52. Turnhout: Brepols, 1981.

Ambrose of Milan. *Apologia David Altera,* in *Sancti Ambrosii Opera Pars 2,* edited by Carolus Schenkl. CSEL 32.2. Vienna: F. Tempsky, 1897. 357–408.

———. *De paenitentia.* In *Sancti Ambrosii Opera Pars 7,* edited by Otto Faller. CSEL 73. Vienna: Hölder-Pichler-Tempsky, 1955. 117–206.

———. *De virginibus, libri tres.* Edited by Egnatius Cazzaniga. Corpus Scriptorum Latinorum Paravianum, new series. Turin: Paravia, 1948.

———. *Expositio Psalmi CXVIII,* in *Sancti Ambrosii Opera Pars Quinta.* Edited by Michael Petschenig and Michaela Zelzer. CSEL 62. Vienna: Verlag des Österreichischen Akademie der Wissenschaften, 1996.

———. *La pénitence.* Edited by Roger Gryson. SChr 179. Paris: Les Editions du Cerf, 1971.

Ambrosiaster. *Commentarius in epistulas Paulinas, Pars III: In epistulas ad Gálatas, ad Efesios, ad Filippenses, ad Colosenses, ad Thessalonicenses, ad Timotheum, ad Titum, ad Filemonem.* Edited by H. J. Vogels. Vienna: Austrian Academy of Sciences Press, 1969. *Summa notarum* in the Library of Latin Texts—Series A, www.brepolis.net. Turnhout: Brepols, 2012.

Augustine of Hippo. *Confessiones.* Edited by Lucas Verheijen. CCSL 27. Turnhout: Brepolis, 1990.

——. *Contra academicos.* Edited by J.-P. Migne. PL 32:903–58. Paris, 1841.

——. *De Genesi ad libri duocecim.* Edited by J.-P. Migne. PL 34:245–486. Paris, 1841.

——. *De Genesi ad litteram imperfectus liber.* Edited by J.-P. Migne. PL 34:219–46. Paris, 1841.

——. *De Genesi ad litteram libri duodecim.* In *Sancti Aureli Augustini Opera,* edited by Joseph Zycha. CSEL 28.1. Vienna: F. Tempsky, 1894. 1–435.

——. *De trinitate.* Edited by W. J. Mountain. CCSL 50. Turnhout: Brepols, 1968.

——. *Ennarationes in Psalmos.* Edited by J.-P. Migne. PL 36:21–1027, 37:1033–1967. Paris, 1842.

——. *In Epistolam Johannis ad Parthos tractatus decem.* Edited by J.-P. Migne. PL 35:1977–2062. Paris, 1841.

——. *Saint Augustine on Genesis: Two Books on Genesis against the Manichees, and On the Literal Interpretation of Genesis: An Unfinished Book.* Translated by Roland J. Teske. The Fathers of the Church, vol. 84. Washington, DC: The Catholic University of American Press, 1991.

Baldwin of Forde. *Spiritual Tractates.* 2 vols. Translated by David N. Bell. CF 41. Kalamazoo, MI: Cistercian Publications, 1986.

Bede. *Explanatio Apocalypsis.* Turnhout: Brepols, 2012. *Summa notarum.* Library of Latin Texts (CLCLT), Series A. www.brepolis.net.

——. *Expositio Apocalypseos.* In *Opera exegetica,* edited by Roger Gryson. CCSL 121A. Turnhout: Brepols, 2001.

——. *In Cantica canticorum.* In *Opera exegetica,* edited by D. Hurst. CCSL 119B. Turnhout: Brepols, 1983.

Bernard of Clairvaux. *Apologia ad Guillelmum Abbatem.* Edited by Jean Leclercq and H. M. Rochais. SBOp 3:61–108. Rome: Editiones Cistercienses, 1963.

——. *Epistolae.* Edited by Jean Leclercq and H. M. Rochais. SBOp 7–8. Rome: Editiones Cistercienses, 1974, 1977.

——. *The Letters of St. Bernard of Clairvaux.* Translated by Bruno Scott James. London: Burns and Oates, 1953.

——. *Liber de diligendo Deo.* Edited by Jean Leclercq and H. M. Rochais. SBOp 3:109–54. Rome: Editiones Cistercienses, 1963.

——. *On Loving God.* With Analytical Commentary by Emero Stiegman. CF 13B. Kalamazoo, MI: Cistercian Publications, 1995.

——. *On the Song of Songs II.* Translated by Kilian Walsh. CF 7. Kalamazoo, MI: Cistercian Publications, 1976.

————. *Sermones in annuntiatione dominica*. Edited by Jean Leclercq and H. M. Rochais. SBOp 5:13–42. Rome: Editiones Cistercienses, 1968.

————. *Sermones super Cantica Canticorum*. Edited by Jean Leclercq and H. M. Rochais. SBOp 1–2. Rome: Editiones Cistercienses, 1957, 1958.

————. *Sermons sur le Cantique*. Vol. 1. Edited by Jean Leclercq, H. M. Rochais, and C. H. Talbot. Translated by Raffaele Fassetta. Introduction and notes by Paul Verdeyen. SChr 414. Paris: Les Éditions du Cerf, 2006.

————. *Sermons sur le Cantique*. Vol. 3. Translated by Paul Verdeyen and Rafaela Fassetta. SChr 431. Paris: Les Éditions du Cerf, 2000.

————. *Vita Sancti Malachiae Episcopi*. Edited by Jean Leclercq and H. M. Rochais. SBOp 3:295–78. Rome: Editiones Cistercienses, 1963.

Biblia sacra: Iuxta Vulgatum versionem. Stuttgart: Deutsche Bibelgesellschaft, 1983.

Caesarius of Arles. *Expositio in Apocalypsim*. In *S. Caesarii Opera Omnia*. Edited by Germain Morin. 2 vols. Bruges: Desclée, Brouwer, et Cie, 1942. 2:210–77.

————. *Expositio in Apocalypsim Beati Joanni*. Edited J.-P. Migne. PL 35:2417–52. Paris, 1841.

Cicero, Marcus Tullius. *Hortensius; Lucullus; Academici libri*. Edited and translated by Laila Straume-Zimmerman, et al. Sammlung Tusculum. Munich: Artemis and Winkler, 1990.

Conrad of Eberbach. *Exordium Magnum cisterciense sive Narratio de initio Cisterciensis ordinis*. Edited by Bruno Griesser. SSOC 2. Rome: Editiones Cistercienses, 1961. Reprinted CCCM 138. Turnhout: Brepols, 1994.

————. *The Great Beginning of Cîteaux: A Narrative of the Beginning of the Cistercian Order: The* Exordium Magnum *of Conrad of Eberbach*. Translated by Benedicta Ward and Paul Savage. Edited by E. Rozanne Elder. CF 72. Collegeville, MN: Cistercian Publications, 2012.

Damian, Peter. *Die Briefe des Petrus Damiani*. Edited by Kurt Reindel. Die Briefe der deutschen Kaiserzeit. 4 vols. Munich: MGH, 1983–1993. *Summa notarum*. The Library of Latin Texts—Series A, www.brepolis.net. Turnhout: Brepols, 2012.

————. *The Letters of Peter Damian*. Translated by Owen J. Blum and Irven M. Resnick. 7 vols. The Fathers of the Church. Washington, DC: The Catholic University of America Press, 1989–2005.

————. *Sanctus Petrus Damianus sermones*. Edited by Ioannis [Giovanni] Lucchesi. CCCM 57. Turnhout: Brepols, 1983.

194 Unity of Spirit

Gregory the Great. *The Letters of Gregory the Great*. 3 vols. Translated by John R. C. Martyn. Toronto: Pontifical Institute for Mediaeval Studies, 2004.

———. *Registrum epistularum*. Edited by Dag Norberg. CCSL 140A. Turnhout: Brepols, 1982.

Guerric of Igny. *Liturgical Sermons*. Translated by Monks of Mount Saint Bernard Abbey. CF 8. Kalamazoo, MI: Cistercian Publications, 1970.

———. *Sermons*. Edited by John Morson and Hilary Costello. 2 vols. SChr 166. Paris: Les Éditions du Cerf, 1970.

Hilary of Poitiers. *De trinitate*. Edited by Pierre Smulders. CCSL 62. Turnhout: Brepols, 1979.

———. *Select Works*. Edited by Philip Schaff and Henry Wace. NPNF 2.9. New York: Scribner, 1899.

Jerome. *Select Letters of St. Jerome*. Translated by F. A. Wright. Loeb Classical Library 262. Cambridge, MA: Harvard University Press, 1933.

Luther, Martin. *D. Martin Luthers Werke; kritische Gesamtausgabe*. 52 vols. Weimar: Hermann Böhlau, 1883.

Novum Testamentum Graece. 27th ed. Edited by Eberhard Nestle, Erwin Nestle, Kurt Aland, et al. Stuttgart: Deutsche Bibelgesellschaft, 1996.

Peter the Venerable. *The Letters of Peter the Venerable*. Edited by Giles Constable. 2 vols. Harvard Historical Studies 78. Cambridge, MA: Harvard University Press, 1967.

Primasius of Hadrumetum. *Commentarius in Apocalypsin*. Edited by A. W. Adams. CCSL 92. Turnhout: Brepols, 1985.

———. *Commentariorum super Apocalypsim*. Edited by J.-P. Migne. PL 68:793–936. Paris, 1841.

Rupert of Deutz. *Commentaria in Evangelium Sancti Iohannis*. Edited by Rhabanus Haacke. CCCM 9. Turnhout: Brepols, 1969.

The Sayings of the Desert Fathers: The Alphabetical Collection, translated by Benedicta Ward. CS 59. London and Oxford: A. R. Mowbray; Kalamazoo, MI: Cistercian Publications, 1975.

Severus, Sulpitius. *The Works of Sulpitius Severus*. Translated by Alexander Roberts. Edited by Philip Schaff and Henry Wace. NPNF. 2nd series. New York: Christian Literature Publishing Company, 1894. 11:1–122.

Terence. *The Phormio of Terence*. Edited by John Bond and Arthur Sumner Walpole. 2nd ed. rev. London: Macmillan, 1884.

Vetus Latina: Die Reste der altlateinischen Bibel. Edited by H. J. Frede. Freiburg: Herder, 1962–1964.

Studies

Adam, André. *Guillaume de Saint-Thierry: sa vie et ses œuvres.* Bourg (France): Impr. du "Journal de l'Ain," 1923.

Adams, Henry. *Mont-Saint-Michel and Chartres.* 1913; Garden City, NY: Doubleday, 1959.

Anderson, John D. Introduction to William of Saint Thierry. *The Enigma of Faith,* translated by John D. Anderson. CF 9. Kalamazoo, MI, and Spencer, MA: Cistercian Publications, 1973. 1–31.

Anderson, Luke. "The Appeal to Reason in St. Bernard's *De Diligendo Deo* (2:2–6)." In *The Chimaera of His Age: Studies in Bernard of Clairvaux,* edited by E. Rozanne Elder and John R. Sommerfeldt. Studies in Medieval Cistercian History 5. CS 63. Kalamazoo, MI: Cistercian Publications, 1980. 132–39.

Bell, David N. *The Image and Likeness: The Augustinian Spirituality of William of St. Thierry.* CS 78. Kalamazoo, MI: Cistercian Publications, 1984.

———. Introduction to William of St. Thierry, *The Nature and Dignity of Love,* translated by Thomas X. Davis. CF 30. Kalamazoo, MI: Cistercian Publications, 1981. 5–43.

———. "Is There Such a Thing as 'Cistercian Spirituality'?" CSQ 33 (1998): 455–71.

———. "The Vita Antiqua of William of St. Thierry." CSQ 11 (1976): 246–55.

Boshof, Egon. *Erzbischof Agobard von Lyon. Leben und Werk.* Kölner Historische Abhandlungen 17. Cologne: Böhlau, 1969.

Bouyer, Louis. *The Cistercian Heritage.* London: A. R. Mowbray, 1958.

Bredero, Adriaan H. *Bernard of Clairvaux: Between Cult and History.* Grand Rapids, MI: William B. Eerdmans, 1996.

———. *Études sur la "Vita Prima" de Saint Bernard.* Rome: Editiones Cistercienses, 1960.

Bressolles, Adrien. *Doctrine et action politique d'Agobard: I. Saint Agobard, Evêque de Lyon (760–840).* L'Église et l'état au Moyen Âge 9. Paris: J. Vrin, 1949.

Brooke, Odo. "The Trinitarian Aspect of the Ascent of the Soul to God in the Theology of William of St. Thierry." RTAM 26 (1959): 85–127.

———. "William of St. Thierry's Doctrine of the Ascent to God by Faith." RTAM 30 (1963): 181–204. [Doctrine 1963]

———. "William of St. Thierry's Doctrine of the Ascent to God by Faith." RTAM 33 (1966): 282–318. [Doctrine 1966]

Brown, Peter. *Augustine of Hippo: A Biography.* 2nd ed. Berkeley: University of California Press, 2000.

Brown, Raymond E. *An Introduction to the New Testament.* New York: Doubleday, 1997.

Cabaniss, Allen. *Agobard of Lyons: Churchman and Critic.* Syracuse, NY: Syracuse University Press, 1953.

Casey, Michael. *Athirst for God: Spiritual Desire in Bernard of Clairvaux's Sermons on the Song of Songs.* CS 77. Kalamazoo, MI: Cistercian Publications, 1987.

Cazes, Denis. *La Théologie Sapientielle de Guillaume de Saint Thierry.* Studia Anselmiana 148. Rome: Pontificio Ateneo S. Anselmo, 2009.

Ceglar, Stanislaus. "William of Saint Thierry and His Leading Role at the First Chapters of the Benedictine Abbots (Reims 1131, Soissons 1132)." In *William, Abbot of St. Thierry,* translated by Jerry Carfantan. CS 94. Kalamazoo, MI: Cistercian Publications, 1987. 34–112.

————. "William of Saint Thierry: The Chronology of His Life with a Study of His Treatise *On the Nature of Love,* His Authorship of the *Brevis Commentatio,* the *In Lacu,* and the *Reply to Cardinal Matthew.*" PhD dissertation. Washington, DC: The Catholic University of America, 1971.

Châtillon, Jean. "William of Saint Thierry, Monasticism, and the Schools: Rupert of Deutz, Abelard, and William of Conches." In *William, Abbot of St. Thierry: A Colloquium at the Abbey of St. Thierry,* translated by Jerry Carfantan. CS 94. Kalamazoo, MI: Cistercian Publications, 1987. 153–80.

Chenu, M.-D. *Nature, Man, and Society in the Twelfth Century: Essays on New Theological Perspectives in the Latin West.* Edited and translated by Jerome Taylor and Lester K. Little. Toronto: University of Toronto Press, 1997.

Como, Giuseppe. *Ignis amoris Dei. Lo Spirito Santo e la trasformazione dell'uomo nell'esperienza spirituale secondo Guglielmo di Saint-Thierry.* Milan: Ed. Glossa, 2001.

Cvetović, Carmen Angela. *Seeking the Face of God: The Reception of Augustine in the Mystical Thought of Bernard of Clairvaux and William of St. Thierry.* Turnhout: Brepols, 2012.

Déchanet, Jean Marie. "A Comment." In *William, Abbot of St. Thierry: A Colloquium at the Abbey of St. Thierry,* translated by Jerry Carfantan. CS 94. Kalamazoo, MI: Cistercian Publications, 1987. 254–57.

————. *Guillaume de Saint-Thierry: Aux sources d'une pensée.* Théologie Historique 49. Paris: Beauchesne, 1978.

————. *Guillaume de Saint-Thierry. L'homme et son oeuvre.* Bruges: Éditions Charles Beyaert, 1942. Translated by Richard Strachan as *William of*

St. Thierry: The Man and his Work. CS 10. Spencer, MA: Cistercian Publications, 1972.

DelCogliano, Mark. "The Composition of William of St. Thierry's *Excerpts from the Books of Blessed Gregory on the Song of Songs.*" *Cîteaux* 58 (2007): 57–76.

Delesalle, Jacques. "L'in-hésion' à Dieu. Un langage de l'union à Dieu dans le traité *Nature et dignité de l'amour* de Guillaume de Saint-Thierry." *Collectanea cisterciensia* 71, no. 4 (2009): 300–14.

Dutton, Marsha L. Introduction to Aelred of Rievaulx, *For Your Own People: Aelred of Rievaulx's* Pastoral Prayer. Edited by Marsha L. Dutton. Translated by Mark DelCogliano. CF 73. Kalamazoo, MI: Cistercian Publications, 2008. 1–35.

Elder, E. Rozanne. "Christologie de Guillaume de Saint-Thierry et vie spirituelle." In *Signy l'abbaye et Guillaume de Saint-Thierry, actes du colloque international d'études cisterciennes 9, 10, 11 septembre 1998, Les Vieilles Forges (Ardennes),* edited by Nicole Boucher. Signy: Association des Amis de l'Abbaye de Signy, 2000. 575–87.

———. "The Christology of William of Saint Thierry." RTAM 58 (1991): 79–112.

———. "Guillaume de Saint-Thierry et le 'Chapitre Général' bénédictin de 1131." *Signy l'abbaye et Guillaume de Saint-Thierry, Actes du colloque international d'études cisterciennes 9, 10, 11 septembre 1998, Les Vieilles Forges (Ardennes),* edited by Nicole Boucher. Signy: Association des Amis de l'Abbaye de Signy, 2000. 487–503.

———. "The Image of Invisible God: The Evolving Christology of William of Saint Thierry." PhD dissertation, University of Toronto, Canada, 1972.

———. Introduction to William of St. Thierry, *The Mirror of Faith,* translated by Thomas X. Davis. CF 15. Kalamazoo, MI: Cistercian Publications, 1979. xi–xxxi.

———. "Making Virtues of Vexing Habits." In *Studiosorum Speculum: Studies in Honor of Louis J. Lekai, O. Cist,* edited by Francis Swietek and John R. Sommerfeldt. CS 141. Kalamazoo, MI: Cistercian Publications, 1993. 75–94.

———. "The Way of Ascent: The Meaning of Love in the Thought of William of St. Thierry." In *Studies in Medieval Culture 1,* edited by John R. Sommerfeldt. Kalamazoo, MI: Medieval Institute Publications, 1964. 39–47.

———. "William of St. Thierry: The Monastic Vocation as an Imitation of Christ." *Cîteaux* 26 (1975): 9–30.

————. "William of Saint Thierry: Rational and Affective Spirituality." In *The Spirituality of Western Christendom*, edited by E. Rozanne Elder. CS 30. Kalamazoo, MI: Cistercian Publications, 1976. 85–105, 197–200.

Falmagne, Thomas. *Un texte en contexte. Les Flores paradisi et le milieu culturel de Villers-en-Brabant dans la première moitié du 13ᵉ siècle.* Turnhout: Brepols, 2001.

France, James. *Medieval Images of Saint Bernard of Clairvaux.* CS 210. Kalamazoo, MI: Cistercian Publications, 2005.

Gilson, Étienne. *The Christian Philosophy of Saint Augustine.* Translated by L. E. M. Lynch. New York: Octagon Books, 1983.

————. *The Mystical Theology of Saint Bernard.* Translated by A. H. C. Downes. CS 120. Kalamazoo, MI: Cistercian Publications, 1990.

Hamilton, Bernard, with P. A. McNulty. "*Orientale lumen et magistra latinitas*: Greek Influences on Western Monasticism (900–1100)." In *Monastic Reform, Catharism and the Crusades (900–1300)*, edited by Bernard Hamilton. London: Variorum Reprints, 1979. 181–216.

Heffernan, Thomas J. *Sacred Biography: Saints and Their Biographers in the Middle Ages.* New York: Oxford University Press, 1988.

Hourlier, Jacques. Introduction to William of Saint-Thierry, *On Contemplating God, Prayer, Meditations*, translated by Sr. Penelope [Lawson]. The Works of William of St. Thierry, vol. 1. CF 3. Spencer, MA: Cistercian Publications, 1971; Kalamazoo, MI: Cistercian Publications, 1977. 1–35, 65–70, 75–86, 179–86.

————. "S. Bernard et Guillaume de Saint-Thierry dans le 'Liber de Amore.'" In *Saint Bernard théologien: actes du congres de Dijon, 15–19 septembre, 1953.* ASOC 3–4 (1953): 223–33.

Javelet, Robert. *Image et ressemblance au XIIᵉ siècle, de saint Anselme à Alain de Lille.* 2 vols. Paris: Letouzey et Ané, 1967.

Kutter, Hermann. *Wilhelm von St. Thierry: Ein Repräsentant der mittelalterlichen Frömmigkeit.* Giessen (Ger): Ricker, 1898.

LeBrun, Freddy. "*Vita Antiqua Willelmi Sancti Theoderici* d'après le manuscrit 11782 de la Bibliothèque Nationale de Paris." *Signy l'abbaye et Guillaume de Saint-Thierry, actes du Colloque international d'études cisterciennes 9, 10, 11 septembre 1998, Les Vieilles Forges (Ardennes)*, edited by Nicole Boucher. Signy: Association des Amis de l'Abbaye de Signy, 2000. 437–59.

Leclercq, Jean. Introduction to *The Spirituality of Western Christendom*, edited by E. Rozanne Elder. CS 30. Kalamazoo, MI: Cistercian Publications, 1976. xi–xxxv.

————. Introduzzione Generale to *Opere di San Bernardo* 4, edited by Ferruccio Gastaldelli. Scriptorium claravallense fondazione di studi cistercensi. Rome: Città Nuova Editrice, 1984, 1986.

————. *Nouveau visage de Bernard de Clairvaux: Approches psycho-historiques "Essais."* Paris: Les Éditions du Cerf, 1976.

————. *A Second Look at Bernard of Clairvaux.* Translated by Marie-Bernard Said. CS 105. Kalamazoo, MI: Cistercian Publications, 1990.

Lekai, Louis J. *The Cistercians: Ideals and Realities.* Kent, OH: Kent State University Press, 1977.

Louth, Andrew. *Maximus the Confessor.* New York: Routledge, 1996.

Mackay, T. W. "Augustine and Gregory the Great in Bede's Commentary on the Apocalypse." In *Northumbria's Golden Age*, edited by Jane Hawkes and Susan Mills. Stroud (UK): Sutton, 1999. 396–405.

McGinn, Bernard. Introduction to William of St. Thierry, "The Nature of the Body and Soul," in *Three Treatises on Man: A Cistercian Anthropology*, ed. Bernard McGinn. CF 24. Kalamazoo, MI: Cistercian Publications, 1977. 30–47.

Metzger, Bruce M. *The New Testament: Its Background, Growth, and Content.* 3rd ed. Nashville, TN: Abingdon Press, 2003.

Meyer, Robert T. Introduction to Bernard of Clairvaux, *The Life and Death of Saint Malachy the Irishman*, translated by Robert T. Meyer. CF 10. Kalamazoo, MI: Cistercian Publications, 1978. 1–7.

Miccoli, Giovanni. *Chiesa Gregoriana. Ricerche sulla riforma del secolo XI.* Storici antichi e moderni n.s. 17. Florence: La Nuova Italia, 1966.

Milis, Ludo. "William of Saint Thierry, His Birth, His Formation and His First Monastic Experiences." In *William, Abbot of St. Thierry: A Colloquium at the Abbey of St. Thierry*, translated by Jerry Carfantan. CS 94. Kalamazoo, MI: Cistercian Publications, 1987. 9–33.

Montanari, Cesare Antonio. *"Per figuras amatorias"*: L'Expositio super Cantica canticorum *di Guglielmo di Saint-Thierry: Esegesi et Teologia.* Analecta Gregoriana 297. Rome: Pontificio Istituto Biblico, 2006.

Morson, John, and Hilary Costello. Introduction to *Liturgical Sermons by Guerric of Igny*, vol. 1, translated by Monks of Mount Saint Bernard Abbey. CF 8. Kalamazoo, MI: Cistercian Publications, 1970. vii–lxi.

Neil, Bronwen. "Two Views of Vice and Virtue: Augustine of Hippo and Maximus the Confessor." In *Prayer and Spirituality in the Early Church 3: Liturgy and Life*, edited by Bronwen Neil, G. Dunn, and L. Cross. Sydney (Aus): St. Paul's, 2003. 261–71.

Panikkar, Raimundo. *Myth, Faith, and Hermeneutics: Cross-Cultural Studies.* New York: Paulist Press, 1979.

Poncelet, Albert. "Vie ancienne de Guillaume de Saint-Thierry." In *Mélanges Godefroid Kurth: Recueil de mémoires relatifs à l'histoire, à la philologie et à l'archéologie*, 2 vols. Liège (Belgium): Vaillant-Carmanne, 1908. 1:85–96.

Posset, Franz. "*Divus Bernhardus*: Saint Bernard as Spiritual and Theological Mentor of the Reformer Martin Luther." In *Bernardus Magister: Papers Presented at the Nonacentenary Celebration of the Birth of Saint Bernard of Clairvaux, Kalamazoo, Michigan*, edited by John R. Sommerfeldt. CS 135. Kalamazoo, MI: Cistercian Publications, and *Cîteaux: Commentarii Cistercienses*, 1992. 517–32.

Rougé, Matthieu. *Doctrine et expérience de l'eucharistie chez Guillaume de Saint-Thierry*. Théologie Historique 111. Paris: Beauchesne, 1999.

Rydstrøm-Poulsen, Aage. *The Gracious God: Gratia in Augustine and the Twelfth Century*. Copenhagen: Akademisk, 2002.

———. "Research on William of Saint-Thierry from 1998 to 2008." *Analecta Cisterciensia* 58 (2008): 158–69.

Sander, Kai G. *Amplexus. Die Begegnung des Menschen mit dem dreieinen Gott in der Lehre des sel. Wilhelm von Saint Thierry*. Quellen und Studien zur Zisterzienserliteratur 2. Langwaden: Bernardus-Verlag, 1998.

Schuck, Johannes. *Das religiöse Erlebnis beim hl. Bernhard von Clairvaux*. Würzburg: C. J. Becker, 1922.

Schwienhorst-Schönberger, Ludger. "Die Hoheliedsauslegung Bernhards von Clairvaux im Gespräch mit neueren Entwicklungen in der Bibelwissenschaft." In *Von der Freude, sich Gott zu nähern: Beiträge zur cisterciensischen Spiritualität*, edited by Wolfgang Buchmüller. Heiligenkreuz (Austria): Be&Be-Verlag, 2010. 77–107.

Sergent, F. Tyler. "'Signs of Spiritual and Divine Realities': The Sources and Originality of William of St. Thierry's Ascetic Language." PhD diss., Roskilde Universitet, Denmark, 2009.

———. "*Vita prima Bernardi*: Portrait of a Spiritual Journey?" Paper presented at the 1998 Cistercian Studies Conference, during the 33rd International Congress on Medieval Studies at Western Michigan University, Kalamazoo, MI, May 8, 1998.

Smulders, Pierre. Introduction to *De Trinitate*, by Hilary of Poitiers. CCSL 62. Turnhout: Brepols, 1979. 1–80.

Southey, Robert. "Art. IX. The Works of the Reverend William Huntington, SS. Minister of the Gospel, at Providence Chapel, Gray's Inn Lane, Completed to the Close of the Year 1806." *The Quarterly Review* 24, no. 48 (1821): 462–510.

Špidlík, Tomáš. *The Spirituality of the Christian East: A Systematic Handbook.* Translated by Anthony P. Gythiel. CS 79. Kalamazoo, MI: Cistercian Publications, 1986.

Standaert, Maur. "La doctrine de l'image chez Saint Bernard." *Ephemerides Theologiae Lovanienses* 23 (1947): 70–129.

Stiegman, Emero. "An Analytical Commentary." In Bernard of Clairvaux, *On Loving God.* CF 13B. Kalamazoo, MI: Cistercian Publications, 1995. 43–219.

————. "Bernard of Clairvaux, William of St. Thierry, the Victorines." In *The Medieval Theologians*, edited by G. R. Evans. Oxford: Blackwell Publishers, 2001. 129–55.

Van Acker, L. Introduction to *Opera Omnia*, by Agobardi Lugdunensis. CCCM 52. Turnhout: Brepols, 1981. v–xvii.

Van Burink, Antony. Introduction to "Excerpta de Libris Beati Ambrosii super Cantica Canticorum." In *Guillelmi a Sancto Theodorico Opera Omina, II: Excerpta de Libris Beati Ambrosii super Cantica Canticorum*, edited by Antony van Burink. CCCM 87. Turnhout: Brepols, 1997. 199–204.

Van Engen, John. "Rupert of Deutz and William of St. Thierry." *Revue Bénédictine* 93 (1983): 327–36.

Vauchez, André. *Sainthood in the Later Middle Ages.* Translated by Jean Birrell. Cambridge (UK): Cambridge University Press, 1997.

Verdeyen, Paul. "En quoi la connaissance de Guillaume de Saint-Thierry a-t-elle progressé depuis le colloque de 1976?" In *Signy l'abbaye et Guillaume de Saint-Thierry, actes du colloque international d'études cisterciennes 9, 10, 11 septembre 1998, Les Vieilles Forges (Ardennes)*, edited by Nicole Boucher. Signy: Association des Amis de l'Abbaye de Signy, 2000. 411–13.

————. "En quoi la connaissance de Guillaume de Saint-Thierry a-t-elle progressé depuis le colloque de 1976?" *Revue de sciences religieuses* 73 [1999]: 17–20.

————. "Guillaume de Saint-Thierry Liège (Belgique), 1075—Signy l'Abbaye (Ardennes), 1148." In *Signy l'abbaye et Guillaume de Saint-Thierry, actes du colloque international d'études cisterciennes 9, 10, 11 septembre 1998, Les Vieilles Forges (Ardennes)*, edited by Nicole Boucher. Signy: Association des Amis de l'Abbaye de Signy, 2000. 409–10.

————. *Guillaume de Saint-Thierry, premier auteur mystique des anciens Pays-Bas.* Turnhout: Brepols, 2000.

————. Introduction to *Guillelmi a Sancto Theodorico Opera Omnia, I: Expositio super epistolam ad Romanos*, edited by Paul Verdeyen. CCCM 86. Turnhout: Brepols, 1989. v–li.

Waddell, Chrysogonus. "The Exegetical Challenge of Early Cistercian Hagiography." CSQ 21, no. 3 (1986): 195–212.

Wilmart, André. "La série et la date des ouvrages de Guillaume de Saint-Thierry." *Revue Mabillon* 14 (1924): 157–67.

Wordsworth, William. "Ode." In *William Wordsworth: Selected Poems*, edited by Sandra Anstey. Oxford: Oxford University Press, 2006. 89–95.

Zwingmann, W. "Der Begriff *Affectus* bei Wilhem von Saint-Thierry." PhD dissertation, Gregorian University, Rome, 1964.

———. "*Ex affectu mentis*: Über die Vollkommenheit menschlichen Handelns und menschlicher Hingabe nach Wilhelm von St. Thierry." *Cîteaux* 18 (1967): 5–37.

Contributors

Fr. Luke Anderson, OCist, is prior of St. Mary's Priory in New Ringgold, Schuylkill County, Pennsylvania. He received a master of theology degree from Princeton Theological Seminary and a PhD from the University of St. Thomas in Rome. In addition to his book, *The Image and Likeness of God in St. Bernard of Clairvaux's Free Choice and Grace* (2005), he has published numerous articles on Saint Bernard. He is also the spiritual advisor to the sisters of the Order of St. Theresa in Mahanoy City, Pennsylvania, and has for many years served the sisters of the order as retreat master and workshop leader in India, Mexico, and the United States.

David N. Bell is professor emeritus of religious studies at the Memorial University of Newfoundland and a fellow of the Royal Society of Canada. He is the author of some twenty books and over one hundred articles, dealing primarily with the history of libraries (especially Cistercian libraries), medieval intellectual history, and the history of Egyptian Christianity.

Mark DelCogliano holds a PhD from Emory University and is assistant professor of Theology at St. Thomas University, St. Paul, Minnesota. His research focuses on the development and influence of patristic thought and exegesis, especially Basil of Caesarea and Gregory the Great. He has written several articles and books, including *Gregory the Great on the Song of Songs* (2012).

Marsha L. Dutton is the Samuel and Susan Crowl Professor of Literature at Ohio University. She is the editorial director of Cistercian Publications; she has published extensively on the works of Cistercian authors, especially Aelred of Rievaulx. Her critical edition of the works of Gilbert of Hoyland will appear soon from Corpus Christianorum, Continuatio Mediaevalis.

James France holds an MA from Oxford University and a PhD from Roskilde University, Denmark. He is the author of *The Cistercians in Scandinavia* (1990), *The Cistercians in Medieval Art* (1998), *Medieval Images of Saint Bernard of Clairvaux* (2007), and *Separate but Equal: Cistercian Lay Brothers 1120–1350* (2012). He is a Fellow of the Society of Antiquaries.

Fr. Brendan Freeman, OCSO, is president of the editorial board of Cistercian Publications. He is the author of *Come and See: The Monastic Way for Today* (2010). After nearly thirty years as abbot of the Abbey of New Melleray in Peosta, Iowa, he is now superior *ad nutum* of Holy Trinity Abbey in Huntsville, Utah.

Marjory Lange is professor of English and humanities at Western Oregon University, where she teaches a broad range of courses, including Bible as Literature, Women Writers, Renaissance Literature, and Shakespeare. She is the author of *Telling Tales in the English Renaissance* (1997) (a volume in the Studies in the History of Christian Thought series) and several articles on works by twelfth-century Cistercian authors. She is also a professional musician, playing violin and viola with various local ensembles, including a douçaine-viola duo.

Bernard McGinn is the Naomi Shenstone Donnelley Professor Emeritus at the Divinity School of the University of Chicago, where he taught for thirty-four years. He has worked extensively in the history of medieval theology, especially in the areas of spirituality and mysticism. His major project is a series on the history of Western mysticism under the general title *The Presence of God*. Five volumes of a projected seven have appeared to date.

Aage Rydstrøm-Poulsen is head of the Department of Theology at the University of Greenland and former visiting scholar at the Medieval Institute and Institute of Cistercian Studies at Western Michigan University. He is the author of a major study of the Augustinianism of the twelfth century (not least among the Cistercians), a book about Richard of Saint-Victor's trinitarian theology, and several articles about the twelfth-century theological renaissance among the Cistercians and the Victorines.

F. Tyler Sergent was a graduate student of Rozanne Elder at the Medieval Institute of Western Michigan University, Kalamazoo. He is visiting assistant professor of history and general studies at Berea College, Kentucky, where he teaches courses in ancient and medieval history and religion as well as research and writing seminars. His own research includes ancient and medieval intellectual history, particularly Christian monasticism and the twelfth-century Cistercian William of Saint-Thierry, the subject of his dissertation at Roskilde University (Denmark) and of several published articles.

John R. Sommerfeldt is professor emeritus of medieval history at the University of Dallas, where he had been president from 1978 to 1980. He was for many years professor of history at Western Michigan University, where he created Cistercian Publications, the Medieval Institute, and what would become the International Medieval Studies Congress. He is the editor of numerous collections of articles on Cistercian topics and author of three books on Bernard of Clairvaux and two on Aelred of Rievaulx as well as more recent books on topics in medieval history and culture.

Emero Stiegman is professor emeritus of religious studies at St. Mary's University in Halifax, Nova Scotia. He has published many studies on Bernard of Clairvaux, including the introductions to five Cistercian Publications volumes of translations of the works of Saint Bernard.

Rose Marie Tillisch has an MA and a PhD in theology from the Faculty of Theology in the University of Copenhagen. She is also a vicar of the Danish Lutheran Church, serving the diocese of Elsinore in the parish of Maglegaard. She is the author of several published articles on Hildegard of Bingen, Bernard of Clairvaux, and Maria Sibylla Merian.

Benedicta Ward, SLG, is a supernumerary fellow and dean of degrees at Harris Manchester College in Oxford (UK) and a member of the Anglican religious community of the Sisters of the Love of God. She has published widely on the history of Christian spirituality and medieval church history. Her books include *The Sayings of the Desert Fathers: The Alphabetical Collection* (2006), *Relics and the Medieval Mind* (2010), and *The Great Beginning of Cîteaux: A Narrative of the Beginning of the Cistercian Order* (2012).

Index A

Names of Ancient, Biblical, Patristic, and Medieval Figures

William of Saint-Thierry does not appear in this index. References are listed by chapter, with page numbers preceding note numbers. *Fore*: Foreword; *Ackn*: Acknowledgments; *Let*: Letters of Appreciation; *Intr*: Introduction; *Aft*: Afterword. Names in the two bibliographies are not indexed.

Index B

Names of Post-Medieval Figures

References are listed by chapter, with page numbers, and note numbers following. *Fore*: Foreword; *Ackn*: Acknowledgments; *Let*: Letters of Appreciation; *Intr*: Introduction; *Aft*: Afterword. Names in the two bibliographies are not indexed.

212   *Unity of Spirit*